Instructor's Guide for

THE LAST DANCE
ENCOUNTERING DEATH AND DYING

THIRD EDITION

Lynne Ann DeSpelder
Albert Lee Strickland
Patrick Vernon Dean

Mayfield Publishing Company
Mountain View, California
London • Toronto

International Standard Book Number: 1-55934-152-1

Manufactured in the United States of America

Mayfield Publishing Company
1240 Villa Street
Mountain View, California 94041

CONTENTS

Preface   ix

CHAPTER 1
ATTITUDES TOWARD DEATH: A CLIMATE OF CHANGE **1**

Objectives **1**
Content Overview **1**
Key Terms and Concepts **3**
Questions for Guided Study and Evaluation **3**
Teaching Strategies   **4**
Comments and Considerations **5**
Resources: Films and Videocassettes **6**

CHAPTER 2
PERSPECTIVES ON DEATH: CROSS-CULTURAL AND HISTORICAL **8**

Objectives **8**
Content Overview **8**
Key Terms and Concepts **9**
Questions for Guided Study and Evaluation **10**
Teaching Strategies   **10**
Comments and Considerations **11**
Resources: Films and Videocassettes **11**

CHAPTER 3
SOCIALIZATION: HOW WE LEARN ABOUT DEATH AS CHILDREN **13**

Objectives **13**
Content Overview **13**
Key Terms and Concepts **14**
Questions for Guided Study and Evaluation **15**
Teaching Strategies **15**
Comments and Considerations **17**
Resources: Films and Videocassettes **17**

CHAPTER 4
HEALTH CARE SYSTEMS: PATIENTS, STAFF, AND INSTITUTIONS **19**

Objectives **19**
Content Overview **19**
Key Terms and Concepts **21**
Questions for Guided Study and Evaluation **21**

Teaching Strategies 22
Comments and Considerations 23
Resources: Films and Videocassettes 23

CHAPTER 5
FACING DEATH: LIVING WITH LIFE-THREATENING ILLNESS **31**
Objectives 31
Content Overview 31
Key Terms and Concepts 33
Questions for Guided Study and Evaluation 33
Teaching Strategies 34
Comments and Considerations 35
Resources: Films and Videocassettes 36

CHAPTER 6
LAST RITES: FUNERALS AND BODY DISPOSITION **41**
Objectives 41
Content Overview 41
Key Terms and Concepts 43
Questions for Guided Study and Evaluation 43
Teaching Strategies 44
Comments and Considerations 46
Resources: Films and Videocassettes 46

CHAPTER 7
SURVIVORS: UNDERSTANDING THE EXPERIENCE OF LOSS **48**
Objectives 48
Content Overview 48
Key Terms and Concepts 50
Questions for Guided Study and Evaluation 50
Teaching Strategies 51
Comments and Considerations 52
Resources: Films and Videocassettes 52

CHAPTER 8
DEATH IN CHILDREN'S LIVES **54**
Objectives 54
Content Overview 54
Key Terms and Concepts 55
Questions for Guided Study and Evaluation 56
Teaching Strategies 56
Comments and Considerations 57
Resources: Films and Videocassettes 57

CHAPTER 9
DEATH IN THE LIVES OF ADULTS 63
     Objectives 63
     Content Overview 63
     Key Terms and Concepts 65
     Questions for Guided Study and Evaluation 66
     Teaching Strategies 66
     Comments and Considerations 67
     Resources: Films and Videocassettes 67

CHAPTER 10
MEDICAL ETHICS: DYING IN A TECHNOLOGICAL AGE 76
     Objectives 76
     Content Overview 76
     Key Terms and Concepts 80
     Questions for Guided Study and Evaluation 80
     Teaching Strategies 81
     Comments and Considerations 82
     Resources: Films and Videocassettes 83

CHAPTER 11
THE LAW AND DEATH 87
     Objectives 87
     Content Overview 87
     Key Terms and Concepts 89
     Questions for Guided Study and Evaluation 89
     Teaching Strategies 90
     Comments and Considerations 93
     Resources: Films and Videocassettes 93

CHAPTER 12
ENVIRONMENTAL ENCOUNTERS WITH DEATH 95
     Objectives 95
     Content Overview 95
     Key Terms and Concepts 98
     Questions for Guided Study and Evaluation 99
     Teaching Strategies 99
     Comments and Considerations 100
     Resources: Films and Videocassettes 100

CHAPTER 13
SUICIDE 110
     Objectives 110
     Content Overview 110

Key Terms and Concepts 112
Questions for Guided Study and Evaluation 112
Teaching Strategies 113
Comments and Considerations 114
Resources: Films and Videocassettes 114

CHAPTER 14
BEYOND DEATH/AFTER LIFE 118
Objectives 118
Content Overview 118
Key Terms and Concepts 120
Questions for Guided Study and Evaluation 120
Teaching Strategies 121
Comments and Considerations 122
Resources: Films and Videocassettes 122

CHAPTER 15
THE PATH AHEAD: PERSONAL AND SOCIAL CHOICES 124
Objectives 124
Content Overview 124
Key Terms and Concepts 126
Questions for Guided Study and Evaluation 126
Teaching Strategies 126
Comments and Considerations 127
Resources: Films and Videocassettes 127

APPENDIX A
COURSE PAPERS 128
Assignment 1: Deathography 128
Assignment 2: I Learned Final Paper 129

APPENDIX B
EXAMINATIONS 130
Part 1: Objective Test Questions 130
Part 2: Essay Examination Construction 139
Part 3: Sample Essay Examination 140

APPENDIX C
FURTHER READINGS: TEACHING STRATEGIES AND RESOURCES 143
Books and Articles 143
Periodicals 149

APPENDIX D
ORGANIZATIONS 152

APPENDIX E
DISTRIBUTORS OF RESOURCES **165**
       University Audiovisual Libraries **165**
       General Listing: Distributors of Resources **166**

APPENDIX F
EXCERPT FROM THE BOG *BY MICHAEL TALBOT* **174**

PREFACE

This *Instructor's Guide*, which accompanies the third edition of DeSpelder and Strickland's *The Last Dance: Encountering Death and Dying*, gives educators creative and flexible tools to aid students in exploring the many aspects of death and dying. The *Instructor's Guide* suggests ways in which the text presentation can be enhanced and supplemented by various teaching strategies, and it provides resources that can facilitate students' mastery of course materials.

The *Instructor's Guide* includes: (1) an overview of resources for teaching death education courses; (2) teaching strategies and other materials pertaining to each of the chapters in the text; and (3) appendices with additional educational resources.

Each chapter presents instructional objectives, a content overview, key terms and concepts, methods for assessing achievement of objectives, teaching strategies, comments and considerations, and an annotated listing of film and videocassette resources. Resource listings generally include format, length, year of production, and distributor. Contact distributors for current price and availability; addresses are listed in Appendix E.

With respect to assessing the achievement of objectives, Questions for Guided Study and Evaluation challenge students to gain information and knowledge at a number of different levels of learning, from memorization to analysis and evaluation. These questions can be distributed at the beginning of a chapter assignment to focus students' thinking, as well as at the end of a unit to assess how well the material was learned. Using study questions when a new unit is introduced can: (1) help students organize their readings in advance and be alert to important information, (2) give students anchor points for learning key concepts and facts, and (3) help students review for quizzes or tests. When students are held responsible for mastering the material presented in the Questions for Guided Study and Evaluation, it frees the instructor from "teaching the text," thus allowing more class time for supplemental materials and discussion.

Two course papers useful in helping students assimilate and synthesize information are described in Appendix A. The first of these, the *Deathography*, is a written loss inventory, or personal history of death experiences: it requires students to identify and assess the impact of various losses they have experienced. The *Deathography* reading assignment also helps build rapport among classmates, which is useful in facilitating class discussion.

The second assignment, the *I Learned* paper, is due toward the end of the term. It provides a means for students to review and synthesize what they have learned. Students are encouraged to ground theoretical concepts in experiential reality and to do so in a personally meaningful way.

Appendix B contains information about objective and essay examinations. Included is a selection of questions from the 600-item test bank, as well as a sample essay examination constructed to measure increasingly complex levels of learning. The objective test bank is available from the publisher in booklet form as well as on computer disk. To obtain the complete test bank, contact Mayfield Publishing Company, 1240 Villa Street, Mountain View, California 94041; (415) 960-3222.

General resources for teaching death education include a bibliography of printed materials relevant to death education (Appendix C), a list of death-related organizations

(Appendix D), and addresses of distributors of film and videocassette resources (Appendix E). Appendix F contains an excerpt from a novel by Michael Talbot to be used with a teaching strategy in Chapter 3.

The authors thank Elisabeth Bright, Tammie Meininger, Tom Langenfeld, and Bei Yao Zheng at the University of Florida at Gainesville for applying their expertise in objective test construction to this project. They have completely revised the test bank from the previous edition of the *Instructor's Guide*, thus creating a more reliable and valid instrument for evaluating student learning. Our thanks also to Professor Judith Stillion of Western Carolina University at Cullowhee for advice and assistance with respect to the Questions for Guided Study and Evaluation, and for providing the model for the sample essay examination in Appendix B. We also acknowledge the contribution of Barbara Jade Sironen, who assisted us with the previous edition of the *Instructor's Guide*.

We welcome your comments and suggestions.

Lynne Ann DeSpelder
Albert Lee Strickland
Ojai, California

Patrick Vernon Dean
Elm Island, Wisconsin

Fall 1991

Chapter 1

Attitudes Toward Death: A Climate of Change

OBJECTIVES

1. To evaluate the usefulness of expanding death awareness through death education.
2. To identify historical antecedents of current attitudes toward death.
3. To list and analyze the factors that have contributed to a lessened familiarity with death.
4. To point out how attitudes toward death are expressed through language, humor, the mass media, literature, the visual arts, and music.

CONTENT OVERVIEW

Chapter 1 introduces the study of death and dying by focusing on individual and societal attitudes toward death. The perception that death is taboo, a subject not to be discussed, is contrasted with the goal of learning about dying and death as a means of increasing personal and social choices about these significant human experiences.

The recent interest in formal education concerning death is traced to its foundation in the contributions made by such pioneers in the field as Herman Feifel, Elisabeth Kübler-Ross, Barney Glaser, Anselm Strauss, Robert Fulton, Geoffrey Gorer, Jeanne Quint Benoliel, and others. The burgeoning of professional and scholarly literature about death in recent decades has been accompanied by the proliferation of courses dealing with death.

The interdisciplinary nature of death education is highlighted, as is its conjoining of both cognitive and affective content, the blending of objective facts and subjective concerns. For professionals who encounter dying and death in the course of their work—including nurses, fire fighters, police officers, and emergency medical technicians—death education is an important adjunct to curricula that impart specific job-related skills.

The experiences of death that most people bring to a class on death and dying, as persons living in the 1990s, are contrasted with those of Americans in the last century. Our tendency to avoid discussion of death and dying is not necessarily so much a matter of individual choice as it is a result of social attitudes and shared practices concerning death. The typical funeral practices of the nineteenth century involved extensive participation by members of the dead person's family; today, the care of our dead is turned over to hired professionals and our participation in rituals surrounding the dead is minimal.

The reasons for this change in the manner of dealing with dying and death are examined, with particular attention given to the social and technological factors that have lessened our familiarity with death. Discussed in this context are such factors as increased life expectancy, reduced mortality rates (especially among the young), geographical mobility, the displacement of death from the home to an institutional setting, and life-extending medical technologies.

Building on the awareness that attitudes and practices relative to death are not static but rather are subject to change, the next section of the chapter introduces the wealth of cultural expressions by which we can discern both individual and social attitudes toward death. Examples are given of how euphemistic language may blur the reality of death or diminish its emotional impact, and of how humor is employed to defuse anxiety toward death or provide relief from painful situations. The mass media's role in both reflecting and shaping attitudes toward death is examined, with examples cited from news reports about death as well as entertainment programs featuring death-related themes. Attention is paid to the issue of whether the images of death circulated by the media accurately reflect the reality of death in human experience. Literature, the visual arts, and music are also examined with respect to what they tell us about our own and other people's attitudes toward death.

The chapter concludes by noting that we are in a period when people are rethinking their assumptions about death. In a pluralistic society, there are many options for dealing with death. Education about dying and death is not simply academic or theoretical. It engages not only our intellect, but also our emotions. The experience of a loved one's death or an encounter with our own mortality makes our quest for a more meaningful understanding of death both practical and intimately relevant.

KEY TERMS AND CONCEPTS

causes of death

death education

death notices

Dies irae

epidemiologic transition

euphemisms

gallows humor

geographical mobility

hibakusha

Holocaust literature

iconography of death

life expectancy

life-extending technologies

"mean world syndrome"

mortality rates

mourning memorials

obituaries

pornography of death

teachable moments

thanatology

tomb art

vigilante literature

QUESTIONS FOR GUIDED STUDY AND EVALUATION

Multiple-choice questions relevant to this chapter can be found in the test bank.

1. Trace the history of death education by citing at least five influential books and at least one professional organization.

2. Contrast nineteenth- and twentieth-century death customs.

3. List and describe at least four factors that have contributed to changes in death customs from the nineteenth to the twentieth century.

4. Compare the death rate at the turn of the century with that of today.

5. Trace the changing causes of death from the turn of the century through today, paying particular attention to the effects of the epidemiologic transition.

6. Explain the ways in which language and humor can be used to distance people from the reality of death.

7. Describe the ways in which the media portray death, citing at least one statistic regarding the amount of coverage given to it.

8. Describe how television portrayals of violent death reflect the "mean world syndrome."

9. Explain and illustrate how attitudes toward death are expressed through the arts.

10. Suggest reasons for studying death and dying, using both the discussion in the text and your own experience.

TEACHING STRATEGIES

1. Ask students to peruse the text, paying attention to the photographs. As they think about how their own life histories relate to the images, have them note the following:
   - Which images are the most provocative?
   - What thoughts and feelings are provoked?
   - In which areas of death and dying do they have little or no information?
   - In which areas do they have extensive information?
   - Which areas would they like to have more information about?

   Alternatively, divide the class into pairs. Have each pair discuss the photographs in the text and then select the two images that elicit the most significant response. This is a good early activity that encourages students to begin talking with one another.

2. Obtain a copy of the questionnaire, "You and Death," which was published in *Psychology Today* (August 1970). After students have completed the questionnaire (or your adaptation of it), you can supplement the results by having students code the questions using the following symbols:

   PE = Answers based on personal experience

   S = Answers about which they feel strongly

   A = Answers about which they feel ambiguous

   SB = Answers based on religious or spiritual beliefs

   Through this analysis, students are afforded the opportunity to think deeply about their responses and thereby expand awareness of their personal attitudes and what gives rise to them. This exercise forms a basis for assimilating information as the course progresses and for assessing attitudinal change at its conclusion.

3. Brainstorm euphemisms about death by having students name those with which they are familiar. List them on the board and discuss their usage and meaning, emphasizing that euphemisms reflect attitudes toward death. Point out that an individual's use of language may also indicate experiences regarding the mode of death or a survivor's belief system. For example: "We lost him" compared to "He passed on." Direct students to the listing in the text for additional items.

4. Have students think about fearful experiences. Make a list of these fears on the board. Then have students identify those related to death. Discuss how such fears may prevent them from "getting the most" from life.

5. Instruct students to select artwork or photographs from magazine covers, newspapers, and other similar sources. Have them bring their selections to class and discuss what, specifically, about each image caught their attention or triggered an emotional response. Alternatively, collect all of the students' selections and distribute them randomly. Pair up students and have them discuss the thoughts and feelings provoked by the images.

6. Have each student bring to class the words and music from a popular song related to dying or death. (Make sure they bring copies of the lyrics for each class member.) Play the music and have students discuss their reactions and interpretations.

7. Present a medley of death-related lyrics that range over a wide selection of musical compositions. Ask students:
   - What kinds of topics are dealt with in the compositions?
   - What attitudes and behaviors are expressed in the lyrics?
   - What do you notice about similarities and differences among the various lyrics?
   - Can you detect changes in the themes at different musical periods or times of composition?
   - Are themes dealt with differently depending on the type of musical genre?

8. Divide the class into small groups. Have each group recall two or three popular jokes about death. Then have them write one or two original jokes. Come back together as a class and have each group share one popular and one original joke. Have students evaluate the function of the humor in each joke.

9. Instruct students to use the table of contents of the text as a guide for going through periodicals to cull related *headlines*. Point out that death-related terms are used in a variety of contexts (sports, for example). Direct the subsequent discussion to illustrate the myriad examples of death-related concerns as well as the frequent use of death-related terms in nondeath contexts.

COMMENTS AND CONSIDERATIONS

1. **Identifying and Assessing Attitudes.** When doing the exercise that involves perusing the imagery in the text, students are usually impressed by one or two photographs. Encourage them to discuss the feelings evoked by the photographs, relating those feelings to their personal histories. They probably will find that the strongest feelings result from perceived similarity (that is, a strong identification with another person's characteristics or the situation). This is a useful teaching moment for discussing the effects of perceived similarity.

2. **Gathering Information.** During the term discussions are often based on intimate experiences, and students may be reluctant to divulge personal information to a class of strangers. This hesitancy often results from a lack of awareness about the death experiences of other students. Students are often surprised and comforted to discover essential similarities in their attitudes and behaviors toward death and dying. The sooner they become comfortable with each other, the easier it will be to initiate meaningful class discussions. One way to achieve this is to have students anonymously fill out a three-by-five card with the following information:

- Side 1: What brings you here?
- Side 2: What would you like to take away from this course when it is over?

This strategy provides an opportunity to determine the composition of the class in terms of experience, curiosity, personal or professional needs, and so on. You can open the next class meeting by reading the cards aloud.

RESOURCES: FILMS AND VIDEOCASSETTES

Amazing Grace with Bill Moyers (videocassette; 90 min.; color; 1990; PBS Video) Characterized as a "courier of the spirit," the song *Amazing Grace* has been a source of hope for millions of people worldwide. The story of the song and its heartfelt effect is interwoven with moving performances by Judy Collins, Jessye Norman, and Marion Williams, among others.

Conscious Living/Conscious Dying: The Work of a Lifetime (videocassette; 8 programs totaling 213 min.; color; 1982; Original Face Video) Work with the dying and the bereaved is highlighted in this series of videotapes drawn from talks by Ram Dass and Stephen Levine. Shown are the interactions of participants during two nine-day retreat-workshops sponsored by the Hanuman Foundation Dying Project. Some participants were terminally ill. Some were health care professionals working with the dying. Some were grieving. All were given an opportunity to confront the reality of death—their own and others'—within the context of a spiritual and philosophic understanding of change and loss based on Eastern psychological and religious traditions. The eight programs consist of: (1) Opening to Grief: The Threshold Task, (2) Purification by Fire: The Passage Through Pain, (3) From Tragedy to Grace: Stages and Transitions in the Process of Dying, (4) The Experience of Dying: A Guided Meditation, (5) Awakening to Life Through Truthful Relationship, (6) On Pain, Perfection, and the Work to Relieve Suffering, (7) Finding a Path to an Open Heart, and (8) Wisdom Has No Fear of Death. Programs 1 and 3 have the broadest appeal.

Death: Coping With Loss (16 mm.; 19 min.; color; 1976; Coronet/MTI Film & Video) A film about American attitudes and practices related to dying and death.

The Death of Ivan Ilych (videocassette & 16 mm.; 28 min.; color; 1979; Mass Media Ministries) The film is in two parts. Part 1 dramatizes Tolstoy's short story, albeit condensed, portraying the pain, doubts, and fear accompanying the dying of Ilych. Part 2 consists of interviews with terminally ill individuals as they relate to Ilych's situation.

Eulogy (videocassette & 16 mm.; 25 min.; color; 1986; IFEX Films) As Ben Gracie practices the eulogy he will deliver at the funeral of his brother and law partner, his wife reacts with disgust, knowing that the fine words do not reflect the reality of the dead man's character and his deceitful actions toward others. In private, Ben and Kathryn share their pain from these old wounds. Based on the play by James Richardson, this production shows how survivors can grow in understanding and in their relationships following a death in the family.

Extending the Warranty: Organ Replacement, Progress Against Cancer, and Alzheimer's Disease (videocassette; 60 min.; color; 1987; PBS Video) A title from the series "The Health Century," this video surveys medical advances in organ transplantation, cancer treatment, and Alzheimer's diagnosis. Featured in the program are the inventor of kidney dialysis, Dr. Willem Kolff, and two pioneers in the work with artificial hearts and heart transplantation, Dr. William Pierce and Dr. Norman Shumway.

Little Big Man (16 mm.; about 2-1/2 hours; color; 1970; Swank Motion Pictures) An historical look at the genocide of Native Americans.

The Lottery (videocassette & 16 mm.; 18 min.; color; 1970; Encyclopaedia Britannica Educational Corp) Based on the short story by Shirley Jackson, this film deals with an unnerving death ritual in a New England town.

Terminal (videocassette; 30 min.; black & white; 1970; Foundation of Thanatology) Symbolic presentation of death attitudes as expressed through the performing arts.

What Man Shall Live and Not See Death? (16 mm.; 57 min. in two parts; color; 1971; Brigham Young University, NBC Educational Enterprises) Depicts the various attitudes of a wide range of people (survivors, terminally ill persons, doctors, nurses, social workers, clergy) toward death and dying.

Chapter 2

Perspectives on Death: Cross-Cultural and Historical

OBJECTIVES

1. To become acquainted with the diversity of death-related rituals and beliefs found in various cultures.
2. To assess the correspondences among various cultures relative to death-related rituals and beliefs.
3. To describe the historical changes in death-related beliefs and practices in the Western world.
4. To analyze the impact of various beliefs and practices and to assess their value for survivors.

CONTENT OVERVIEW

Chapter 2 broadens our perspective by examining how people have dealt with death in cultural and historical settings other than our own. The discussion begins with an examination of the functions of traditional mythologies, or beliefs about death. The relationship between beliefs and practices is examined in the context of phenomena that many traditional societies associate with the power of the dead. A society's attitude toward the dead is frequently seen in its naming practices, either avoiding or memorializing the name of the deceased. The explanations offered by traditional societies of the causes of death and of its ultimate origin are discussed with an emphasis on the central themes that still have currency in our struggle to understand death, even though the specifics of the story may differ.

Three cultures are highlighted for more extensive investigation of their death-related beliefs and practices—those of the native peoples of North America, the LoDagaa of Africa, and the peoples of Mexico, whose celebration of the Day of the Dead reflects a blending of indigenous and European traditions. The text encourages us to look for commonalties as well as differences with respect to the way human beings in different cultures relate to death.

Finally, attention is drawn to the death-related beliefs and practices that have existed through the history of Western civilization. Changes over the centuries in the manner of dying are discussed in the context of the dying person's anticipation of death and the scene around the deathbed. The attitude of survivors toward the dead is traced by examining the changing fashion in burial customs, with particular attention to the contrast between anonymous burial in charnel houses and the development of individual graves and memorialization of the dead. Similarly, changing attitudes about death are charted by reviewing the evolution of the Dance of Death.

Our survey of cross-cultural and historical perspectives on death concludes with a discussion of "invisible death," a term that characterizes the way that death and dying have been dealt with during most of the present century by people living in modern, technological societies. It refers to the practice of delegating care of the dying and the dead to professionals and to the emphasis on delaying death by all means available, as well as to the comparative lack of social or cultural supports for placing death and dying within a meaningful context as an intrinsic part of human experience. The chapter closes by citing the words of several commentators, who point out that ultimate fulfillment, the sense of having lived one's life well, may be possible only within a community that acknowledges the significance of death. The examples of other cultures—more or less distant from our own in time or space—may offer us insights and inspiration for creating such a community.

KEY TERMS AND CONCEPTS

All Souls' Day
ancestor worship
ancestral shrine
anticipated death
Black Death
charnel houses
cult of martyrs
danse macabre
death knell
death songs
effigies
El día de los Muertos

fear of the dead
invisible death
journey of the soul
liber vitae
mourning restraints
name avoidance
origin-of-death myths
rites of passage
shaman
speculum mortis
tamed death

QUESTIONS FOR GUIDED STUDY AND EVALUATION

Multiple-choice questions relevant to this chapter can be found in the test bank.

1. Compare four different cultural explanations of how death came to be.

2. Contrast Hopi and Cocopa funeral rituals. Decide which you find more positive and explain why.

3. Explain the meanings of the LoDagaa death ceremonies, including the practices surrounding mourning restraints, the mourning companion, and grave digging. Compare LoDagaa rituals with ours.

4. Analyze the apparent ambivalence of Mexican attitudes toward death as revealed in customs surrounding the Day of the Dead.

5. Develop a brief historical summary based on Ariès' work concerning the ways death has been viewed for the past thousand years or so in the Western world, including at least four distinctive periods.

6. Describe the origin and evolution of the Dance of Death.

7. Contrast the views of death in the seventeenth, eighteenth, and early nineteenth centuries with those of today.

TEACHING STRATEGIES

1. As a class, compare and contrast the cultures discussed. Place the name of each culture as a heading on the board and leave space to record student comments. Have students name the beliefs and practices of each culture, identifying those that either attract or repulse them. List their responses under the appropriate heading for each culture. This activity stimulates discussion about beliefs as they relate to the function of ritual practices for each culture. For example, the opening chapter photograph illustrates a cultural belief manifested in a burial custom: A belief in a return of the body's elements to the "natural world" is actualized in platform burial. Ask students what our own customs of body disposition might suggest in terms of belief systems.

2. Divide the class into small groups. Have each group develop a list of death customs they have participated in or heard about. Come together as a class and have them compare and contrast these customs with those of the cultures described in the text. Have students discuss the functions served by these customs and the beliefs associated with each. Pointing out the importance of contextualizing customs within the wider belief system of a culture makes unfamiliar practices seem less bizarre or exotic.

3. Have students break into small groups. Tell them to compare and contrast the various customs and practices they have read about in the chapter. Then have them design their own "survivor strategy package" based on their discussion.

COMMENTS AND CONSIDERATIONS

1. **Expanding Awareness of Cultural Relativity.** A primary goal of this chapter is to help students recognize the validity of the diverse cultural responses to the basic human experience of death and dying. In this way, they learn how to suspend judgment and recognize the value of these various ritual practices in terms of their benefit to survivors. For example, while name avoidance may seem to be a rather exotic practice, correlations can be drawn between this practice as it exists in other cultures and the practice of not mentioning the name of the deceased to the recently bereaved in our own culture. Note, however, that the beliefs behind these two practices may be different.

2. **Recognizing One's Own Cultural Patterns As Unique.** Students can learn to recognize that their own beliefs and practices are no less bizarre than the beliefs and practices of other peoples. This recognition allows them to evaluate the degree to which their own beliefs and practices benefit them.

RESOURCES: FILMS AND VIDEOCASSETTES

Day of the Dead (16 mm.; 15 min.; color; 1957; Pyramid Film & Video, UCLA Instructional Media Library) Looks at preparations for Mexico's Day of the Dead by highlighting the remembrance of a dead girl.

Dead Birds (videocassette & 16 mm.; 83 min. in three parts; color; 1963; Brigham Young University, Phoenix/BFA Films & Video, Portland State University, UCLA Instructional Media Library) This extraordinary film documents in detail the way that death permeates the lives of the Dani, a Papua New Guinea people. Viewers are privy to the daily lives of the men, women, and children of this tribe and to the way in which beliefs surrounding death, dying, and revenge color their everyday activities, particularly those of the men, for it is only in taking the life of an opposing tribal member that the death of a loved one is avenged. Consequently, the Dani are continually at war. The film depicts this warfare and ultimately the death of a tribal member, a young boy, murdered while caught off guard near his village. We see the ritual preparation of the body, its cremation, and the impassioned grief and mourning of tribal members.

Dreamspeaker: Society Fails a Troubled Youth (videocassette & 16 mm.; 75 min.; color; 1979; Filmakers Library) The film depicts an encounter between an old Nootka shaman, his comrade, and a young Canadian boy whose life has been full of trouble. With the two men, the youth finds acceptance despite his failure and enjoys a measure of understanding not bestowed upon him by his own culture. The film ends in tragedy when the boy returns to his community where he kills himself. The shaman, seeing that his own life is at its end, also chooses to die. His view of death, however, presents the understanding of this human experience as a necessary part of the cycle of nature; the young boy's death is precipitated by his feeling that there is no other way out—that death is his only choice.

Eduardo the Healer (16 mm.; 54 min.; color; 1978; Pennsylvania State University) A film about a Peruvian shaman as he plies his trade.

Emergence (videocassette & 16 mm.; 14 min.; color; 1981; Barr Films) An animated depiction of the Navajo creation myth, revealing the necessity of restoring homeostasis should the cosmological system be upset.

Goodbye Old Man (videocassette & 16 mm.; 70 min.; color; 1979; UCB Extension Media Center) A look at the beliefs, values, and practices of an Australian aboriginal tribe, the Tiwi, as they prepare for and carry out the funeral of one of their members. The film is especially important for grounding the mortuary practices of the Tiwi in their belief system by relating these practices to their myth of the origin of death.

How Death Came to Earth (16 mm.; 14 min.; color; 1971; CRM Films) An East Indian story that recounts the events leading to the condition of death for humankind.

I Heard the Owl Call My Name (16 mm.; 78 min.; color; 1974; Learning Corporation of America) A look at the contrasting belief systems of a dying Anglican priest and native British Columbians. Sent by his superiors to a remote village, the young priest deepens his philosophical understanding of life in the face of death by looking at the beliefs and values of these people.

Joseph Campbell and the Power of Myth (videocassette; 60 min. each segment; color; 1988; PBS Video) In this highly acclaimed six-part series hosted by Bill Moyers, Joseph Campbell introduces the viewer to the riches of myth and its application to our own lives. Campbell touches upon such topics as the concept of the transcendent and the spiritual potentialities of human life, the importance of accepting death, the value of ritual, the role of sacrifice, the awakening of compassion, and the love that is created out of our suffering and care for others. Individual titles include: The Hero's Adventure, The Message of the Myth, The First Storytellers, Sacrifice and Bliss, Love and the Goddess, and Masks of Eternity.

Mourning for Mangatopi (videocassette & 16 mm.; 56 min.; color; 1977; UCB Extension Media Center) A detailed account of the funerary rituals surrounding the death by murder of Mangatopi, a tribal leader of the Tiwi peoples of Melville Island, Australia. Due to his status, the funeral is well attended and elaborate.

The Parting (16 mm.; 16 min.; color; 1973; Wombat Productions) A film depicting Yugoslavian death rituals.

The Spirit Possession of Alejandro Manani (videocassette & 16 mm.; 30 min.; color; 1974; Filmakers Library) With English subtitles, this film documents the final stage of life of an aged Aymara Indian. His change of status has left him feeling rejected and lonely. Believing himself possessed by evil spirits, he ultimately chooses suicide.

The Three Worlds of Bali (videocassette; 60 min.; color; 1980; PBS Video) Explores the pageantry of daily life on the Indonesian island of Bali, where offerings of art, poetry, and song are designed to maintain a balance between the forces of growth and the forces of dissolution.

Chapter 3

Socialization: How We Learn About Death as Children

OBJECTIVES

1. To identify the components of a mature concept of death.
2. To describe the psychosexual, psychosocial, and cognitive models of development and to demonstrate their value in comprehending a child's understanding of death.
3. To identify the factors that influence a child's understanding of and attitude toward death.
4. To design responses to children's questions about death at different stages of development.

CONTENT OVERVIEW

Chapter 3 deals with the way that individuals in a given society learn about death as children; that is, it focuses on the process of socialization as it relates to the understanding of death. (Chapter 8, by contrast, deals with losses experienced during childhood.) This process of learning about death is one of continuous adjustment and refinement, as new experiences cause children to reexamine their values and responses. Eventually, children arrive at what is known as a mature concept of death—an understanding of death shared by the adults in a particular culture. Within modern societies, a mature concept of death includes five components:

1. Death involves the *cessation* of all physiological functioning, or signs of life.
2. Death is biologically *inevitable*.
3. Death is *irreversible*; organisms are unable to return to biologic life after death.
4. Death involves *causality*; there are biological reasons for the occurrence of death.
5. Death is *universal*; it eventually comes to every living organism.

A child's understanding of death is influenced by his or her level of psychosocial and cognitive development, as well as by attitudes and experiences encountered in the environment. The role of developmental factors is explored by focusing particularly on the models of child development devised by Erik Erikson (psychosocial development) and Jean Piaget (cognitive transformation). These models are applied to children's understanding of death at various periods of development, beginning with infancy and toddlerhood, through the early and middle years of childhood, to adolescence—by which time children have generally acquired a mature concept of death. There is evidence that the essential elements of a mature concept of death may be recognized by much younger children, although more abstract or symbolic thoughts about death usually take longer to develop.

Parental messages, general cultural influences, and particular life experiences also play an important role as environmental influences on a child's understanding of death and attitude toward it. Sometimes these influences are communicated to children subtly or unconsciously, as with the notion of replaceability when, without acknowledging the grief resulting from the loss, the suggestion is made that a dead pet can be replaced. Children's literature and television programs also communicate cultural expressions and attitudes relevant to the child's attempt to understand death. Deaths that are widely reported by the media—such as the death of President John F. Kennedy and the deaths of the *Challenger* astronauts—also set into motion processes that affect how children learn about death. Finally, the significant experiences in a child's life can have great impact on his or her understanding of death. The death of a close family member, for example, may cause a child to come to an understanding of death that generally would be associated with a later period of development.

The concluding section of the chapter presents guidelines for talking with children about death. Even in the absence of significant death-related experiences, children are naturally curious and inquisitive about death. Adults who are prepared to discuss the subject openly and honestly, and in a way appropriate to the child's level of understanding, can play a crucial supportive role in the child's efforts to come to terms with the reality of death and the emotions engendered by loss.

KEY TERMS AND CONCEPTS

autonomy vs. shame
cognitive transformations
concrete operational
fear of death
formal operational
identity vs. role confusion
industry vs. inferiority
initiative vs. guilt
magical thinking
mature concept of death
metaphorical explanation

parental messages
preoperational
protothanatic
psychoanalytic theory
psychosexual model
psychosocial development
replaceability
reversibility
sensorimotor
trust vs. mistrust

QUESTIONS FOR GUIDED STUDY AND EVALUATION

Multiple-choice questions relevant to this chapter can be found in the test bank.

1. Name the three components of a mature understanding of death.

2. Describe the Freudian view of death anxiety in children, with particular attention to the separation-individuation processes.

3. Explain Erikson's theory of psychosocial development in terms of the kinds of issues children may pay particular attention to at different times in their lives.

4. Identify Piaget's stages of cognitive development and explain how each relates to particular understandings of death.

5. Evaluate death education for children and describe how you would suggest that children be introduced to the topic of death.

6. List three major sources of attitudes toward death and give examples of each.

7. Distinguish between the "healthy-minded" and "morbidly minded" arguments regarding the presence of a fear of death in human beings.

8. Imagine that a fifth-grade teacher has called on you as someone knowledgeable on the topic of death and dying. There is a child in class whose mother is dying. The children know about it and are expressing feelings of anxiety. You are invited to come and talk to them about death and dying. Would you go? Why or why not? If you went, what would you say? If you did not go, what advice might you give to the teacher? Explain your answer in detail.

TEACHING STRATEGIES

1. Divide the class into groups. Each group will consider themselves as either Freudian, Eriksonian, or Piagetian experts and will spend from fifteen to twenty minutes discussing the most important elements of their particular school of thought as applied to children's understanding of death. Bring the class together and have each group explain, in their own words, how their model relates to comprehending death.

2. Have students pair off. Ask them to compare their earliest childhood death memories. Have them include in the discussion the kinds of children's games they played relative to death and dying.

3. Just as attitudes about death and dying are rooted in childhood, so are attitudes toward the aging process and the aged. Have students interview a number of children asking:

   • Who is the oldest person you know?

   • What does he or she most like to do?

   Ask each child to draw a picture of the oldest person he or she knows and to describe the picture. In class, have students present the information gathered through these interviews and drawings. Have them note similarities and differences between the two methods of eliciting information. [Adapted from *Understanding Death and Dying: An Interdisciplinary Approach*, 3d ed., by Sandra G. Wilcox and Marilyn Sutton (Palo Alto, Calif.: Mayfield, 1985), p. 317. Reprinted by permission.]

4. Invite to class three children who have experienced the death of a pet. Interview them and allow their discussion to range freely. Ask questions only when necessary. After the children leave, have students analyze each child's response to the loss in terms of his or her developmental understanding of death. [Adapted from *Understanding Death and Dying: An Interdisciplinary Approach*, 3d ed., by Sandra G. Wilcox and Marilyn Sutton (Palo Alto, Calif.: Mayfield, 1985), p. 317. Reprinted by permission.]

5. You can use selections from popular literature containing descriptions of a child's response to death to help students synthesize and apply their learning. For each selection, the appropriate developmental responses can be evaluated. As an example, duplicate and distribute the excerpt from Michael Talbot's *The Bog* (Appendix F), and then have students respond to the following questions:

   - Which euphemism does the father use when describing what happened to Ben? (Underline each appearance in the excerpt.)
   - Review Table 1-2 in Chapter 1 of *The Last Dance*. Pick another euphemism and substitute it for the one in the story excerpt. How does the excerpt read now?
   - Using Piaget's model of cognitive development (discussed in Chapter 3 of *The Last Dance*), identify the developmental phase that is presumed in the father's explanation.
   - What age range is associated with this developmental phase?
   - What are the characteristics of this phase?
   - Summarize the parental message that is communicated about death in this story.
   - Based on the information given in your text and in class, evaluate the parental communication. Use specific examples to identify the elements you find appropriate as well as the elements you believe to be inadequate.
   - Given that the child in this story is the survivor of a high-grief death, identify at least five possible benefits to him resulting from this conversation.
   - Do you find that instances of characters talking with children about death are rare in contemporary paperback novels?
   - What editorial advice would you give the author if you knew that the child in this story was five years old?

COMMENTS AND CONSIDERATIONS

1. **Handling Complex Developmental Models in One Class Period.** Be sure that students grasp the points of each model as they relate to a child's developmental understanding of death and dying—for instance, separation-individuation and magical thinking in the psychosexual model. Teaching strategy 1 helps provide the needed focus.

2. **Personalizing Students' Death Experiences.** Talking about early childhood memories of death and dying is a useful exercise. It allows students to apply the developmental theories to their own lives.

RESOURCES: FILMS AND VIDEOCASSETTES

Annie and The Old One (16 mm.; 16 min.; color; 1976; Phoenix/BFA Films & Video) A superb story of a young Navajo girl's confrontation with the inevitability of death. As her grandmother is dying, Annie learns about her culture's deepest values, attitudes, and beliefs with respect to death. Most of all, she learns the value of loving and letting go.

Children's Conceptions of Death (videocassette; 30 min.; color; 1986; Health Sciences Consortium) Presents the general process a child goes through in arriving at a mature concept of death by focusing on three "stages": perceiving the causes of death, recognizing death as final, and acknowledging that it is inevitable. Notes that children may not follow a strict age-stage correlation and that a child may regress to a previous stage of understanding during times of stress and anxiety.

The Day Grandpa Died (videocassette; 12 min.; color; 1978; Phoenix/BFA Films & Video) This vignette of a boy's first experience with the death of a loved one can be used to create an opportunity for adults and children to discuss death together. We watch David's struggle with the reality of death, from denial of the fact to acceptance of death as part of life.

The Dead Bird (16 mm.; 13 min.; color; 1971; AIMS Media) Children's attitudes toward death are depicted in this short animation of Margaret Wise Brown's story.

Death: How Can You Live with It? (16 mm.; 19 min.; color; 1977; Disney Educational Productions) An excerpt from the Disney film *Napoleon and Samantha* depicting a young boy's reaction to his grandfather's dying.

Death and Dying: A Teenage Class (16 mm.; 10 min.; color; 1980; CRM Films) Dan Leviton, a leading death educator, provides commentary as high school students learn about death and dying through group discussions and a field trip to a funeral home.

Emily: The Story of a Mouse (16 mm.; 5 min.; color; 1975; Benchmark Films) An animated film of the life and death of a field mouse, highlighting her relationship to her offspring.

Everybody Rides the Carousel (videocassette & 16 mm.; 72 min. in three parts; color; 1976; Pyramid Film & Video, UCLA Instructional Media Library) This animated film consists of three 24-minute parts presenting Erik Erikson's theory of personality development. Part 1 deals with infancy, toddlerhood, and early childhood; part 2 with school age, adolescence, and young adulthood; and part 3 with adulthood and old age.

The Garden Party (16 mm.; 24 min.; color; 1974; AIMS Media, Portland State University) Based on the novel by Kathryn Mansfield, this film contrasts upper- and lower-class attitudes toward death, dying, and funerals, looking specifically at the death experience of a young girl.

Mr. Rogers' Neighborhood: Death of a Goldfish (videocassette & 16 mm.; 28 min.; color; 1970; Family Communications) The death of a goldfish provides an opportunity to present young children with a model for dealing with loss and sadness. This classic episode of the children's television program is especially appropriate for preschoolers.

My Turtle Died Today (videocassette; 8 min.; color; 1968; Phoenix/BFA Films & Video) In this first-person story for young children, a boy recalls the death of a pet. His father, his teacher, and the pet store owner are unable to help his sick turtle, and it dies. Creates an opportunity to discuss with children the inevitability of death and the continuity of life.

Nine-Year-Olds Talk About Death (videocassette & 16 mm.; 15 min.; black & white; 1977; International Film Bureau) Fourth-grade children are interviewed by their teacher regarding their feelings about death. An interesting and informative discussion by the children, which reveals developmental awareness and socialization patterns, even though the teacher's questioning style is weak.

Talking about Death with Children (videocassette; 13 min.; color; 1979; Batesville Management Services) For elementary school-age children. This film is based on the book by Earl Grollman and covers such issues as how to tell children about death, what death is, and what to expect at funerals.

Talking with Young Children about Death (videocassette & 16 mm.; 28 min.; color; 1978; Family Communications) Examines the lives of three aged Black Alabamians who, despite various difficulties, have a positive attitude toward life.

To Be Aware of Death (16 mm.; 13 min.; color; 1974; University of Minnesota) A multimedia presentation of the attitudes and understandings of death as discussed by young people.

Chapter 4

Health Care Systems: Patients, Staff, and Institutions

OBJECTIVES

1. To list the three components of a health care system and to explain how their interrelationship influences the effectiveness of patient care.
2. To describe the characteristics of an optimal patient–caregiver relationship.
3. To summarize the factors influencing the onset of stress among health professionals who care for dying patients and to point out ways of alleviating such stress.
4. To describe and assess the public health response to AIDS.
5. To identify the various types of health care for terminally ill patients and to differentiate between their functions and purposes.
6. To explain the factors influencing the social role of the dying patient and to create an ideal model.

CONTENT OVERVIEW

Chapter 4 examines the American health care system as it relates to care of persons with life-threatening and terminal illnesses. Following an introduction to the history of modern hospital care, current issues concerning health care financing are discussed; these focus particularly on methods of prospective payment, the high cost of innovative medical technologies, and pressures to ration scarce resources. The issues raise questions about the limits of medical progress and how to achieve a balance between the extension of life and the quality of life.

Modern health care embodies a tripartite relationship among patient, institution, and staff. Each of these entities contributes to the overall shape and quality of care. Excessive bureaucratization and making death taboo can cause care of the dying to be impersonal, undermining the subjecthood of the patient. In such cases, biological death may be preceded by social death. Alternatives to such depersonalization and abstraction require that we break the illusion of immortality and recognize that all our lives have an end. Compassionate care also requires sensitivity to issues of communication between caregivers and patients. Good communication between caregiver and patient helps to motivate the patient's own healing system, thereby creating the potential for a positive outcome regardless of the ultimate prognosis.

Caregivers who work in environments where death occurs frequently are subject to high levels of stress. Decisions involving life or death may have to be made under extreme time pressures. Caregiving professionals may face the task of delivering bad news to relatives and handling their reactions. Medical and nursing professionals need to operate within a supportive environment that allows death to be discussed openly among those involved in patients' care. They must also be confident that the care they provide is appropriate, beneficial, and in patients' best interests.

Emergency care for life-threatening injury or other trauma is another area that involves significant issues related to the study of death and dying. Accidental injury is the leading cause of death for persons under age 35. Many of the advances in emergency medicine have come about by focusing on the critical "golden hour" following injury. The use of the helicopter air ambulance and the triage system for evacuating casualties have increased the chances of surviving many types of injury, as has development of specialized trauma centers, where needed surgery and other medical interventions can be provided expeditiously. More lives could be saved, however, if funding were available to provide such emergency services on a broader scale.

Questions about the allocation of economic, medical, and social resources have also marked the history of AIDS, a disease that hampers the body's natural defenses against infection and for which there is currently no cure. The AIDS epidemic has put great pressure on medical resources and institutions, and the disease has caused more than 85,000 deaths. Coping with the disease remains a major challenge to the health care system and to society as a whole, as well as a personal challenge to the individuals directly affected.

Although hospitals remain the primary setting for care of terminally ill patients, other options for such care have become increasingly available. Hospice care, for example, is oriented specifically toward the needs of the dying patient and his or her family. Home care is also being recognized as an appropriate alternative for some patients and their families. Even within the institutional setting of the conventional hospital, there is a new emphasis on providing palliative care for dying patients—that is, care intended to alleviate pain and other symptoms as opposed to measures intended to extend life. Many terminally ill patients use some combination of all these forms of care, depending on the stage of illness and their particular situation. Organized support groups that focus on specific interests and needs of patients have also become an important part of the overall health care system used by terminally ill patients.

Until about the middle of the twentieth century, a social role for the dying person was more or less fixed by custom and circumstance. Since then, rapid and pervasive social and technological changes have largely eliminated the traditional role of the dying, but have offered few guidelines for replacing it. As people become more willing to face the issues of dying and death squarely, and as hospice and other forms of palliative care become more widely available, a social role for the dying that is appropriate for our own time is being created. Such a role does not require the patient to sustain false hope or to maintain an appearance of expecting to live forever. As the prospect of death nears, there is cooperation among caregivers, family members, and the patient to nurture a sense of empowerment and self-determination. Farewells are communicated, and attention is given to the special physical, psychological, and spiritual needs that arise at the end of life.

KEY TERMS AND CONCEPTS

acute care
AIDS (acquired immune deficiency syndrome)
bureaucratization of death
chronic care
classic and ideal caring situations
covenantal relationship
DOA (dead on arrival)
DRGs (diagnosis-related groups)
emergency/trauma care
grief room
health care rationing
HIV (human immunodeficiency virus)
home care
hospice care

hospital
hospitium
intermediate care
medical eschatology
medical paternalism
nursing home
palliative care
skilled nursing care
social death
support groups
terminal care
triage
will to live

QUESTIONS FOR GUIDED STUDY AND EVALUATION

Multiple-choice questions relevant to this chapter can be found in the test bank.

1. Discuss the extent and cost of health care, citing at least three statistics.
2. Analyze the impact of DRGs and related forms of prospective payment on the American health care system, especially on care of the dying.
3. Describe the usual treatment of the dying and the bereaved in a hospital or other health care institution. Compare this description to the ideal treatment that could be instituted.

4. Describe the five strategies identified by Robert Kastenbaum that staff members may use when responding to a patient's desire to discuss death.

5. Evaluate the importance of the patient–caregiver relationship, including the impact of medical paternalism.

6. State at least three reasons why caregivers may experience stress in caring for the dying. Discuss how caregivers can decrease this stress.

7. Summarize the qualities of care suggested by Jeanne Quint Benoliel and add as many others as you can that would enhance the quality of care for a dying person.

8. Summarize the public health response to AIDS and suggest ways that it could be improved.

9. Contrast the roles, types of care, and philosophical differences between hospice and hospital care.

10. Describe at least three different models of hospice care.

11. Evaluate the dying person's bill of rights. Do you agree with each item? Why or why not? Is it a realistic and practical document? Can you suggest changes or additions?

12. Describe a support group for the dying.

13. Differentiate the social role of dying patients from that of patients who anticipate recovery.

TEACHING STRATEGIES

1. Elicit students' experiences of different health care settings from three perspectives: family member, patient, and health care professional. For example, from the perspective of a family member, discuss students' experiences with acute care facilities, nursing homes, and hospices. What were the written and unwritten rules for behavior in each setting? List them on the board. Compare and contrast these rules. Ask for a show of hands indicating how students would rate each of the three health care settings in meeting the needs of the dying. Make sure that views from all three perspectives are included in the discussion. (As an alternative for gathering information, divide the class into three groups. Assign one group to interview family members, another group to interview patients, and the third group to interview health care professionals. Have students bring the results of their interviews to class and proceed as described above.)

2. Instruct students to watch three different medical programs on television, paying attention to how terminally ill patients, their doctors, nurses, other caregivers, family, and friends are portrayed. Have them answer the following questions and bring their responses to class:

    • What was the patient's age, sex, and socioeconomic level?

- Describe his or her personality.
- How was he or she treated by family members and medical personnel?
- Was the death presented in a realistic context?
- What was the cause of death?
- In what ways was the death similar or different from your own experiences with death?
- Was the death realistic?
- What life values were expressed in the death?
- What program suggestions would you make to the writers?

Have students discuss their findings with the class. [Adapted from *Thanatopics: A Manual of Structured Learning Experiences for Death Education,* by J. Eugene Knott, Mary C. Ribar, Betty M. Duson, and Marc R. King (Kingston, R.I.: SLE Publications, 1982), pp. 30–31. Reprinted by permission.]

COMMENTS AND CONSIDERATIONS

The Quality of Care. It is important for students to recognize that there is nothing inherently bad or good about any particular health care system. What makes a setting good or bad are the values, beliefs, and practices of the people involved. Consequently, through education any health care system can become more responsive to the needs of dying patients.

RESOURCES: FILMS AND VIDEOCASSETTES

A Hand to Hold (videocassette; 23 min.; color; 1991; Filmakers Library) A look at hospice and its goal of optimizing quality of life before death through pain management, companionship, and help with daily chores. A personal, in-depth look at hospice and loving care.

A Nursing Support Group: Dealing with Death and Dying (videocassette; 31 min.; color; 1984; American Journal of Nursing Co) An oncological nursing group offers peer support.

AIDS (videocassette; 29 min.; color; 1988; PBS Video) From the series "Life Matters," this program focuses particularly on the social stigma of AIDS and on the efforts of caregivers to help patients live with dignity.

AIDS Babies (videocassette; 58 min.; color; 1990; The Cinema Guild) This documentary examines the plight, care, and hope of babies born with AIDS. Includes interviews with Mother Hale, founder of Hale House in New York City, and Dr. Elisabeth Kübler-Ross.

AIDS in the Barrio: Eso No Me Pasa a Mi (videocassette; 28 min.; color; 1990; The Cinema Guild) Examines the impact of AIDS within Mexican-American communities where the disease is often considered a taboo subject and where education and social support systems have been slow to materialize.

The AIDS Movie (videocassette & 16 mm.; 26 min.; color; 1986; New Day Films) For students from early adolescence to college age, this film focuses on AIDS through discussions with three people who have the disease.

The AIDS Quarterly (videocassette; 60 min. per segment; color; 1990; PBS Video) This series of news updates and documentary programs focuses on a variety of issues surrounding AIDS, including its impact on society. Individual programs in the series focus on the federal government's response (AIDS 101), research into an effective treatment and efforts to stop the spread of the disease (AIDS 102), the impact of AIDS on women and minorities (AIDS 103), conventional and underground testing of potential drug treatments (AIDS 104), and the social-political issues that have arisen in small towns as they cope with the AIDS epidemic (AIDS 201). In addition to coverage of a primary topic, most segments include brief reports of the disease's impact on individuals and families.

AIDS Ward (videocassette; 56 min.; color; 1988; Films for the Humanities & Sciences) An examination of the burdensome cost of AIDS to the health care system. Wards are filled with incurably ill patients who require many times the care of other hospital admissions. Caregivers are exhausted. Funding for out-of-hospital services is seriously deficient. Patients, medical staff, and experts in a range of pertinent fields talk about the problem.

As Long as There Is Life (videocassette & 16 mm.; 40 min.; color; 1980; Hospice Institute) Portrays a young family from just before the death of the mother to follow-up bereavement care. Shows hospice care both within the home and the hospital.

Bailey House: To Live as Long as You Can (videocassette; 55 min.; color; 1990; Filmakers Library) An intimate portrait of the people who live at Bailey House, a 44-room residence in New York City for homeless people with AIDS. Bailey House was created out of a former gay luxury hotel. The filmmaker spent several months working as a volunteer, and his camera records the daily lives, courage, conflict, and kindness found in the setting, as well as the deaths of several residents. A powerful film about living with terminal illness.

Born in Africa (videocassette; 60 min.; color; 1990; PBS Video) The remarkable story of Philly Bongoley Lutaaya who left his country of Uganda in 1984 as a political refugee. When he returned in 1988 as a singer and musician, his song, "Born in Africa," became an anthem for his countrymen and he was embraced as a national hero. One year later, Lutaaya shocked his fans when he announced that he was dying of AIDS, the first prominent African to publicly disclose that he had the disease, contracted through sexual contact with a woman. This video chronicles Lutaaya's last months as he traveled across Uganda in a crusade to help stop the spread of AIDS, even as his body was ravaged by the disease. Viewers learn that about 90 percent of Africans with AIDS contract the virus through heterosexual sex, blood transfusions, or transmission from mother to child in the womb.

The Broken Cord with Louise Erdrich and Michael Dorris (videocassette; 30 min.; color; 1990; PBS Video) Authors Louise Erdrich and Michael Dorris are husband and wife, and both are half Indian. In this program, they talk about the devastating effects of fetal alcohol syndrome on their adopted son and on the Native American community. Alcohol abuse, they note, is cited as the number one health hazard of Indians, and the prevalence of fetal alcohol syndrome among Native Americans is placing a whole generation at risk of impairment.

Cancer Care (videocassette; 60 min.; color; 1980; Boulder County Hospice) In a training film for hospice workers, an oncologist discusses cancer and its treatment, including alternative care.

Care of the Caregiver: Coping with Perinatal Death (videocassette; 15 min.; color; 1990; Altschul Group) Although the setting concerns perinatal death, the principles discussed in this program apply to all caregivers. Examines the causes of stress among caregivers and suggests methods of coping with it. Applies the principles of grief intervention to the needs of caregivers.

Caring for the Dying Patient (videocassette; 28 min.; color; 1985; Health Sciences Consortium) A round table discussion between two nurse oncologists, a medical oncologist, a medical social worker, and a patient about the importance of the nurse's role in the psychosocial care of dying patients. Emphasizes the need for nurses to be aware of their own feelings about death and to avoid undermining the beliefs about death held by patients. Includes a discussion of levels of acceptance and problems that may impede a patient's ability to deal with his or her situation.

Caring for Tomorrow's Children (videocassette; 60 min.; color; 1989; PBS Video) Focusing on care for infants and young children, this award-winning program explores infant mortality, changes in the Medicaid program, and increasing health insurance costs as they affect the young. The history of the government's interest in child health care is chronicled, and examples of present maternal and child health programs are shown.

Chuck Solomon: Coming of Age (videocassette & 16 mm.; 57 min.; color; 1987; The Cinema Guild) An intimate portrait of one man, his community, and their courage despite the reality of AIDS. Solomon, a co-founder of the Gay Men's Theater Collective and a mainstay of the San Francisco theatrical community, was diagnosed with AIDS in 1985. His friends came together to celebrate his life in an enormous, flamboyant fortieth birthday party, attended by over 350 friends and family members. Includes interviews with Chuck's friends and colleagues, as well as an extensive interview with Chuck himself about his life and his experience in facing AIDS.

Classroom AIDS (videocassette; 27 min.; color; 1989; Carle Medical Communications) Focuses on the issues surrounding an HIV-positive child in a public school setting.

Communication and Counseling Skills for Hospice Care (videocassette; 13 min.; color; 1980; Southern Illinois University School of Medicine) A training film for hospice nurses that addresses concerns such as verbal and nonverbal communication, awareness of feelings, attitudes toward death and dying, and patient anxiety.

Coping with AIDS (videocassette; 60 min.; color; 1990; UCB Extension Media Center) This British-produced training program is designed to raise awareness about HIV- and AIDS-infected persons. Social service agencies and health care providers are the target audience.

Death and Dying: The Physician's Perspective (videocassette; 29 min.; color; 1982; Fanlight Productions) A candid look at how nine physicians in varying specialties handle death and dying from both a personal and professional perspective. Interviews reveal these doctors as human beings and not simply medical automatons. An excellent insider's view of a physician's perspective.

Death and the Family (16 mm.; 15 min.; color; Professional Research) This film, for professionals working in the field of death and dying, looks at various family systems and the impact of death on them. Dramatizes actual family experiences, showing how family roles are changed and reorganized.

The Detour (videocassette & 16 mm.; 13 min.; color; 1977; Phoenix/BFA Films & Video) A rather tongue-in-cheek look at hospital care and the institutional setting through the eyes of an elderly woman who, although mute, tries to make her needs and desires known to an insensitive staff.

Doctors Are People, Too (videocassette; 30 min.; color; 1987; Coronet/MTI Film & Video) This program profiles doctors under stress, including Dr. James H. "Red" Duke, professor of surgery at the University of Texas Medical Center at Houston. The camera follows Duke through a typical day as trauma surgeon at Houston's Hermann Hospital while he discusses how long workdays, malpractice suits, patient expectations, and family pressures contribute to physician burnout.

Exploring the Heart of Healing in AIDS (videocassette; 2 hours; color; 1986; Daniel Barnes) This collaborative effort between Ram Dass and Stephen Levine addresses many aspects of the dying process.

Family Centered Care (videocassette; 60 min.; color; 1980; Boulder County Hospice) A training film for hospice workers that looks at family dynamics and the role of family members in hospice care.

Family Therapy Techniques for Nurses, Parts I and II (videocassette; 18 min. & 12 min., respectively; color; 1980; Southern Illinois University School of Medicine) Through role-playing techniques, this film educates nurses about care for the terminally ill and their families.

Grief and Bereavement, Parts I and II (videocassette; 75 min.; color; 1980; Boulder County Hospice) A training film for hospice workers that looks at bereavement support for survivors.

Health Care on the Critical List: Containing Medical Costs (videocassette; 55 min.; color; 1985; Filmakers Library) Patients, doctors, hospital administrators, and health policy experts share their perspectives on the crisis in health care financing. Examines the role of HMOs, DRGs, and similar programs of cost containment, and looks at their impact on the quality of health care.

The Heart of the New Age Hospice (videocassette; 28 min.; color; 1989; Carle Medical Communications) Through candid interviews with patients, families, and staff members, this video examines the full spectrum of hospice services.

Hospice (16 mm.; 38 min.; color; 1976; Michigan Media) Looks at St. Christopher's Hospice in England.

Hospice: Introduction, Parts I and II (videocassette; 60 min.; color; 1980; Boulder County Hospice) Part 1, *History and Philosophy of Hospice,* looks at the history and philosophical foundations of hospice care. Part 2, *Hospice Care in the Context of Human Needs,* looks at the needs of dying patients through Abraham Maslow's model.

Hospice: Medical Care for the Dying (videocassette; 17 min.; color; 1986; Health Sciences Consortium) Explores the concept of hospice care and physicians' responsibilities relative to home care, pain control, and the team approach. Includes discussion of the issues of terminal care by hospice program directors, a hospice patient, and a patient's wife.

Hospice Encounters: Mental Health Training Film (videocassette; 17 min.; color; 1981; Lawren Productions) A training film for hospice workers that focuses on the development of counseling skills.

Hospital (videocassette; 84 min.; black & white; 1970; Zipporah Films) Shows the daily activities of a large urban hospital, with the emphasis on the emergency ward and outpatient clinics. Illustrates the way that medical expertise, availability of resources, institutional considerations, and the nature of communication among staff and patients affect the delivery of appropriate health care. This documentary by Frederick Weisman won two Emmy awards (Best News Documentary and Best Director).

I Want To Die At Home (videocassette; 46 min.; color; 1990; Filmakers Library) An incredible journey with the family and friends of a young woman dying at home of cancer. A story of love and compassion.

If I Should Die . . . (videocassette; 47 min.; color; 1986; Daniel Arthur Simon Productions) The inspiring story of Sandy Simon who, at age 47, was diagnosed with chronic myelogenous leukemia. She became involved with the hospice movement and helped to establish the Hospice of Los Angeles and the Hospice Program at Cedars Sinai Medical Center. This film, by Sandy's son, is both a declaration of support for hospice practices and a testimony to the courage of one human being in her encounter with death. This award-winning film provides an intimate and loving glimpse into the last months of Sandy's life, honestly showing the tensions and conflicts experienced within the family setting. Includes interviews with other terminally ill patients, their families, hospice staff, and volunteers.

Into Thy Hands (videocassette; 30 min.; color; 1977; Great Plains National Instructional Television Library) Presents an alternative health care system at Burnswood Institutional Fellowship in England, where healing is of a spiritual nature, with patient-intensive care. The laying on of hands is one example of treatment.

Issues in Dying and Death (videocassette & 16 mm.; 15 min.; color; Sandoz Pharmaceuticals) A film directed toward physicians and others who work with terminally ill patients.

Jory Graham Talks About Cancer (videocassette; 9 min.; color; 1981; Southern Illinois University School of Medicine) Jory Graham, who has had two mastectomies, discusses her experience as a cancer patient and the importance of a good patient–doctor relationship.

The Last Days of Living (videocassette & 16 mm.; 58 min.; color; 1980; American Journal of Nursing Co., National Film Board of Canada) The Palliative Care Unit of the Royal Victoria Hospital in Montreal is the focus of this film, which portrays terminally ill patients as they receive the care they wish in their last days. The types of care include being on a ward for the terminally ill, home care, bereavement counseling, volunteer support, and outpatient treatment. Each scenario is illustrated by glimpses into the lives of patients, reflecting both seriousness and humor.

Living with AIDS (videocassette & 16 mm.; 24 min.; color; 1987; Carle Medical Communications) Focusing on the psychosocial care of AIDS patients, this documentary chronicles the last weeks in the life of Todd Coleman. Interviews with Todd, his lover, and his caregivers point up the pain of those who care but cannot stop the progress of the disease. Emphasizes the value of community support and nonjudgmental caring.

Mending Hearts (videocassette; 59 min.; color; 1990; Carle Medical Communications) Documentary of a two-year period in the lives of four individuals diagnosed as HIV-positive. Included are interviews with friends and health professionals.

Near Death (videocassette; 5-3/4 hours; black & white; 1989; Zipporah Films) Focusing on the Medical Intensive Care Unit at Boston's Beth Israel Hospital, this film provides a comprehensive look at how people face death. It presents the complex interrelationships among patients, families, doctors, nurses, hospital staff, and religious advisors. In particular, it shows these individuals confronting the personal, ethical, medical, psychological, religious, and legal issues involved in making decisions about life-sustaining treatment for dying patients. A documentary by acclaimed filmmaker Frederick Wiseman.

Other Faces of AIDS: An Indiscriminate Disease (videocassette; 60 min.; color; 1989; PBS Video) A response to the notion that AIDS is a "homosexual disease," with special emphasis on the effect of the disease among minorities. Features interviews with former Surgeon General C. Everett Koop, Reverend Jesse Jackson, and other political, medical, and educational leaders.

Overcoming Irrational Fear of AIDS: A Coping Strategy for Health Care Providers (videocassette; 22 min.; color; 1987; Carle Medical Communications) Explores the issue of anxiety on the part of health care providers when dealing with AIDS patients and offers a training model for overcoming counterproductive thinking that can affect work performance as well as personal lives.

Priory: The Only Home I've Got (videocassette; 29 min.; color; 1980; Phoenix/BFA Films & Video) The Priory is a public extended-care hospital in Victoria, British Columbia, where the treatment includes some innovative approaches designed to stimulate interest in living and a sense of self-worth when a person needs constant care.

Psychosocial Care: The Artistry of Medicine (videocassette; 22 min.; color; 1985; Southern Illinois University School of Medicine) The importance of psychosocial care for patients is exemplified through clinical scenes and interviews. Norman Cousins is among the commentators.

Psychosocial Interventions in AIDS (videocassette; 22 min.; color; 1987; Carle Medical Communications) Explores counseling issues around AIDS for both clients and caregivers. Particular attention is given to the stages in the course of the disease that are likely to present special challenges with respect to psychological distress, including suspected high-risk contact, HIV antibody testing, development of symptoms, confirmed diagnosis, recurrence of symptoms, and imminent death.

Remember My Name (videocassette; 52 min.; color; 1989; Films for the Humanities & Sciences) The story of the AIDS Quilt—and, by extension, the story of the AIDS epidemic—is told by focusing on the lives and deaths of eleven individuals whose names are memorialized in the quilt.

Roger's Story: For Cori (videocassette; 28 min.; color; 1989; Fanlight Productions) This documentary tells the story of Roger, a forty-four-year-old recovering heroin addict diagnosed with AIDS. We see Roger at home with his wife and daughter, and we learn about his efforts to overcome addiction only to face a life-threatening battle with AIDS. The strength of Roger's character, his honesty in facing both his past mistakes and present challenges, and the support of his family are highlighted.

Role of the Volunteer (videocassette; 60 min.; color; 1980; Boulder County Hospice) A training film for hospice workers that looks at the role of the hospice volunteer, including his or her motivation.

The Savvy Patient (videocassette; 30 min.; color; 1987; Coronet/MTI Film & Video) This look at the doctor–patient relationship offers viewers suggestions about how to actively collaborate with their physicians.

Spiritual Care Concerns (videocassette; 60 min.; color; 1980; Boulder County Hospice) A training film for hospice workers that looks at how to provide spiritual care in the hospice setting.

This Is My Garden (videocassette; 26 min.; color; 1989; Filmakers Library) Through the stories and memories of five men whose partners died of AIDS, the viewer is treated to an intimate, nonsexual look at real caring, sharing, and love.

Too Little, Too Late: A Program About Families of AIDS Patients (videocassette; 48 min.; color; 1987; Fanlight Productions) Portrays the reality of AIDS as it affects patients and families. Examines the impact of ignorance and fear on those afflicted with the disease and on their families.

The Transition Services Videotape Series (videocassette; 111 min.; color; 1978; University of Washington Health Sciences Center for Educational Resources) Using the advanced cancer experience as a prototype for any patient–family situation in which life-threatening disease brings people face to face with existential concerns and practical problems in daily living, these videotapes were designed to help health care providers gain perspective on the complexities of offering palliative care. The series is composed of three programs: *Goals, Needs, and Concerns* (29 min.), *Communication with the Family* (33 min.), and *Support at the Time of Death* (49 min.). The series was inspired by and created to accompany an innovative graduate nursing program entitled Transition Services, directed by Ruth McCorkle and Jeanne Quint Benoliel.

Who Lives, Who Dies: Rationing Health Care (videocassette; 55 min.; color; 1987; Filmakers Library) Surveys the state of American health care and examines the manner in which health care is effectively rationed by the ability to pay. Includes a discussion by medical ethicist Arthur Caplan on organ transplantation and the allocation of scarce organs.

Why Won't They Talk to Me? How to Break Bad News (videocassette; 30 min. each segment; color; 1986; International Tele-Film Enterprises) This five-part series presents medical caregivers with effective strategies for communicating "bad news." Covers techniques for giving information and reassurances, truth telling, and talking with dying patients and the bereaved.

Willard Gaylin (videocassette; 30 min.; color; 1989; PBS Video) Interviewed by Bill Moyers, Gaylin discusses issues of medicine and ethics as they affect the well-being of individuals and communities, particularly with respect to growing populations and limited medical resources.

Chapter 5

Facing Death: Living with Life-Threatening Illness

OBJECTIVES

1. To list the personal and social costs of life-threatening illness.
2. To describe and assess patterns of coping with life-threatening illness.
3. To define and evaluate therapeutic strategies for patients with life-threatening illness.
4. To design a personal strategy for health care (both physical and psychological) should one be faced with a life-threatening illness.
5. To identify psychosocial factors influencing one's relationship with a loved one who is dying.

CONTENT OVERVIEW

Chapter 5 focuses on the experience of living with life-threatening illness, and its personal and social costs. The issue of terminal illness being perceived as taboo is addressed in terms of how others view the terminally ill person as well as how the terminally ill person views himself or herself. The terminally ill person may assume responsibility for the illness through the medium of magical thinking or similar self-questioning. Fatal diseases are often accompanied by an unjustified social stigma—as when heart disease is seen as a disease of overachievers or AIDS as a "gay" disease. The reality is that such life-threatening illnesses affect people in all walks of life.

The personal and social costs of life-threatening illness are immense. They include not only the direct financial costs attributable to the disease, but also the burden of disrupted lives, damaged self-concept, and anxiety about the future. Positive approaches to dealing with life-threatening illness include education, counseling, and social support. Although these techniques are not likely to remove the threat of serious illness, they can promote understanding, place the crisis in a more affirmative context, and restore a sense of personal control over a confusing situation.

A typical pattern associated with persons coping with life-threatening illness is illustrated by an anecdotal presentation that takes the reader from the initial discovery of symptoms through diagnosis and treatment, the ups and downs of changing circumstances, and finally the confrontation with death. Building on this introduction, the emotional and psychological response to life-threatening illness is discussed, using as a model Elisabeth Kübler-Ross's pioneering work with terminal patients. At various times, and in varying order, patients may experience denial, anger, bargaining, depression, and acceptance or resolution.

Even though certain general patterns can be distinguished, it must be recognized that different individuals cope with life-threatening illness differently. Furthermore, the way we imagine the events leading to death is not necessarily an accurate reflection of how those events are experienced by most dying persons. The idealized version of dying often leaves out the pain, nausea, constipation, bed sores, and insomnia, as well as the loneliness, anxiety, and fear—all frequent concomitants of the dying process.

The options available for treating life-threatening illness depend not only on the nature of the disease and the medical technologies available, but also on decisions made by society as a whole. Not all diseases and interventions can occupy the place of highest priority. Ethical issues are increasingly important in setting priorities for managing various diseases and determining appropriate treatments. Focusing primarily on cancer as the prototypic life-threatening illness, the discussion turns to the main types of therapy employed against the disease—surgery, radiation therapy, and chemotherapy—as well as the role of experimental, unorthodox, or alternative therapies. The role of "symbolic healing"—often as an adjunct to conventional therapies—is discussed in terms of its value in mobilizing a patient's inner resources and will to live.

The discussion of treatments for life-threatening illness concludes with an examination of two important topics: infection and pain management. Because of the diminished immune response associated with diseases like AIDS, and also some forms of cancer (often resulting from the treatment regimen), infection itself can be life-threatening. Pain is the most common symptom of terminally ill patients, and managing it effectively is a chief goal of palliative care. The perception of pain differs between individuals and cultures, and the phenomenon of pain is increasingly being addressed by interdisciplinary approaches that relate to the terminally ill patient's total pain—physical, psychological, social, and spiritual.

Successfully coping, mentally and emotionally, with life-threatening illness involves maintaining a "coping potency" that sustains the will to live in the face of death. Visualization and affirmation are examples of techniques designed to enhance the patient's sense of self-worth, dignity, and empowerment even when there is no hope for recovery from illness. The Japanese psychotherapeutic technique known as "meaningful-life therapy" postulates that it is in our control over our own behavior that hope lies.

Despite fears, we can take responsibility for what we do in the time remaining to us. We can accept the inevitability of dying and live alongside it.

Being with someone who is dying may cause uncomfortable feelings to arise, uncertainty about what to say or do. This discomfort may be manifested by excessive sympathy or by obsessive avoidance. Eventually, it becomes clear that it is all right not to know how to respond or what to say. Being there with our friend or relative means simply being sensitive to the demands of the moment and responding as our heart dictates. This is not meant to suggest that it's easy for friends or family members to live with the paradox of caring for a dying loved one while carrying on with the normal business of living. The perception of a patient's "fading away" may be accompanied by a task of redefinition, during which individuals and families begin to deal with the burden of letting go before picking up the new. Being with someone who is dying can help us recognize just how precious life is, and how uncertain. We learn that we cannot expect ourselves to have all the answers.

KEY TERMS AND CONCEPTS

artificial heart	oncologist
biopsy	pain management
cancer	prognosis
chemotherapy	radiation therapy
coping mechanisms	relapse
diagnosis	remission
heart disease	surgery
infection	symbolic healing
interferons	tumor
life-threatening illness	type A behavior
malignancy	unconventional therapy
metastasis	visualization

QUESTIONS FOR GUIDED STUDY AND EVALUATION

Multiple-choice questions relevant to this chapter can be found in the test bank.

1. Summarize how the statistics relative to cancer and heart disease are changing.
2. Identify the financial, personal, social, and psychological costs of life-threatening illness.
3. Describe the possible reactions of the patient, friends, and family to news of a life-threatening diagnosis.
4. Suggest at least five different ways of coping with life-threatening illness.

5. Assess the relative benefits of surgery, radiation therapy, and chemotherapy in treating cancer, and describe how each one works to eradicate cancer cells.

6. Evaluate the role of symbolic healing techniques in an overall treatment plan.

7. Identify and give examples of three basic approaches to pain management.

8. Describe methods of helping a loved one who has a life-threatening illness.

TEACHING STRATEGIES

1. Statements like the following provide an opportunity to elicit attitudes and beliefs about life-threatening illness. Have students respond to each statement by indicating:

    SA = Strongly agree

    A = Agree

    U = Undecided

    D = Disagree

    SD = Strongly Disagree

    - A physician's decision to inform a patient about his or her terminal illness should be made on a case-by-case basis.

    - A close family member should be the one to inform the patient about his or her life-threatening illness.

    - A patient who is prematurely informed about his or her terminal illness will lose the will to live.

    - A child with life-threatening illness should not be told about the possibility of his or her death.

    - I would not want the responsibility of informing a member of my family about the nature of his or her life-threatening illness.

    - If I had a life-threatening illness, I definitely would want to be informed by my physician.

    - A person can make important changes in his or her life when given knowledge of his or her terminal illness.

    - Knowledge of impending death gives both the patient and his or her family an opportunity to communicate about important matters.

    - Sudden death is much easier for an individual and his or her family than is death resulting from a lingering degenerative illness.

    - Overwhelming and unrelenting physical pain would be the worst aspect of coping with a life-threatening illness.

You can add other statements. Divide students into groups and have them discuss their responses. Then, as a class, discuss the range of responses.

2. This exercise is designed to help students confront fears related to dying. To identify the sources of these fears, have them respond to each statement with yes, no, or maybe.

   • I am afraid of nothingness—the end of everything.
   • I am afraid of abandoning the people who depend on me.
   • I am afraid of making those who love me unhappy.
   • I am afraid of not having time to make amends for all my sins of commission and omission.
   • I am afraid that death will be the end of feeling and thinking.
   • I am afraid of losing control over what is being done to my body.
   • I am afraid of the pain of dying.
   • I am afraid of punishment after death.
   • I am afraid of losing those I care about.
   • I am afraid of being helpless and having to depend completely on others.
   • I am afraid of dying because I don't know what happens after death.
   • I am afraid of dying before I am ready to go.
   • I am afraid of taking a long time to die.
   • I am afraid of dying suddenly and violently.
   • I am afraid of dying alone.

   When students finish responding, have them go through all the items marked yes and complete the sentence: "I am afraid of . . ." by stringing together all the responses marked yes. Have them do the same thing with the items marked no and maybe, completing the sentences "I am not afraid of . . ." and "I might be afraid of . . ." Have students pair off and discuss their answers. (As an alternative, assign this activity as homework. Have students write papers reflecting on their experiences of completing the questionnaire.) [Adapted from *Nursing the Dying Patient*, by Charlotte Epstein (Reston, Va.: Reston Publishing Co., 1975), p. 122. Reprinted by permission.]

COMMENTS AND CONSIDERATIONS

Whose Death Is It Anyway? This chapter emphasizes the importance of patient choice based on individual needs to achieve a sense of control and empowerment. Students sometimes judge too quickly and harshly the dying styles and options chosen by the terminally ill. It is important to alert them to the fact that, although a patient's choices may seem wrong to them for any number of reasons, the most important aspect of a choice is that it be the patient's and not solely that of health professionals or family members.

RESOURCES: FILMS AND VIDEOCASSETTES

AIDS: Caring for the Caregiver (videocassette; 28 min.; color; 1990; American Journal of Nursing Co.) This video explores the psychological stressors that affect those who care for AIDS patients: fear of contagion, feelings and attitudes about homosexuality or drug abuse, physical and emotional care demands, identification with the patient, helplessness, and grief related to the disease's high mortality. Presents strategies to promote healthy coping and to ensure optimal care of patients.

An Ancient Form of Care (videocassette; 30 min.; color; 1987; Coronet/MTI Film & Video) Examines the growing popularity of alternative therapies such as acupuncture and other forms of folk and traditional medicine.

Cancer: A Family Journal (videocassette & 16 mm.; 57 min.; color; Social Work Oncology Group) Chronicles the grieving of a young family as they witness the death of the father. The film focuses not only on the family's response to his dying, but also on his care at home during part of the treatment. The narrative is chronological and concludes six weeks after the father's death with comments by family members.

Castles in the Sand (videocassette; 52 min.; color; 1987; Films for the Humanities & Sciences) The story of Josh Littman, a television reporter who turned the camera on himself after being diagnosed with leukemia. Shows how a patient lives with the fear and pain of dying, and how the patient's family can provide encouragement and support when death can no longer be denied. An Emmy-award winner.

Controlling the Behavioral Effects of Chemotherapy (videocassette; 16 mm.; color; 1983; Carle Medical Communications) Focuses on the psychological experience of patients undergoing chemotherapy.

A Conversation with Leslie (videocassette; 45 min.; color; Louis E. LaGrand) A young college student faces her mortality as she deals with third-stage Hodgkin's disease.

Coping with Cancer (videocassette; 24 min.; color; 1981; Professional Research) Looks at ways of helping patients and families cope with the psychological and emotional struggles of living with cancer.

Coping with Serious Illness (videocassette & 16 mm.; 30 min. per program; color; 1980; Ambrose Video Publishing) A series of filmed sequences excerpted from *Joan Robinson: One Woman's Story*, in which a number of issues related to dying from cancer are discussed candidly, with further commentary by professionals. Includes Finances/Insurance, Doctor-Patient Relationships, Facing Death, Relationships and Stress, Pain, and Sexuality.

Death: Dying in a Hospital (videocassette; 43 min.; black & white; 1971; Filmakers Library) By focusing on 52-year-old Albo Pearsall, dying of cancer at Calvary Hospital in New York, this film examines the responses of staff, family, and patient to terminal illness. Particular attention is given to the process of communication between the dying person, the family, and professional caregivers.

Death and Dying: A Conversation with Elisabeth Kübler-Ross, M.D. (videocassette; 29 min.; color; 1976; PBS Video) Elisabeth Kübler-Ross discusses her work and philosophy. She describes how she handles death in her own family and shares her views on euthanasia and death with dignity, as well as her beliefs about life after death.

Dialogue with Elisabeth Kübler-Ross and Tom McCormick: Caring for the Dying (videocassette; 60 min.; color; 1984; Elisabeth Kübler-Ross Center) Elisabeth Kübler-Ross discusses the patient's "intuitive knowledge" of his or her disease, the importance of an open and honest relationship with one's physician, and how unfinished business regarding death can interfere in one's relationship with a dying patient. A discussion designed for health care professionals, patients, and survivors of life-threatening illness.

Dying (videocassette & 16 mm.; about 1-1/2 hours; color; 1976; King Features, UCLA Instructional Media Library) Sandra Bertman's classic documentary depicting the effects of terminal cancer on four families, each of which responds uniquely. Excellent exploration of the influence of attitudes and beliefs.

The End (16 mm; 1-3/4 hours; color; 1978; United Artists Pictures) Burt Reynolds stars in this poignant comedy about one man's attempt to come to terms with his terminal illness. A tongue-in-cheek presentation of the psychological and emotional responses evoked.

Essie: A Cancer Patient Asserts Herself (videocassette & 16 mm.; 55 min.; color; 1982; Filmakers Library) Documents the life of a thirty-one-year-old woman who has been living with cancer for four years. Essie participates in a number of experimental protocols for the treatment of her disease. Included are discussions about her relationships with her husband, family, and friends.

Feeling Good Again: Coping with Breast Cancer (videocassette; 20 min.; color; 1987; Carle Medical Communications) A frank discussion by five women who have successfully recovered, physically and emotionally, from surgery for breast cancer.

Finding Your Way: Managing the Discomfort of Treatment (videocassette; 22 min.; color; 1989; Fanlight Productions) Documents the Dana-Farber Cancer Institute's use of behavioral techniques to help patients reduce anxiety and cope more effectively with pain. Patients are seen learning techniques of breathing control, affirmation, and visualization, and then using them to minimize discomfort while undergoing treatment. Staff members explain how and why these techniques help patients feel more in control of their medical treatment.

From Both Ends of the Stethoscope (videocassette; 30 min.; color; 1985; Scripps Memorial Hospital Cancer Center Films) A film that looks at the issues of living with dying from the perspective of the patient as well as the doctor, for the speaker is both. Dr. David Peters died at the age of thirty-eight a few weeks after the film was made. He talks about his newfound awareness of working with dying patients and the importance of being willing to communicate with them, as well as about the changes in his relationships with friends and family.

How Could I Not Be Among You? (videocassette & 16 mm.; about 1-1/2 hours; color; 1971; Benchmark Films, UCLA Instructional Media Library) An artistic presentation of a young poet's thoughts and feelings as he faces the fact that his illness is terminal. It expresses diverse emotions—

depression, fear, and anger, tempered with humor—and discloses his changed philosophy toward life; one that allows him more freedom than before his illness.

Ikiru (16 mm.; about 2-1/2 hours; black & white; 1952; Films, Inc.) A Japanese setting is the backdrop for witnessing the changes that occur as a man lives the last months of life knowing that he will soon die.

Lana's Story (videocassette; 25 min.; color; 1986; Health Sciences Consortium) Chronicles the last six months in the life of Lana Beach, who died of cancer at the age of forty-three. Explores the impact of terminal illness on patients and their families, as well as the role of hospice care in the dying process and in follow-up bereavement care.

The Last Laugh (videocassette; 57 min.; color; 1988; Fanlight Productions) A three-day comedy workshop for patients with AIDS, emphasizing that laughter is a component of coping.

Letter to My Uncle (16 mm.; 14 min.; black & white; Deborah Lefkowitz) After her uncle's death, Deborah discovers that he had recorded a number of journal tapes revealing his reflections as he faced his death. As a death educator, he shares many thoughts about his professional experience.

Life, Death and the Dying Patient, Parts I & II (videocassette; 60 min.; color; 1982; Elisabeth Kübler-Ross Center) In Part 1, Elisabeth Kübler-Ross talks with a medical student about personality development. In Part 2, she focuses on repression and unfinished business.

Living with Cancer: The Windstorms of Life (videocassette; 28 min.; color; 1990; Filmakers Library) An inspirational true story of Dr. Fred Lee, a noted prostate cancer researcher, who discovers the disease in himself. A highly personal tale of courage, love, understanding, spiritual growth, and healing.

Living with Death: Unfinished Business (16 mm.; 30 min.; color; 1983; Coronet/MTI Film & Video) This film presents Elisabeth Kübler-Ross showing how dying patients can be helped to prepare for death. Includes scenes from her workshops, in which terminally ill people are counseled.

Living Time: Sarah Jesup Talks on Dying (16 mm.; 15 min.; color; Concern for Dying) A few weeks before her death at age forty-one, Sarah Jesup, a single mother of two children, discusses the complexities of living with dying, including her relationships with doctors, friends, and children.

Make Today Count (16 mm.; 30 min.; color; 1978; Brigham Young University) Documentation of a self-help group for people facing life-threatening illness, narrated by Orville Kelly, the group's founder.

The Mark Waters Story (videocassette & 16 mm.; 26 min.; color; 1969; National Audiovisual Center) Mark Waters, who is dying of lung cancer and who writes his own obituary, is the subject of this documentary.

Mastering Pain (videocassette; 30 min.; color; 1987; Coronet/MTI Film & Video) Presents research on patients' perceptions of pain, including ethnic differences in how pain is perceived, and information about treating acute and chronic pain.

Nothing Final (videocassette; 60 min.; color; Elisabeth Kübler-Ross Center) A film about the work of Elisabeth Kübler-Ross produced by the BBC. She is shown in her early work, making house calls to dying patients.

On Death and Dying (videocassette & 16 mm.; 58 min.; color; 1974; Films, Inc.) Elisabeth Kübler-Ross talks about helping the terminally ill, including children, face death without fear. She discusses the stages of dying as well as the importance of effective communication, including nonverbal communication.

Pain and Physical Care Concerns (videocassette; 60 min.; color; 1980; Boulder County Hospice) A training film for hospice workers concerning types of pain and pain management.

Quality of Mercy: A Case for Better Pain Management (videocassette; 53 min.; color; 1988; Filmakers Library) An investigation of pain management (or lack thereof) in American hospitals, specifically in pediatric surgery, cancer care, and burn treatment. Includes footage of actual surgical procedures.

Soon There Will Be No More Me (videocassette & 16 mm.; 10 min.; color; 1972; Churchill Films, Portland State University) Through her last written words and photographs, the feelings of a young mother dying of bone cancer are shared with her infant daughter.

Terminal Illness (also known as the "Leinback-Eisdorfer Series") (videocassette; six parts totaling 201 min.; black & white; 1972; University of Washington Press) This six-part series looks at the last months of Dr. Gary E. Leinbach's life, as he faces death from intestinal cancer. Part 1 (25 min.) looks at the emotional response to imminent death, as Dr. Leinbach discusses his reactions with his psychiatrist. Part 2 (41 min.) examines the role of the physician in treating the terminally ill. Part 3 (37 min.) discusses pain management. Part 4 (35 min.) consists of interviews between Dr. Leinbach and clergy from different religious backgrounds. Parts 5 (25 min.) and 6 (45 min.) discuss the grieving process.

Terminal Illness: The Patient's Story (videocassette; 28 min.; color; 1987; Films for the Humanities & Science) The story of Joan Robinson, filmed during five years, from her diagnosis with ovarian cancer through six operations, hospitalization, chemotherapy, and radiation therapy, to her death. Adapted from a Phil Donahue show.

A Time to Die (videocassette & 16 mm.; 49 min.; color; 1983; Coronet/MTI Film & Video) Omega, a support group for people with life-threatening illness, is the subject of this film. Interviewed are a number of people who candidly disclose their concerns about the importance of keeping communication open so that they can better face the reality of their illnesses.

To Die Today (videocassette & 16 mm.; 50 min.; black & white; 1972; Filmakers Library) Through interviews and discussion, Elisabeth Kübler-Ross talks about the fears and concerns of patients facing terminal illnesses and delineates stages of dying.

To Think of Dying (videocassette; 58 min.; color; 1974; PBS Video) Orville Kelly, a terminal cancer patient, and Lynn Caine, a widow, discuss their experiences and understandings about cancer.

Particular attention is paid to the phases of grief over the death of a loved one and issues of one's own mortality. Effects on friends and family are also examined.

Until I Die (videocassette & 16 mm.; 30 min.; color; 1970; American Cancer Society, American Journal of Nursing Co., UCLA Instructional Media Library) Elisabeth Kübler-Ross interviews a terminally ill patient, with follow-up discussion by caregivers.

We Want to Have It All (videocassette; 41 min.; color; 1986; Health Sciences Consortium) One man's thoughts and feelings about his terminal illness emphasize how the illness has changed his way of thinking about the future. He now plans days in advance, where he used to plan weeks or months in advance before the illness.

When Your Loved One Is Dying (videocassette; 16 min.; color; 1981; Batesville Management Services) Based on the book by Earl Grollman, this film explains how to relate sensitively to dying people.

Why Me? (videocassette & 16 mm.; 10 min.; color; 1979; Pyramid Film & Video) An animation depicting the reaction of a patient to knowledge of imminent death.

Chapter 6

Last Rites: Funerals and Body Disposition

OBJECTIVES

1. To describe the function of funeral rituals, including their psychosocial aspects.
2. To describe the historical changes in American funeral rituals and to assess the relevance of criticism of current practices.
3. To examine practices and costs of various mortuary and cemetery options.
4. To design a personally meaningful funeral ritual for oneself.

CONTENT OVERVIEW

Chapter 6 examines the structure, symbolic content, and function of funeral rituals as they pertain to the change in status of both the deceased and his or her survivors. In some societies (as we saw in Chapter 2), the funeral is primarily a rite of passage, denoting a change of status for the deceased. In modern societies, however, it is primarily a mechanism for providing social support to the survivors. The social aspects of last rites begin with the notification of death, a process that extends outward from relatives and close friends to those who were less intimately related to the deceased. Gathering together to support and comfort the bereaved during the events of the visitation and funeral provides reassurance that the death of an individual and the survivors' subsequent grief are part of a larger whole, that these rites of passage take place within a caring community.

Although funerals fulfill an important function as a mechanism for coping with loss, the modern funeral has been criticized for its cost as well as its tendency to "prettify" or deny death by cosmetically restoring the corpse, engaging in euphemistic language to describe the facts of death, and creating a "staged" ceremony. Studies have shown that most people are satisfied with current funeral practices and feel they have been treated fairly by those in the funeral industry. Nevertheless, there is a sense of concern that customers of funeral establishments could be easily taken advantage of since most people are unfamiliar with the activities and costs surrounding funeral and mortuary services.

Gaining familiarity with the antecedents of present funeral practices helps explain why the funeral industry has been criticized over the past few decades. Initially a tradesman who supplied funeral paraphernalia, usually as a sideline to some other business, the undertaker simply provided a service to families who were, in effect, their own funeral directors. Increasing urbanization and other social changes altered this traditional relationship, with professional morticians taking on an ever larger role in caring for the dead while family involvement diminished. Indeed, it is perhaps stretching things only a bit to suggest that the main involvement of families in modern funeral rituals is to pay for the services provided by professional funeral directors.

Even for those persons who have no desire to assume a larger role in designing their own funerals or creating appropriate farewells for their deceased loved ones, it is prudent to become acquainted with the options available in funeral services. The purpose of the funeral—as an occasion for acknowledging publicly that a member of the community has died and to effect closure on that person's life for the bereaved—can be realized whether it is garnished with diamonds and rubies, or with poetry and a song. As a transaction unique in commerce, the contract for funeral services is usually entered into during a time of crisis, and the decision, once made, is final. Thus, preparing oneself in advance by acquiring knowledge of the types of funeral service charges and their approximate costs can help greatly in making meaningful decisions.

An itemized listing of funeral service charges will include categories for professional services (covering mortuary staff services and general overhead), intake charges (for transporting remains), embalming or refrigeration of the body, other body preparation (cosmetology, hairstyling, dressing the corpse, and the like), the casket (of which there is a wide range of choices), facilities (use of a visitation or viewing room, or the mortuary chapel), vehicles (hearse, family cars), and a miscellaneous category that might include the costs of newspaper death notices, acknowledgment cards, floral arrangements, honoraria for pallbearers or clergy, and burial garments purchased from the mortuary. The purchaser of mortuary services is also advised to understand something of the options for body disposition—burial, entombment, and cremation being the most commonly employed in North America. Finally, the costs associated with placing grave markers or erecting more elaborate memorials to the deceased ought to be considered, as well as endowments or fees for "perpetual care" assessed by cemeteries.

As a response to death, funerals range from the simple to the elaborate, from the essentials needed for quick and proper disposal of the body to ornate ceremonies that span several days, or even longer. Some people choose a minimal involvement in caring for their dead loved ones; others seek more active participation. In a pluralistic society, there are many ways of dealing meaningfully with death. Becoming aware of the available alternatives enables us to make more informed, and more gratifying, choices about last rites.

KEY TERMS AND CONCEPTS

burial
casket
cemetery
crypt
coffin
columbarium
condolences
cosmetic restoration
funeral director
funeral parlor
funerary artifacts
grave liner
grave marker
itemized pricing
last rites
mausoleum
memorial society

cremation
cremation society
crematory
cryonics
embalming
entombment
FTC Funeral Rule
funeral director
memorialization
mortician
mortuary
notification of death
pallbearers
psychological closure
single-unit pricing
undertaker

QUESTIONS FOR GUIDED STUDY AND EVALUATION

Multiple-choice questions relevant to this chapter can be found in the test bank.

1. Describe the psychosocial functions of death notification and funeral rites. Identify how these social activities fulfill the psychological needs of the bereaved.

2. Summarize the major criticisms of the American funeral and assess their validity.

3. Describe the major requirements of the FTC Funeral Rule.

4. Describe the four categories of charges that constitute the total cost of a funeral and body disposition.

5. Compare the various methods of body disposition and discuss the advantages and disadvantages of each.

6. Explain the functions of cremation and memorial societies and contrast them with conventional practices.

7. Define the purpose of the funeral, and assess current funeral practices in light of that definition.

8. Write a detailed description of the funeral you would plan for yourself, giving reasons for your choices.

TEACHING STRATEGIES

1. An interview with a mortician provides an opportunity for students to learn firsthand about the business of funeral directing, including the services offered by a mortuary. The class can meet at the mortuary for the interview and a tour. The interview may be followed by a question and answer period. Students should not feel limited in their choice of questions. Make sure that the interviewee is aware of this before the interview and feels comfortable responding "pass" or "no comment." This freedom allows the students to ask questions and the mortician to maintain his or her privacy. The following questions relate to three areas: personal history, services offered, and business realities.

   Q: Many children say what they want to be when they grow up. I would imagine they don't often say "a mortician." When did you know that you wanted to be a mortician? What prompted you to choose this career over, say, being a firefighter or a doctor?

   Q: Will you tell us about the first time you saw a dead body? What were the circumstances and how did you feel?

   Q: What allows you to handle so much exposure to death? How do you cope?

   Q: How are you perceived by the public? For example, how do children react to your occupation? What about acquaintances, close friends, and relatives?

   Q: What training did you receive for your job?

   Q: Did you receive training in grief counseling?

   Q: Would you describe the embalming process? Is it required by law and, if so, under what circumstances?

   Q: Can refrigeration substitute for embalming? How do the costs compare?

   Q: What is the longest period of time you've kept a body before final disposition?

   Q: Would you say something about body viewing? For example, under what circumstances would you recommend not viewing a body? When do you think body viewing is most beneficial for survivors? What are your feelings about the importance of viewing the body?

   Q: Should children view a body? Have there been situations when you thought they should not have viewed the body? What were the circumstances?

   Q: What about cosmetics? Are they required? What do you think are the advantages? Any disadvantages?

   Q: Making funeral rituals personally meaningful can be valuable for survivors. What requests do people make? What would be an unconventional request?

   Q: Could survivors handle all the details of a funeral themselves? How would it be done and what would be the costs?

Q: What do you find to be the most difficult deaths? How do you personally cope?

Q: What are some of the costs in operating this business?

Q: Do you think the stereotype of the rich mortician making money from others' pain is ever accurate?

Q: What kinds of malpractice suits is a mortuary subject to?

Q: How do funeral directors build their businesses?

2. Direct students to visit a cemetery. Have them use newsprint and crayons to make a rubbing of a headstone that they find especially interesting. Hang the rubbings around the classroom and discuss them as a group. Ask: What was the deceased remembered for? How do you know? What image or belief of death is presented? Which tombstone would you want for yourself? What would your inscription read?

3. Have students indicate their funeral wishes by completing these sentences:

- I would like my body to be (embalmed, viewed at home, not viewed, cremated, buried, entombed . . .) _____.

- I'd like to be wearing _____.

- Please transport my body in a _____.

- The mortuary, crematory, or memorial society I prefer is _____.

- The price range I would want spent on my funeral is _____.

- I would like the final disposition of my body to be at _____.

- If I were cremated, I would want my remains _____.

- I'd like a tombstone or marker that reads _____.

- I would/would not like flowers sent _____ and donations could be made to _____.

- I would like a funeral or memorial service led by _____ at _____.

- I'd like a religious/secular service that would include (open casket, flowers, music, quotes, speakers...) _____.

- I'd prefer to leave the arrangements for my funeral to _____.

After they finish this activity, have students date, sign, and give this information to appropriate family members. As a class, discuss reactions to completing this activity.

COMMENTS AND CONSIDERATIONS

1. **Touring the Mortuary.** Some students have expressed in "ughs" and "sighs" a disinterest in touring a mortuary. Find out what they are uncomfortable about and assure them that the experience probably will not match their worst expectations. They may be afraid of seeing a dead body, embalming equipment, or the like. The tour should be arranged with the mortician beforehand so that students will have some choices about what they see. Remind students to exercise common courtesy while at the mortuary since mourners may be present.

2. **Exercising Choice.** One way to help students become aware of choices they have as consumers is to play a "coffin game." Prearrange with the mortician for the casket prices to be temporarily removed, and have students go to the display area as part of the mortuary tour. Have them guess the cost of each casket. Which do they think is the most expensive? Which is the least? Which would they prefer for themselves? The funeral director can then reveal the actual prices of caskets and discuss the reasons for varying costs with students.

RESOURCES: FILMS AND VIDEOCASSETTES

Arranging Cremation Services—A Guide for the Consumer (videocassette; 6 min.; color; 1985; Batesville Management Services) Discusses, among other things, a number of ways of handling cremation, common misconceptions about this practice , cremation services, and the role of the funeral director.

Death: A Time to Remember (videocassette & 16 mm.; 28 min.; color; 1977; Mass Media Ministries) A historical look at funeral practices, tracing the inception of many modern rituals.

An Equal Knock on Every Door (videocassette; 30 min.; color; WKYC-TV) Looks at funerary rituals and accoutrements, including casket selection. Discusses aid for survivors.

Funeral Customs Around the World (videocassette; 22 min.; color; 1977; Batesville Management Services) A cross-cultural look at funeral customs that highlights similarities as well as differences.

Funeral Service in the 1990s: Serving People, Serving Needs (videocassette; 8 min.; color; 1985; Batesville Management Services) Discusses body disposition, the importance of the funeral for survivors, and tailoring the service to individual needs and desires.

The Great American Funeral (16 mm.; 55 min.; black & white; Mass Media Ministries) A consumer-oriented film that looks at the recent history of the American funeral in terms of services and goods provided, as well as costs and economics of the funeral industry.

The Loved One (16 mm.; about 2 hours; black & white; 1965; Films, Inc.) An adaptation of Evelyn Waugh's satirical novel about the American funeral industry.

Pyramid (videocassette; 60 min.; color; 1988; PBS Video) An interdisciplinary approach to the Great Pyramid at Giza, this video explores the geography, history, mythology, and religions of the ancient Egyptians, including the mythology of the Egyptian god Osiris, ruler of the underworld.

Sallie, 1893–1974 (16 mm.; 54 min.; color; 1975; Portland State University) Shows an actual nontraditional funeral.

Chapter 7

Survivors: Understanding the Experience of Loss

OBJECTIVES

1. To define bereavement, grief, and mourning.
2. To describe the experience of grief.
3. To list the somatic, perceptual, and emotional symptoms of grief and to assess its impact on morbidity and mortality.
4. To describe and evaluate different models of the phases and duration of grief.
5. To explain the variables that influence grief.
6. To list various coping mechanisms and assess the value of each.
7. To draw conclusions regarding bereavement support.
8. To assess how bereavement may provide an opportunity for growth.

CONTENT OVERVIEW

Chapter 7 provides a comprehensive inquiry into the human experience of loss. We are all survivors of loss, whether of the "little deaths" exemplified by endings and changes that occur throughout the normal course of life, or of the more significant impact on our lives brought about by the deaths of loved ones. Understood in their primary meanings, *bereavement* refers to the objective event of loss, *grief* to the total emotional response engendered by loss, and *mourning* to the process of incorporating the experience of loss into our ongoing lives. In practice, however, these terms are often used more or less interchangeably.

The experience of grief can be examined from a number of viewpoints. We can inquire into its duration, and question what might constitute prolonged or pathological grief. We can observe and catalog the physical, emotional, and behavioral symptoms associated with grief, noting the great variability of symptomatology found among different individuals and circumstances. We can distinguish the patterns in how grieving changes over time, delineate its various phases, and establish a model of the process for resolving the loss successfully. We can also examine the effects of severe grief on our physical and psychological functioning, and probe into the possible mechanisms by which grief may cause morbidity and even mortality in someone who has experienced a significant loss. Each of these four approaches to understanding grief adds to our knowledge and contributes detail to the portrait of grief developed in this chapter.

Many variables must also be considered in order to arrive at an adequate understanding of grief. Important variables include the survivor's *model of the world* (involving personality, social roles, the perceived importance of the deceased, and the survivor's value structure), the *mode of death* (whether natural, accidental, homicide, or suicide; whether it occurred suddenly or was anticipated; whether the death is perceived as having been preventable or not), the *relationship of the survivor to the deceased* (its actual nature and degree of intimacy as well as its external form; whether the relationship was central or peripheral to the survivor), the amount of *unfinished business* between the deceased and the survivor, the degree of *conflict between intellectual and emotional responses* to the death, and the amount of *social support* available.

In coping with loss, survivors usually find social support to be of incalculable value. Funeral rites and other leave-taking rituals provide a framework within which survivors can receive the social support they need during the period immediately following a loss. Support groups for specific bereavements offer grieving persons another opportunity to share their concerns and empathy with one another. The composition and structure of such groups varies, but they share an emphasis on offering needed social support while the bereaved person adjusts to the loss.

Bereavement often creates significant change in many details of a person's life: The family unit is different, the social realities have changed, there are legal and financial matters that require attention. In each of these areas, the survivor is challenged to adjust and manage successfully. Despite the burden of loss and the pain of grief, bereavement can be an opportunity for growth, though this may be hard to believe at first. As movement toward resolving the loss continues, however, creative energy is released. The tragic event of the loved one's death is reformulated in a way that offers new opportunities. The loss is transformed. Many bereaved persons describe themselves as stronger, more competent, more mature, more independent, and better able to face other crises as a result of their journey through grief. It's not as if they would wish their grief on others, but that their lives are testimony to the possibility of turning negatives into positives, for viewing loss within a context of growth. For these survivors, grief has become a unifying rather than alienating experience, and the lost relationship is viewed as changed, but not ended.

KEY TERMS AND CONCEPTS

acute grief
anniversary reaction
anticipatory grief
attachment theory
bereavement
central or peripheral relationship
deathbed promises
disenfranchised grief
grief
grief work
secondary morbidity
somatic symptomatology
survivor guilt
survivor support groups

high grief vs. low grief
linking objects
little deaths
loss
mater dolorosa
mortality and morbidity of grief
mourning
pathological grief
perceived similarity
prolonged grief
tasks of mourning
trigger events
unfinished business

QUESTIONS FOR GUIDED STUDY AND EVALUATION

Multiple-choice questions relevant to this chapter can be found in the test bank.

1. Differentiate among bereavement, grief, and mourning.
2. List Erich Lindemann's three primary tasks in managing grief.
3. Give examples of physical, perceptual, and emotional symptoms of grief.
4. Describe the Freudian theory of grief.
5. Contrast Geoffrey Gorer's model of the phases of grief with those of James Kavanaugh and Beverly Raphael.
6. Identify the four tasks of mourning postulated by William Worden.
7. Name illnesses that survivors may experience and explain why bereaved persons are physiologically at higher risk.
8. List factors that may result in a high-grief bereavement.
9. Explain the phenomenon of anticipatory grief and give an example of a situation in which it might occur.
10. Define the term *unfinished business* as applied to grief and its resolution.
11. Evaluate the advice for the bereaved given in the chapter, adding at least one more suggestion designed to optimize bereavement as an opportunity for growth.
12. List and evaluate at least three coping mechanisms for survivors.

13. Imagine you are a professional who will soon meet with a newly bereaved person. What information about the circumstances of the bereavement would be important for you to have before the meeting? What emotions or behaviors might cause you to feel uncomfortable in the situation? What kind of resolution would you like to see this person make and how soon?

TEACHING STRATEGIES

1. This is the ideal class period for exploring the deathographies (see Appendix A). Have students break into small groups for about 15 minutes to discuss their answers to the questions outlined in the description of the deathography. Then come together as a class and ask students to talk about: (1) their general experience of reading a number of deathographies, and (2) the particulars of the individual deathographies.

2. Interview a survivor, either a guest speaker or a volunteer from the class. Questions can include:

    Q: What circumstances led to the death? Tell us about the actual event itself.

    Q: Will you describe the moment you knew how significantly your life had changed?

    Q: What other losses accompanied this bereavement experience?

    Q: How did you cope? Who and what did you turn to for help?

3. This activity investigates the concept of unfinished business. Have students think of an important person in their lives and imagine that that person were to die tomorrow. Ask students to write responses to the following questions:

    • What was the happiest moment you recall sharing?

    • What was the saddest moment the two of you shared?

    • What would you miss most?

    • What do you wish you would have said to that person?

    • What do you wish that person would have said to you?

    • What would you have wanted to change in the relationship?

    • What circumstances (time, place, event) do you expect will elicit the most painful memories?

    Have students share their responses as a group. [Adapted from *Understanding Death and Dying: An Interdisciplinary Approach*, 3d ed., by Sandra G. Wilcox and Marilyn Sutton (Palo Alto, Calif.: Mayfield, 1985), p. 245. Reprinted by permission.]

COMMENTS AND CONSIDERATIONS

Take Time for Emotions. The possibility exists that stories will be emotionally charged, not only in the interview but also during activities and discussions. Voices may become choked and tears shed. Don't cut someone off simply because he or she is expressing difficult emotions. Direct the student (or interviewee) to pause and take a couple of slow, deep breaths; the rest of the story will come out.

RESOURCES: FILMS AND VIDEOCASSETTES

Advice for Friends of the Bereaved (videocassette; 10 min.; color; 1988; Batesville Management Services) Survivors discuss behaviors of friends and family during and after the funeral; what did and did not help.

The Anguish of Loss (slides and audiocassette; 15 min.; color; 1987; Julie Fritsch) The human dimension of loss is movingly captured in a series of sculptures created by artist Julie Fritsch as an outlet for her pain following the death of her son Justin. The program consists of 59 slides—photographs of the clay sculptures—and an audiocassette of background music. A useful resource for bereavement counselors, the bereaved themselves, and others who wish to understand the nature and effects of loss.

Coping with Loss (videocassette; 18 min.; color; 1985; Health Sciences Consortium) Tells the story of Larry Castleberry, whose left leg was amputated above the knee. Interviews with Larry, his wife, his doctors, and his physical therapists convey the shock, disorientation, and grief experienced at the loss of his limb.

Coping with Special Days (videocassette; 14 min.; color; 1990; Batesville Management Services) Survivors offer advice about anniversary grief reactions.

Feelings (videocassette; 10 min.; color; 1983; Batesville Management Services) Focuses on the emotional reaction to bereavement.

The Forgotten Mourner (videocassette; 28 min.; color; 1987; Films for the Humanities & Sciences) Calls attention to the needs of "neglected" mourners, including siblings and grandparents, the families of women who suffer miscarriage, and men whose lovers have died of AIDS or other causes. A clinical psychologist describes how mourners can be comforted. Adapted from a Phil Donahue show.

Going On: The Aftermath of Suicide (videocassette; 29 min.; color; 1989; Films for the Humanities & Sciences) Designed to help persons who have experienced the death by suicide of a friend, family member, or classmate. Through interviews with survivors, this program highlights the common physical and emotional symptoms of survivors and the different ways people express or hide their feelings.

Grief Therapy (videocassette & 16 mm.; 20 min.; color; 1976; Michigan Media, UCLA Instructional Media Library) A doctor treats a grieving mother whose daughter died two years earlier. His confrontative therapy demonstrates a number of techniques for the resolution of prolonged grief.

Invincible Summer: Returning to Life After Someone You Love Has Died (videocassette; 16 min.; color; 1989; Willowgreen Productions) A discussion of the commonalties of grief with the message of hope and healing. Set to beautiful scenes of nature. Good discussion starter for a support group of newly bereaved people.

A Journey Back: Coping with a Parent's Suicide (videocassette; 24 min.; color; 1989; Filmakers Library) A daughter's efforts to cope with her father's suicide provides an intimate look at death in the family. Each family member shares his or her own conflict about the death and understanding of the father, his life, his death. An extraordinary look at adult children's grief.

The Last Taboo (videocassette; 25 min.; color; 1985; St. George's Hospital Medical School) Cameos a group of survivors who are mentally handicapped. Focuses on how to recognize bereavement symptoms in this population.

The Legacy of Suicide (videocassette; 55 min.; color; 1986; La Mariposa Press) Although Eunice Cunningham was a professional psychiatric social worker, this did not diminish her grief when her husband of forty years committed suicide. Moreover, those who counseled her during the early period of loss held misconceptions about the aftermath of suicide that were not helpful to Ms. Cunningham's efforts toward recovery. Five years after her loss, Ms. Cunningham speaks about her initial shock, her self-destructive behaviors, and her path of healing.

Living—When a Loved One Has Died (videocassette; 19 min.; color; 1979; Batesville Management Services) An adaptation of Earl Grollman's book, this film provides information about bereavement reactions and practical advice on how to incorporate loss into one's life.

The Long Valley: A Study of Bereavement (videocassette & 16 mm.; 59/50 min.; color; 1978/80; Films, Inc.) Based on C.S. Lewis's *A Grief Observed*, Colin Murray Parkes discusses with health care professionals his "four-stage" process of grieving. Includes interviews with bereaved persons.

Suicide Survivors (videocassette; 26 min.; color; 1989; Films for the Humanities & Sciences) Explores the special needs of suicide survivors and the role of support groups in helping survivors cope with their grief.

Chapter 8

Death in Children's Lives

OBJECTIVES

1. To list the major causes of death in childhood and adolescence.
2. To describe the child's perception of illness.
3. To explain how a terminally ill child's fears and anxieties are developmentally related.
4. To identify the various coping mechanisms used by terminally ill children and to assess the value of each.
5. To identify factors influencing a child's experience of grief.
6. To illustrate ways of helping children cope with death.

CONTENT OVERVIEW

Chapter 8 examines experiences of loss during the years of childhood. In providing a lifespan approach to the issues, this chapter builds on material presented in earlier chapters—particularly those dealing with how children are socialized concerning death, experiences related to serious illness, and survivors' patterns of coping with bereavement. Change is a common component of children's lives. They may experience separations from friends and neighborhoods to which they have become attached. Changes in the composition of the family unit—through death, divorce, or the departure of a sibling—bring about the need for children to adapt to unfamiliar and sometimes painful circumstances.

When a child receives a life-threatening injury or is diagnosed with a serious and possibly life-threatening illness, confusion and emotional upheaval are the usual accompaniments—for the child as well as for his or her family. A child's curiosity about the seriousness of a traumatic injury or illness may meet with silence or attempts to avert disclosure on the part of adults. Hospitalization and the need to comply with a discomforting medical regimen typically add to the sick child's fears and anxieties. As with adults, children use a range of coping strategies in seeking to adjust to difficult and painful circumstances. How a child perceives an illness and the manner in which he or she responds to it depends on such factors as age (or developmental level), patterns of social interaction, family relationships, and past experiences, as well as the nature of the illness and its treatment (including the child's perception of its meaning and consequences).

Although not all children experience serious injury or illness, most do experience themselves as survivors of a death—whether it be the death of a pet, a parent or grandparent, a sibling, or some other close relation. A child's response to such losses will reflect the influence of such factors as his or her stage of mental and emotional development as well as previous experiences with death. Among children of the same age, significant differences may be observed in their abilities to comprehend death and cope with its effects on them as survivors. Experiencing a close death may also stimulate the development of more mature concepts about death as a child copes with the fact of loss in his or her life.

Children typically look to parents and other adults as examples of how to deal with loss. Children should be given opportunities to express their grief. Feelings of guilt or blame as well as of sadness need to be openly explored in a supportive atmosphere. Children seem to cope more easily with their feelings about a close death or other traumatic event when they are allowed to participate in the unfolding experience. When children are excluded, or when their questions go unanswered, it usually adds to their confusion and pain.

Foremost among the guidelines for helping a child cope with crisis is a willingness to listen. Acknowledge the child's feelings, and discover what he or she thinks and feels. Questions should be answered honestly and directly, without overwhelming the child with information that is beyond his or her ability to comprehend. Age-appropriate books dealing with various situations involving the topic of dying and death can provide opportunities to explore issues and experiences with children. Various organizations also provide social support to children who are coping with life-threatening illness or with a significant death. As much as we might wish it were otherwise, children cannot finally be shielded from painful experiences involving loss. Given the reality, the material covered in this chapter can provide a basis for helping children cope with their experiences of change and loss.

KEY TERMS AND CONCEPTS

art therapy
bibliotherapy
distancing strategies
goal substitution
parent death
pet death
rationalization

regression
selective memory
separation anxiety
sibling death
spontaneous drawings
sublimation

QUESTIONS FOR GUIDED STUDY AND EVALUATION

Multiple-choice questions relevant to this chapter can be found in the test bank.

1. Discuss historical changes in the major causes of death in childhood and adolescence. Suggest how the incidence of death from current major causes might be reduced.

2. Describe and give examples of the developmental phases as related to terminally ill children's understandings and fears.

3. List and evaluate at least four mechanisms that children use to cope with terminal illness.

4. Explain how children of differing ages understand the concept of death and describe how these understandings help children cope with bereavement.

5. Discuss the range of emotions children might experience after the death of a pet, parent, or sibling.

6. Develop a detailed plan for helping a child through the initial period following a specific type of bereavement.

TEACHING STRATEGIES

1. Bring to class a selection of children's books that deal with death. Divide the class into groups of three to five students. Circulate the books from group to group, having one person read each book or parts of it aloud. After each reading, have the group discuss:

   • What age group might benefit from this book? Why?

   • What concept of death is presented? Is the author most concerned with the emotional, biological, social, or philosophical understandings of death?

   • Under what circumstances would this book be useful?

2. Provide students with paper and crayons. Ask them to recall an early childhood memory of death. Guide them into recalling sensory details—picturing the sight, hearing the sounds, smelling the odors. Tell them to recall who, what, where, and when. Then instruct them to draw a picture of that early death experience, choosing colors carefully and avoiding stick figures. Allow 10 to 15 minutes. Then have students pair off to share and discuss their drawings. Come together as a group and talk about the value of spontaneous drawings. Refer to the drawing, "The Crooked Day," in the text.

3. Instruct students to create their own sympathy cards designed for a specific loss and a particular age group. The questions posed in strategy 1 can be used to guide the subsequent class discussion.

COMMENTS AND CONSIDERATIONS

Eliciting Verbal Communication. Some students may contend that it is difficult to elicit information from children about grief related to their terminal illness or the loss of a loved one. Emphasize that one way to do this is to use spontaneous drawings as a vehicle for communication. Note that the primary purpose is not interpretation by an adult, but an explanation from the child that can form the basis of a discussion.

RESOURCES: FILMS AND VIDEOCASSETTES

Adjusting to Amputation (16 mm.; 14 min.; color; 1976; Polymorph Films) Interviews with three adolescents focus on their adjustment to the loss of limbs. At issue are concerns of masculinity and femininity, prejudice in the workplace, and the wearing of prosthetic devices.

Adolescents Living with Cancer (videocassette; 56 min.; color; 1980; University of Arizona) This longer version of *Living With Cancer* includes the addition of a panel discussion by adolescents who are ill. Topics include family relations, truth telling, and the particular effects of cancer on adolescents.

And We Were Sad, Remember? (videocassette & 16 mm.; 29 min.; color; 1978; Lawren Productions, National Audiovisual Center, Portland State University) A film that discusses the importance of making children aware of death and the problems created by hiding the realities. Discussions of grandparental and parental death are included.

Angels Don't Have Headlights: Children's Reactions to Death in the Family (videocassette; 25 min.; color; 1989; Filmakers Library) An opportunity to sit in on clinical counseling sessions with several different grieving children, ages three to eleven, as we hear of their reactions to losses endured in their lives.

Anna and Poppy (videocassette & 16 mm.; 15 min.; color; 1977; The Media Guild, University of Illinois) Depicts the death of Anna's grandfather, Poppy, and her emotional struggle to come to terms with the fact of his death.

Billy (videocassette & 16 mm.; 11 min.; color; 1985; Wise-Currant Productions) A positive look at cancer through the eyes of Billy, as he lives in remission and then faces the return of his disease. The camera captures vignettes of medical treatments, social activities, and private time.

Blackberries in the Dark (videocassette; 26 min.; color; 1988; Coronet/MTI Film & Video) Based on the novel of the same name by Mavis Jukes, this video tells the story of nine-year-old Austin and his grandmother, and their personal struggle to come to terms with the recent death of Austin's grandfather.

Can It Be Anyone Else? (videocassette & 16 mm.; 32 min. & 54 min. versions; color; 1980; Pyramid Film & Video) A film showing how three children and their families, friends, and physicians work together to cope with leukemia. The children comment on their disease and are shown undergoing uncomfortable treatment.

Child's Eyes (16 mm.; 9 min.; color; CRM Films) Five- and six-year-old children narrate this film, which highlights pictures they drew in response to the death of President Kennedy.

Childhood Cancer: Emotional Effects (videocassette; 58 min.; color; 1975; Biomedical Communications) A training program for medical professionals produced by the M. D. Anderson Hospital and Tumor Institute.

Childhood Cancer: Patients Speak Out (videocassette & 16 mm.; 17 min.; color; 1984; Carle Medical Communications) Kids with cancer talk openly about their treatments and fears.

Children and the Grief Process (videocassette & 16 mm.; 21 min; color; 1983; Coronet/MTI Film & Video) Presents a child's perspective on death and shows how the attitudes of adults may result in a child being excluded from the grieving process. Shows how to help children deal with grief in a positive manner. Rabbi Earl Grollman of Temple Beth El in Belmont, Massachusetts, discusses these issues with a group of young children.

Coping with Death (videocassette; 30 min.; color; 1986; PBS Video) Six high school students share their personal stories about the death of a loved one. They discuss how they learned to cope with loss and how such a confrontation with death changed their attitude toward life.

Coping with Loss (videocassette; 19 min.; color; 1987; Films for the Humanities & Sciences) Using the Challenger tragedy as a starting point to describe the reactions of children to loss, this program explores how children cope with death, sudden or otherwise. Suggests how children can be helped to cope with death and emphasizes the importance of grieving.

The Death of a Friend: Helping Children Cope with Grief and Loss (videocassette & 16 mm.; 15 min.; color; 1985; New Dimension Media) Through puppetry, elementary school children are helped in coming to terms with the accidental death of a friend.

Death of a Gandy Dancer (videocassette & 16 mm.; 26 min.; color; 1977; Coronet/MTI Film and Video, Learning Corporation of America) This fictional account of a retired man's struggles with cancer looks at issues of open communication and family relationships, particularly the relationship between grandfather and grandson.

Don't Cry For Me (videocassette; 54 min.; color; Umbrella Films) Documents the lives of five young people with cystic fibrosis and their feelings about life and death.

Dying Child (videocassette; 42 min.; color; 1975; Medical College of South Carolina) Elisabeth Kübler-Ross presents her work with dying children and offers specific ways of encouraging them to talk about their experiences through such activities as play, art, and writing poetry.

The Early School Years (videocassette; 36 min.; color; 1983; American Journal of Nursing Co.) Through play therapy, including the use of puppets and hospital equipment, a nine-year-old girl and an eight-year-old boy, both cancer patients, explore their experiences.

The Fall of Freddie the Leaf (videocassette & 16 mm.; 16 min.; color; 1986; AIMS Media) This story by Leo Buscaglia tells the life story of Freddie, from his beginning as a small, healthy sprout on top of a tall tree, through the balmy days of spring and summer, to the first frost, the cold that frightens and causes Freddie to shiver in fear. His friend Daniel helps Freddie to answer the question, "Why are we here at all, if we only have to fall and die?" An award-winning film that Buscaglia dedicated to all children who have suffered a permanent loss, and to the grownups who could not find a way to explain it.

A Family Again (videocassette; 47 min.; color; 1989; Coronet/MTI Film & Video) Produced by Henry Winkler (of "Happy Days" fame) and with a cast that includes Jill Eikenberry and Michael Tucker, this dramatization depicts a family's coming to terms with the death by accidental drowning of their oldest daughter. Focusing on the surviving middle daughter, this video points up the need for social support in dealing with loss, especially when it seems that the larger society would deny the reality of loss and discourage emotional expression of grief.

The Giving Tree (videocassette & 16 mm.; 10 min.; color; 1973; Churchill Films) This animated presentation of Max Silverstein's book depicts the life cycle of a boy and his relationship to a tree, as he progresses from child to adult.

Grandma Didn't Wave Back (videocassette; 24 min.; color; 1987; Films for the Humanities & Sciences) This drama about senility and Alzheimer's disease focuses on the tender relationship between a senescent grandmother and her eleven-year-old granddaughter. Emphasizes the pain and confusion experienced within family relationships.

Griff Gets a Hand (videocassette; 30 min.; color; 1986; Beacon Films) An episode from the "Kids of Degrassi Street" series, this program explores children's grief by focusing on Griff, a sixth grader, who is devastated by the death of a school crossing guard with whom he had become friends. Griff's reaction to the death brings up his grief at another loss two years earlier—the death of his parents in an accident.

The High School Years (videocassette; 37 min.; color; 1983; American Journal of Nursing Co.) Six teenage cancer patients discuss their disease and its impact on their lives, especially their interactions with friends, family, and teachers.

I'm Still the Same Person (videocassette; 29 min.; color; 1980; Michigan Media) Two high school students, a boy and a girl, discuss their experiences with life-threatening illness, including how they are treated by their families and classmates and their plans for the future.

Jenny's Song (videocassette; 90 min.; color; 1986; Films for the Humanities & Sciences) Starring Ben Vereen and Jessica Walter, this drama tells the story of how one young girl and her family deal with the death of her father. Describes the process of grief and the social setting in which it occurs. Sandra Fox of Boston's Good Grief program consulted in the preparation of this program.

Kübler-Ross Interviews Adolescent Amputees (videocassette; 60 min.; color; 1984; Elisabeth Kübler-Ross Center) Elisabeth Kübler-Ross talks with adolescent cancer patients about how they live with physical disabilities.

Living with Cancer: A Conversation with Six Adolescent Cancer Patients (videocassette; 25 min.; color; 1979; University of Arizona) A documentary about six adolescent cancer patients who are living with life-threatening illness. At issue are such typical adolescent concerns as body image and appearance. Cancer treatment is particularly threatening for them because of its potential disfigurement. The reactions of friends and family to the disease are also discussed.

The Magic Moth (16 mm.; 22 min.; color; 1976; Portland State University) The death of a sibling and changed family relations as seen through the eyes of a six-year-old boy.

The Middle School Years (videocassette; 36 min.; color; 1983; American Journal of Nursing Co.) Three cancer patients, ages twelve to fourteen, discuss their experiences of being ill.

My Grandson Lew (16 mm.; 13 min.; color; 1976; Barr Films) Depicts the reaction of a young boy to his grandfather's death some time after it occurred. The mother and son are able to share happy memories of the grandfather.

No Greater Gift (videocassette; 30 min.; color; 1986; Coronet/MTI Film & Video) A fine drama about the friendship between two young boys hospitalized with life-threatening illness. Relationships with parents and caregivers are also touched upon.

Old Friends . . . New Friends—Gerald Jampolsky, M.D. (videocassette; 28 min. per episode; color; 1981; Family Communications) Gerald Jampolsky shows how love and hope can inspire children with life-threatening illness, as he introduces Fred Rogers to patients at the Center for Attitudinal Healing in California.

Rocket Gilbraltar (videocassette; 100 min.; color; 1988; RCA/Columbia Pictures Home Video) Stars Burt Lancaster as Levi Rockwell, a seventy-seven-year-old patriarch, whose children and grandchildren come to visit at his estate on the shores of Saggaponack, New York. After telling the grandchildren an ancient Viking myth about warriors achieving immortality at their death by being placed in a ship that is set adrift and set afire, the children overhear a doctor informing their grandfather that he is terminally ill. Working in secret from the adults, the children prepare an old boat for the ceremony and, when their grandfather dies, they place his body inside and perform the Viking rites that will ensure his immortality as a proud warrior, thus honoring Levi's most cherished wish.

Ryan White Talks to Kids About AIDS (videocassette; 28 min.; color; 1989; Films for the Humanities & Sciences) Ryan White, a hemophiliac who contracted AIDS from contaminated blood products, had become an expert on the disease by the age of sixteen. When he died at eighteen, his courage in facing the disease was well-known. This specially adapted Phil Donahue program shows an articulate White offering insights and information about AIDS and answering questions from an audience of teens and preteens.

The Sibling Perspective (videocassette; 20 min.; color; 1983; American Journal of Nursing Co.) Siblings of cancer patients, ages six to sixteen, discuss their experiences of living with a sibling who has a life-threatening illness.

Siblings of Children with Cancer (videocassette; 30 min.; color; 1980; University of Arizona) Four siblings from different families discuss learning about a brother's terminal illness, living with the disease, and coping with death. They offer advice to patients, their families, and health care professionals.

The Street (videocassette & 16 mm.; 10 min.; color; 1978; National Film Board of Canada, Portland State University, UCLA Instructional Media Library) Based on the book by Mordecai Richler, this animation depicts a nine-year-old Jewish boy's perspective on his family's experience of the grandmother dying at home.

The Tenth Good Thing About Barney (videocassette & 16 mm.; 13 min.; color; 1987; AIMS Media) Based on the book of the same name, this film tells the story of a pet's death and a young boy's efforts to come to terms with the loss.

Thumpy's Story: A Story of Love and Grief Shared, by Thumpy, the Bunny (videocassette; 9 min.; color; Prairie Lark Press) A story for children of all ages about Thumpy's experience of grief when his sister, Bun, dies unexpectedly. The whole Bunny family reacts to the loss, and Thumpy's parents model sharing their grief and support with the children. Although Thumpy's pain eases over time, he does not forget Bun.

A Time to Live . . . A Time to Die (videocassette; 41 min.; color; 1987; Batesville Management Services) Geared toward adolescents, this film examines death as a part of the life cycle, with an emphasis on the process of grieving.

Two of a Time (videocassette; 8 min.; color; 1990; American Journal of Nursing Co.) This short program depicts an elderly man and a young boy, both with cancer. They talk about their feelings, worries, and hopes. The young boy shares his family's reaction of withdrawal and his feeling of wanting to protect them. Emphasizes the importance of open communication.

Uncle Monty's Gone (videocassette & 16 mm.; 16 min.; color; 1976; University of Illinois) An animated film in which Bill Cosby tells the story of Uncle Monty's death through Fat Albert and the Cosby Kids. Uncle Monty's niece is despondent over her uncle's death and reacts by withdrawing from her playgroup. A discussion with her mother results in the young girl's rejoining the group.

Understanding AIDS: What Teens Need to Know (videocassette; 19 min.; color; 1990; Batesville Management Services) A dialogue between adolescents and professionals about the transmission and prevention of AIDS.

Understanding Grief: Kids Helping Kids (videocassette; 14 min.; color; 1988; Batesville Management Services) Children who have lost a companion animal or loved one discuss their feelings.

Very Good Friends (videocassette & 16 mm.; 29 min.; color; 1977; Learning Corporation of America) A film about sibling death and the importance of sharing feelings as part of the grieving process. The accidental death of an eleven-year-old is witnessed by her thirteen-year-old sister.

Warrendale (16 mm.; 1-3/4 hours; black & white; Grove Press) A documentary that examines the grief reactions of emotionally disturbed children when someone close to them dies.

What Do I Tell My Children? How To Help a Child Cope with the Death of a Loved One (videocassette; 30 min.; color; 1990; Lifecycle Productions) Highlights a group discussion of parents coping with loss and includes input from children and professionals, including Elisabeth Kübler-Ross, Earl Grollman, Sandra Fox, and Sandra Bertman.

When Children Grieve (videocassette; 20 min.; color; 1987; Churchill Films) Interviews with children in three households wherein a parent is dying, has died, or has cancer. The production was supervised and narrated by Dr. Art Ulene, a medical consultant for NBC. Includes scenes of a grief support group attended by the children.

When Friends Die (videocassette; 30 min.; color; 1989; PBS Video) Adolescents who have survived the death of a friend discuss how they learned to cope, and talk about the role of family and friends in recovering from tragedy.

Where Is Dead? (videocassette & 16 mm.; 19 min.; color; 1975; Encyclopaedia Britannica Educational Corp.) When her brother is accidentally killed in an automobile accident, six-year-old Sarah must come to terms with his death. Her parents and grandfather explain how David "lives on" as a memory.

You Don't Have to Die: Jason's Story (videocassette; 40 min.; color; 1989; Ambrose Video Publishing) The story of Jason Gaes and his writing of *My Book for Kids with Cansur*. Includes scenes of Jason being treated in the hospital and interviews with his family.

Chapter 9

Death in the Lives of Adults

OBJECTIVES

1. To list and describe Erik Erikson's psychosocial stages of adult development.
2. To identify the kinds of losses adults experience.
3. To distinguish the particular characteristics of parental bereavement and to identify the types of support available.
4. To compare and contrast the emotional responses to miscarriage, abortion, stillbirth, neonatal death, sudden infant death syndrome, and the loss of the "perfect" child.
5. To describe disenfranchised grief, with examples of its occurrence, and to identify how grief resulting from such losses can be facilitated.
6. To explain family interactional patterns that may be observed when a child is terminally ill.
7. To compare and contrast ways of caring for the dying child.
8. To identify the factors influencing the response to the death of an adult child.
9. To describe the factors influencing spousal bereavement and to summarize the types of social support available.
10. To distinguish the factors influencing the response to the death of a parent.
11. To summarize the physiological and psychological symptoms of aging.
12. To compare and contrast types of institutional care and community support programs for the aged.
13. To give examples of the losses that occur through institutionalization.
14. To assess the value of death education for the aged.

CONTENT OVERVIEW

Chapter 9 continues the lifespan perspective of the previous chapter by focusing on loss experiences during adulthood. As with the years of childhood, particular psychosocial concerns—or developmental crises—are emphasized during the various stages of adulthood: Young adulthood is characterized by concerns involving intimacy versus isolation, middle adulthood by concerns involving generativity versus stagnation, and maturity by concerns involving integrity versus despair. The meaning given to a loss event— that is, how it is interpreted—depends in significant measure, therefore, on the nature of the developmental issues being dealt with by the individual experiencing the loss.

In the normal course of events, the incidence of loss increases as we grow older. Besides confronting the prospect of our own mortality as a result of the bodily signs of aging, growing older increases the chances that we will experience the death of our parents, and, conversely, that, as parents, we may experience the death of a child. For most parents, a child's death is devastating. It represents not only a loss of the potential and unique future envisioned for the child, but also the loss of a kind of genetic and social immortality for the parent.

In coping with the death of a child, the individuals within a couple relationship may well have different styles of grieving the loss, and both may be overwhelmed by a sense of general chaos, confusion, and uncertainty. Each partner may feel isolated and unsupported by the only other person in the world who shares the magnitude of the loss. Behavior that is meant to be supportive may be interpreted by one's mate as being quite otherwise. Conflict is reduced and positive interactions promoted when couples engage in open and honest communication, share emotional responses as well as information, and validate one another's perception of the loss.

Miscarriage, induced abortion, stillbirth, and neonatal death are examples of child-bearing losses that sometimes go unrecognized, unsupported, and unresolved. Yet the grief experienced by parents following such losses may be just as devastating as that resulting from the death of an older child. This is true also of individuals who give up a child for adoption or who find themselves unable to have children because of sterility or infertility. In mourning unlived lives, grief is felt not only for the physical loss, but also for the symbolic loss. When a person's identity as a nurturing parent has been thwarted, healing the grief requires honoring the archetypal bonds between parent and child. It also requires that the loss be acknowledged by the wider community so that the necessary solace and social support can be offered to the bereaved person.

When a child's life is threatened by serious illness, it affects the whole of family life. Awareness of the illness is likely to be reflected in one of four patterns of communication and interaction: closed, suspected, mutual pretense, or open. The awareness context may change as the severity of the prognosis or problems related to care and treatment change during the course of illness. Caring for a seriously ill child involves attending not only to physical needs but also to emotional and psychological needs. While medical care is best provided by trained personnel, family members can participate in the crucial nontechnical aspects of care, such as those involving the provision of emotional support and encouragement.

Spousal bereavement has been termed the most disruptive of all the transitions in the life cycle. The aftermath of a mate's death requires a multitude of adjustments. Occurrences that were once shared pleasures become occasions for individual pain. Age, gender, and the survivor's patterns of interactions with the mate who is now deceased are among the important factors influencing the experience of spousal bereavement. For example, research indicates that individuals who have lived out traditional sex roles find the transition especially difficult: New skills must be learned to manage the needs of daily life. The availability of a stable social network appears to be crucial in determining how bereaved spouses adjust to their changed status. Besides maintaining the continuity of relationships with friends, neighbors, and family, one of the most valuable resources for the recently widowed has been found to be contact with other bereaved persons who have lost a mate and who can serve as role models during the period of adjustment.

Adult survivors of a parent's death often encounter not only the loss of security represented by a parent's love and support, but also a thought-provoking reminder of their own mortality. Studies indicate that, for most midlife adults, the death of a parent is an important symbolic event, one that triggers a period of self-examination accompanied by a transition to a more mature stance toward life.

For the older adult, the experience of aging typically involves losses related to a variety of physical and mental declines. Although the debilitating effects of aging are being steadily pushed toward the end of the human lifespan, thus "compressing" morbidity and extending "active" life expectancy, the processes of senescence—the aging of the human organism—eventually result in greater frailty and susceptibility to illness and injury. To receive adequate care, many frail elderly require institutional or community support, such as that provided by personal care homes, skilled nursing facilities, and home health care agencies. Yet, growing old is not essentially a medical problem. The latter part of life has its own distinct challenges, most notably the question of human mortality. Facing death has been characterized as the final developmental task of old age.

KEY TERMS AND CONCEPTS

abortion
adoption
atherosclerosis
awareness contexts
childbearing losses
chronic illness
congregate housing
degenerative diseases
domiciliary care home
elder daycare center
generativity vs. stagnation
home health care
hypertension
infertility
institutional neurosis

miscarriage
mizuko
neonatal death
parental bereavement
peer support groups
perinatal death
personal care home
postmortem photography
reframing behavior
senescence
SIDS (sudden infant death syndrome)
skilled nursing facility
social support network
spousal bereavement
stillbirth

integrity vs. despair
intimacy vs. isolation
life cycle
lifespan

stroke
symbolic loss
widowhood

QUESTIONS FOR GUIDED STUDY AND EVALUATION

Multiple-choice questions relevant to this chapter can be found in the test bank.

1. Explain how each psychosocial stage of adulthood relates to the experience of loss.

2. Review your adult life and list the losses that have occurred, evaluating the relationship between the type of loss and the age at which it was experienced.

3. Describe why the death of a child may evoke a high-grief response from parents.

4. Distinguish between parental bereavements relative to the loss of the "perfect" child, stillbirth and perinatal death, abortion, sudden infant death syndrome, death preceded by a chronic illness, and the death of an adult child. Point out the kinds of peer support available for these losses.

5. Compare the four patterns of family interaction identified by Glaser and Strauss and analyze the pros and cons of each.

6. Explain the effects of age and gender on spousal bereavement.

7. Assess how the death of a parent may affect the adult child.

8. Describe life-style possibilities for the aged, commenting on the impact of illness and institutionalization, and explain how older people may regard death and dying.

TEACHING STRATEGIES

1. Distribute three-by-five cards to students. Have each student write one stereotype about the elderly. Collect the cards. Divide the class into small groups and distribute the cards evenly among them. Ask students to discuss the origin and validity of these stereotypes. Have them share at least one story or anecdote that contradicts each of the stereotypes. Then, as a class, discuss what students learned about stereotypes of the aged. (As an alternative to the use of three-by-five cards, you can have students collect pictures of the aged from magazines and newspapers. Limit pictures to those that depict older people engaged in some kind of activity. Continue the activity as described.)

2. Have students role-play family interactional patterns as follows: Divide the class into groups of six. Each group consists of a mother, father, dying child, sibling, a professional caregiver, and a close relative. It can be useful to give the same situation—for example, a discussion in the child's hospital room about plans for Christmas or Hanukkah—to each group. Have each group create a scene depicting an

interaction in one of the following modes: open awareness, closed awareness, suspected awareness, or mutual pretense. Bring the class together and have each group act out its situation.

COMMENTS AND CONSIDERATIONS

1. **Students as Adults Currently Involved in Dealing with the Loss Issues Presented.** A class may include survivors of the various losses discussed in this chapter. Formal or informal interviews of students who have experienced one of the following may be appropriate both for educating the class and for helping the student process his or her grief: death of a mate or intended mate, miscarriage, abortion, perinatal death, death of a child, death of a parent.

2. **Survivor Support Groups.** This is an appropriate time to present information about local support groups, either by requesting literature from them or by inviting a representative to make a short presentation to the class.

RESOURCES: FILMS AND VIDEOCASSETTES

Aging in Japan: When Traditional Mechanisms Vanish (videocassette; 45 min.; color; 1989; Films for the Humanities & Sciences) This program examines a society in flux, wherein the traditional mechanisms for looking after the aged are breaking down. Once considered the most important members of the family, Japan's elderly are finding themselves increasingly isolated and alone.

Agnes Escapes from the Nursing Home (videocassette; 4 min.; color; 1989; Fanlight Productions) An animated film that, with dreamlike images, aims to depict the thoughts and emotions of an elderly woman who repeatedly wanders away from the nursing home where she resides. Can be used as a discussion starter for dealing with the topic of nursing home care for the aged.

Alive Again (videocassette; 31 min.; color; 1985; Health Sciences Consortium, Southern Illinois University School of Medicine) Perinatal death is examined from the perspective of a couple who experienced the death of two newborn babies. Emphasizes the different grief reactions of the mother and father.

All the Way Home (16 mm.; 107 min.; black & white; 1963; Films, Inc.) A dramatic presentation of James Agee's story about aging, death, and family relationships.

Alzheimer's Disease (videocassette; 29 min.; color; 1988; PBS Video) The impact of Alzheimer's on sufferers and family members is depicted in this documentary showing the daily struggles of Lee and Mary Rose as they cope with Lee's deteriorating condition and loss of memory.

Alzheimer's Disease: Coping with Confusion (videocassette & 16 mm.; 28 min.; color; 1985; American Journal of Nursing Co.) Describes care of the Alzheimer's patient at various stages of the disease.

Alzheimer's Disease: Discharge Planning (videocassette & 16 mm.; 28 min.; color; 1985; American Journal of Nursing Co.) Presents the emotional, psychological, and physical struggles of patients and families living with Alzheimer's disease with an emphasis on preparing for discharge from the hospital.

An Alzheimer's Story (videocassette; 28 min.; color; 1986; Filmakers Library) Portrays the painful effects of Alzheimer's disease on the patient's family.

And I Want Time (16 mm.; 28 min.; color; 1977; Portland State University) An excerpt from the film *Love Story*, which portrays the life of a young couple from their marriage to the wife's untimely death.

Are You Listening: Widows (videocassette & 16 mm.; 28 min.; color; 1979; Martha Stuart Communications) The issues of widowhood as seen through the eyes of women of differing ages and ethnicity whose husbands died of various causes.

Babies at Risk (videocassette; 60 min.; color; 1989; PBS Video) An examination of infant mortality in the United States, which has a poor record compared with other Western industrialized nations, with particular attention to the role of inadequate prenatal care and drug addiction in causing this national tragedy. Notes that as little as $450 worth of prenatal care might avoid later costs, absorbed by taxpayers, of as much as $1200 per day for special infant care in hospitals.

Because Somebody Cares (videocassette & 16 mm.; 27 min.; color; 1980; Filmakers Library) Examines the efforts of a volunteer program whereby people of varying ages and backgrounds provide services and companionship for the elderly, either in their own homes or in nursing homes. Emphasizes the rewards of such relationships for all who are involved.

Beginning Again: Widowers (videocassette; 30 min.; color; 1981; WHA-TV) A narrative discussion of spousal bereavement based on interviews with three articulate and candid men: one retired, the others left with growing families. All openly express emotion as they narrate the details of their wives' deaths as well as the funerals and subsequent adjustments. All talk about the difficulties of being alone.

Bereaved Parents (videocassette; 28 min.; color; 1987; Films for the Humanities & Sciences) Addresses the issues of loss and guilt that accompany parental bereavement. Emphasizes the importance of social support and sharing one's grief with others. Adapted from a Phil Donahue program.

Brittle Bones (videocassette & 16 mm.; 22 min.; color; 1983; Filmakers Library) Presents the medical understanding of osteoporosis, including its prevention and treatment. Also examines its impact by focusing on a woman with the disease who organized a number of self-help groups.

The Business of Aging (videocassette & 16 mm.; 27 min.; color; 1981; Filmakers Library) Examines both privately and publicly funded nursing homes and raises issues of patient care, including the economics of institutional care.

Can't Afford to Grow Old (videocassette; 55 min.; color; 1990; Filmakers Library) Narrated and hosted by Walter Cronkite, this program provides a cogent analysis of the impact of aging on the American health care system. Focuses on financial problems associated with aging, particularly as they relate to a system of public funding that forces old people into poverty before they can receive governmental aid. Includes an account of innovative programs that allow the aged some options as they experience frailty.

Caring for the Elderly (videocassette; 19 min.; color; 1987; Films for the Humanities & Sciences) An overview of the various methods of care available for aged persons, from day care centers and group housing to respite care and nursing homes. Profiles a middle-aged couple searching for the best mode of care for their parents. Includes discussion by social workers, nursing home administrators, and advocates for the elderly to clarify the available options and the emotional and financial impact on adult children and their parents.

A Child Dies (videocassette; 28 min.; color; 1987; American Journal of Nursing Co.) Produced as a training film for nurses, this video highlights two nurse clinicians with extensive experience working with dying children and their families. They explain typical grief responses and emphasize the importance of listening.

Childhood Cancer: A Day at a Time (videocassette; 59 min.; color; 1983; Filmakers Library) This program documents the lives of four families wherein a child is living with cancer. Ambiguity, honesty, and adaptation are key themes in each family. The children's coping mechanisms are also discussed.

Chillysmith Farm (videocassette & 16 mm.; 55 min.; color; 1981; Filmakers Library) An account of birth, life, and death in one extended family. Still photographs show the grandfather's dying over a period of three years, and film footage shows the grandmother's final days followed by the birth of a new family member. Emphasizes the importance of the extended family.

Companions: Pets and the Elderly (videocassette & 16 mm.; 11 min.; color; 1982; Filmakers Library) Focuses on the therapeutic effect of pets on the elderly.

Coping with Terminal Illness (videocassette; 36 min.; color; 1983; American Journal of Nursing Co.) Portrays the struggle of one family as the father, diagnosed at age forty-one with ALS, dies at the age of forty-three. His wife and teenage children discuss their experiences of his dying and death.

A Cradle Song (videocassette; 29 min.; color; 1989; Fanlight Productions) Historically based perspective from ancient times to the present. Includes interviews with both medical professionals and grieving parents. Filled with informative facts about what SIDS is and is not. Also includes perspectives of surviving siblings and grandparents.

Crib Death (videocassette; 59 min.; color; 1990; Films for the Humanities & Sciences) Shows the mourning process of the filmmaker, as he copes with the loss of his seven-month-old son. Provides information about SIDS and looks at the experiences of other families.

David (videocassette & 16 mm.; 28 min.; color; 1980; Filmakers Library) David, an adolescent with Down's syndrome, leads a full and productive life, which he discusses in an interview. His family also participates. Focuses on the loss of the "perfect" child.

Dear Little Lightbird (16 mm.; 19 min.; color; Viewfinders) The grieving parent of a terminally ill boy is the subject of this film.

Death Be Not Proud (16 mm.; about 1 hour & 40 min.; color; 1975; Learning Corporation of America) A film version of John Gunther's novel, telling the story of his son's terminal illness and death.

Death Is Afraid of Us (videocassette & 16 mm.; 26 min.; color; 1980; Filmakers Library) Cameos the lives of a number of Soviet Georgian centenarians. An interesting twist on lifespan development, as we look at "older" individuals enjoying a life of seemingly extended adolescence.

Death of the High Risk Infant (videocassette; 30 min.; color; 1985; American Journal of Nursing Co.) Intended primarily for nurses and other hospital staff working with bereaved parents, this video provides information about parental grief at the death of an infant, with emphasis on the process of grief and how caregivers can encourage healthy grieving.

Death of a Wished-For Child (16 mm.; 28 min.; color; OGR Service Corp.) Glen Davidson discusses how to meet the psychological needs of mothers whose wished-for babies die. Emphasizes avoiding pathological responses by early and appropriate intervention. One mother is cameoed as she responds to the well-intentioned but unhelpful advice of caregivers.

The Elder (videocassette; 8 min.; color; 1989; Fanlight Productions) Containing no dialogue, this short film depicts a family's decision to place an elderly relative in a nursing home. Sequences convey a sense of the characters' feelings and their relationships. Beautiful imagery that helps to elicit the viewer's feelings about old age and nursing home care.

Empty Arms: The Caregiver's Role—Pregnancy and Infant Loss (videocassette; 120 min. each segment; color; 1988; Wintergreen Press) A video presentation of a day-long seminar presented by Sherokee Isle at Vanderbilt University Hospital. Consists of three two-hour videotapes covering the range of issues pertaining to reproductive and perinatal losses. Designed for training medical professionals, funeral directors, clergy, mental health personnel, and support group leaders.

Empty Arms: Reaching Out to You (videocassette; 30 min.; color; 1988; Wintergreen Press) Produced by Sherokee Ilse, this video addresses the reactions and needs of parents in the first hours after perinatal bereavement. Offers advice about seeing and holding the deceased infant, creating mementos, saying goodbye, planning a memorial service, and going home to face an empty nursery. The importance of social support for the loss is emphasized. Recommended for professionals as well as for survivors of perinatal loss.

Epitaph: The Lingering Heart (16 mm.; 25 min.; color; 1975; WKYC-TV) A young man dies of leukemia, and we witness the reactions of his wife and daughters to life without him.

A Family in Grief: The Ameche Story (videocassette; 26 min.; color; 1987; Research Press) This documentary has become a modern classic for its sensitive portrayal of a family's grieving following the sudden death of a twenty-two-year-old son and sibling. Father (Alan Ameche, a Heisman trophy winner and former star fullback for the NFL champion Baltimore Colts), mother, and the five siblings share their feelings about the loss and describe the family's process of coping with it. The elements, or phases, of the bereavement process are placed into the context of a family's journey through grief.

The Father (16 mm.; 28 min.; black & white; 1970; New Line Cinema) A fictional account of a father's need to talk to strangers about his recently deceased son. Burgess Meredith plays the role of a cab driver in New York City who interacts with his passengers concerning his loss.

Fool's Dance (videocassette & 16 mm.; 30 min.; color; 1988; Carle Medical Communications) Into the stereotypical surroundings of an extended care facility filled with aged residents comes the "fool," an eccentric who disrupts the institutional status quo while revitalizing the lives of the residents. Emphasizes the power of philosophy, spirituality, and wit to enrich life.

Grieving: Suddenly Alone (videocassette & 16 mm.; 26 min.; color; 1982; Churchill Films) The grief of widowhood is examined, including typical emotions such as anger and guilt—anger at the deceased for abandonment, displaced anger at the living, and guilt at the possibility of not having done enough to prevent the death. Intrafamilial relationships are also explored, as are relationships with co-workers. The film concludes by focusing on the importance for some of joining a self-help group.

The Grieving Family (videocassette; 28 min.; color; 1987; American Journal of Nursing Co.) Designed as an accompaniment to the training film for nurses entitled *A Child Dies*, this video focuses on the actions that caregivers can take to assist grieving families, including helping survivors to say goodbye, dealing with funeral arrangements, and attending to the other decisions that must be made following a death in the family.

Growing Old in America (videocassette; 30 min.; color; 1980; Michigan Media) A gerontologist and a sociologist interview author May Sarton about her visits to nursing homes while researching a book.

Halftime: Five Yale Men at Midlife (videocassette; 90 min.; color; 1988; The Cinema Guild) This award-winning documentary profiles five men from Yale's class of 1963, who look back on their lives at midlife. The five men—a Hollywood producer, a psychotherapist, a prosecutor, a former corporate executive, and a bank president—struggle to come to terms with their failures and successes in love and marriage, parenting and professions, and, especially, with the disparities between what they dreamed their lives would be like and the reality of what they've become.

How Do I Go On? Redesigning Your Future After Crisis Has Changed Your Life (videocassette; 21 min.; color; 1989; Willowgreen Productions) Scenic images and serene music greet viewers of this video designed for people whose futures appear limited by circumstance, accident, or illness.

Interviews with Childhood Cancer Patients and Their Families (videocassette; 60 min.; color; 1983; Elisabeth Kübler-Ross Center) Along with three- and eight-year-old cancer patients, parents, grandparents, and siblings talk about their experiences.

The Jilting of Granny Weatherall (videocassette & 16 mm.; 57 min.; color; 1980; Coronet/MTI Film & Video, Guidance Associates) Geraldine Fitzgerald stars in this teleplay depicting the deathbed thoughts of a crusty old woman who has one major regret about her life.

Larry: An Amputee's Story (videocassette; 58 min.; color; 1984; Southern Illinois University School of Medicine) Looks at the physical, social, and psychological impact of amputation from the time of Larry's accident to a year and a half later.

Letting Go (videocassette; 29 min.; color; 1990; American Journal of Nursing Co.) Designed to help parents and caregivers cope with the death of a child. Includes the viewpoints of terminally ill children as well as of two families going through the difficult time surrounding the death of a child.

Leukemia Panel Discussion (videocassette; 32 min.; color; 1975; Stanford University School of Medicine) Parents discuss with doctors the emotional and psychological impact of leukemia on their children.

The Mailbox (16 mm.; 24 min.; color; 1977; Brigham Young University) The struggles of an elderly woman are depicted as she tries to maintain a relationship with her grown children; she dies waiting to hear from them.

Memories (videocassette; 27 min.; color; 1982; Health Sciences Consortium, Southern Illinois University School of Medicine) The feelings and experiences of parents whose babies have died through miscarriage, stillbirth, or neonatal death are examined. The parents are from SHARE, a peer support group.

Michael Cardew (videocassette; 29 min.; color; 1983; Barr Films) Five months prior to his death, a master potter talks about his art and his philosophy of life.

Mirror, Mirror on the Wall (videocassette & 16 mm.; 28 min.; color; 1978; Mass Media Ministries) A presentation of lifespan development that focuses on the impact of body images. Two lives are cameoed: a woman who had surgery for breast cancer and a survivor of heart attack. Both discuss the new awareness resulting from their respective experiences.

The Most Neglected Resource (videocassette; 20 min.; color; 1987; Ideal Communications) This program, narrated by John Houseman, depicts low-income, healthy seniors providing home care to frail elderly. The healthy seniors receive a tax-free stipend for their services and they develop strong relationships with the frail elderly, who are able to continue living in the familiar surroundings of their homes.

No Place Like Home: Long Term Care for the Elderly (videocassette; 55 min.; color; 1987; Filmakers Library) This documentary with Helen Hayes focuses on home care for the elderly, emphasizing that public policies can be formed that allow old people to stay in their own homes rather than being forced into institutional care. Examples of alternatives to institutionalization in New York, Appalachia, San Francisco, and England are shown.

Old, Black, and Alive (16 mm.; 28 min.; color; 1975; New Film Co.) Examines the lives of three aged Black Alabamians who, despite various difficulties, have a positive attitude toward life.

Open House: Shared Living for the Elderly (videocassette & 16 mm.; 19 min.; color; 1989; Filmakers Library) Focuses on viable living alternatives for the elderly person who no longer wants to live alone but is too independent to live in an institution. "Shared housing" combines privacy and companionship while it saves dollars and promotes the well-being of the sharers. A variety of such housing arrangements are shown, as Maggie Kuhn, founder of the Gray Panthers, provides commentary.

Parenting Our Parents (videocassette; 26 min.; color; 1987; Films for the Humanities & Sciences) As the elderly population increases, many middle-aged people are feeling as if they are the "sandwich generation"—staggering under the double burden of raising children and caring for chronically ill or disabled parents. This program examines ways of coping with the stress of caring for aging parents and suggests personal and political mechanisms for easing the burden.

Parents Who Have Lost Children (videocassette; 29 min.; color; 1981; University of Arizona) This program documents the lives of a number of parents after the deaths of their children. It is intended to help health care professionals recognize what is at issue and thereby help parents during the grief process.

Peege (videocassette & 16 mm.; 28 min.; color; 1974; Phoenix/BFA Films & Video) The life of a nursing home resident is depicted through a series of flashbacks experienced by her grandson when he and his family pay her a Christmas visit. Looks at both familial relationships and individual responses. An excellent film.

A Perspective of Hope: Scenes from the Teaching Nursing Home (videocassette & 16 mm.; 29 min.; color; 1988; Fanlight Productions) Examines an ongoing demonstration project aimed at improving the health care of elderly Americans. The project's goal is to encourage schools of nursing to establish clinical affiliations with nursing homes, much as those between medical schools and teaching hospitals.

The Pitch of Grief (videocassette; 30 min.; color; 1985; Fanlight Productions) Four men and women of varying ages are interviewed about the deaths of their loved ones. Examines the phases of grieving, detailing the physiological and psychological symptoms.

Portraits of Aging (videocassette & 16 mm.; 28 min.; color; 1979; Portland State University) Presents a positive view of aging by older people.

Rose by Any Other Name (16 mm.; 15 min.; color; 1980; Tricepts Productions) Discusses attitudes toward the relationship between Rose Gordon and Mr. Morris, aged residents in a nursing home.

The Silent Epidemic: Alzheimer's Disease (videocassette & 16 mm.; 25 min.; color; 1982; Filmakers Library) Examines the difficulties of living with an Alzheimer's patient and the questions surrounding the institutionalization of such patients, as well as the emotional confusion resulting from the loss of a loved one with Alzheimer's disease.

Smiles (16 mm.; 29 min.; color; 1973; Portland State University) A documentary about college students working with the elderly. A positive attitude forms the basis for a University of Maryland program that pairs students with the elderly in activities ranging from physical exercise to talent shows.

Softfire (videocassette & 16 mm.; 19 min.; color; 1984; Barr Films) The last days in the life of an eighty-eight-year-old woman named Ethyl are characterized by an open and honest discussion of her life and impending death. Staff members at the Dana Home Care Service of Boulder, Colorado, discuss the philosophical foundation of a program that encourages people to live with dignity until they die.

Some Babies Die (videocassette; 16 mm.; color; 1986; UCB Extension Media Center) Remarkable documentary chronicling a hospital-based counseling team's work with families experiencing neonatal loss. Directly confrontational techniques include encouraging even the youngest children to hold the body of their dead sibling.

Sudden Infant Death Syndrome: A Family's Anguish (videocassette; 15 min.; color; 1986; Colorado SIDS Program) Designed for parent support, professional training, and community education, this video presents medical and statistical information about SIDS as well as interviews with parents concerning family issues.

Sudden Infant Death Syndrome: The Unfulfilled Promise (videocassette; 19 min.; color; 1982; Batesville Management Services) Discusses the impact of sudden and inexplicable infant death on survivors.

Sudden Infant Death Syndrome and the Pediatrician (videocassette; 43 min.; color; 1974; University of Arizona) A training film for physicians working with parents of potential SIDS babies. Looks at how this type of death affects parents.

The Syndrome of Ordinary Grief (videocassette; 32 min.; color; 1971; Videotape Library of Clinical Psychiatric Syndromes) An interview with a young medical student whose only child, a two-year-old, was killed one month before in an automobile accident. Examines acute grief and its somatic and psychological symptomatology.

Tales of Tomorrow: Our Elders (videocassette & 16 mm.; 22 min.; color; 1982; Filmakers Library) Shows the lives of a number of physically and mentally handicapped elders, attending to both the positive and negative aspects of institutionalization.

There Was a Child (videocassette; 32 min.; color; 1990; Fanlight Productions) Interviews with bereaved parents, including a Black American couple. Open, honest reflections by people who have experienced miscarriage, stillbirth, or perinatal death.

Three Grandmothers (16 mm.; 28 min.; black & white; 1963; Brigham Young University) A cross-cultural look at the roles of grandmothers in Brazil, Canada, and Nigeria. A common pattern is discerned even though the cultures are different.

Valley of the Shadow: A Journey Through Grief (videocassette & 16 mm.; 38 min.; color; 1980; Creative Marketing) Parents discuss their grief after the sudden deaths of their two children. The morbidity of grief is discussed in light of the father's having developed cancer after the deaths.

We Can Help (videocassette & 16 mm.; 20 min.; color; Case Western Reserve University) A training film for hospital staff who care for pediatric cancer patients and their families. Concerned with both the physical and emotional well-being of patients, who range from young children to older adolescents.

What About Mom and Dad? (videocassette; 60 min.; color; 1985; PBS Video) An award-winning "Frontline" program describing the plight of many elderly, who find their savings eroded by the costs of nursing home care. The difficult emotional and financial issues facing both the aged and their families are explored.

Widows (videocassette & 16 mm.; 41 min.; black & white; 1972; Documentaries for Learning) A series of interviews with bereaved wives of varying ages and backgrounds as they discuss widowhood, including what was most helpful to them. Looks at members of a "widow-to-widow" self-help group. Special emphasis is placed on young widows and their children.

Widows and Widowers—Problems and Adjustments (videocassette; 20 min.; color; 1981; Batesville Management Services) Looks at the first year of widowhood and offers advice about how to help survivors.

You Are Not Alone (videocassette & 16 mm.; 27 min.; color; 1976; National Audiovisual Center, SIDS Alliance) Discusses the fact that little is known about the prevention or cause of SIDS and looks at ways to help bereaved families.

Chapter 10

Medical Ethics: Dying in a Technological Age

OBJECTIVES

1. To explain how the fundamental ethical principles of autonomy, beneficence, and justice apply to medical ethics.
2. To describe the factors affecting truth telling in cases involving terminal illness.
3. To assess patients' rights with respect to self-determination and informed consent.
4. To identify the consequences of withholding the truth from the point of view of both patient and physician.
5. To evaluate the ethical issues involved in euthanasia.
6. To explain how issues regarding competency affect decisions to withhold treatment from infants or comatose patients.
7. To describe the emotional, physical, and ethical components of organ transplantation.
8. To name four approaches to the definition of death and to evaluate the usefulness of each.
9. To give an example of a practical definition of death and its application to making a determination of death.

CONTENT OVERVIEW

Chapter 10 deals with the central issues in medical ethics, issues that have become prominent with advances in biomedical technology. Modern techniques of cardiopulmonary resuscitation and organ transplantation, for example, make possible life-sustaining interventions that were unavailable just a few decades ago. Yet such technologies present us with difficult questions about how they should be used. In circumstances where sophisticated and innovative medical technologies have the power to dramatically alter the course of dying and to challenge the traditional definition of death, the Hippocratic obligation to keep people alive can lead to confusing consequences. Coming to terms with these consequences and arriving at a satisfactory guide to behavior means grappling with fundamental ethical principles involving autonomy, beneficence, and justice.

Although these ethical principles have been a topic of intelligent discourse by moral philosophers for hundreds if not thousands of years, their application to the practice of medicine has varied, reflecting changes in public attitudes and social situations. Studies indicate, for example, that as recently as three decades ago most physicians tended to withhold information about a terminal prognosis. Telling the unadulterated truth was viewed as possibly harmful to the patient's best interest. Thus, patients with incurable cancer were told that they had a "lesion" or "mass," and adjectives such as "suspicious" or "degenerated" were used to temper the impact of the diagnosis. Within a period of about twenty years, however, a very different climate of truth-telling emerged. While not abandoning their concern with the patient's welfare, physicians became much more likely to reveal the true nature of a terminal diagnosis.

In tracing the causes for this change in the practice of truth telling, we can discern the influence of consumer attitudes as well as improvements in the medical outlook for patients with life-threatening disease. As consumers began to demand a greater voice in decisions affecting their own welfare, medical practitioners were increasingly being held accountable for the services provided to patients. Medical paternalism with respect to decisions about patient care opens the door to allegations of malpractice when outcomes differ from expectations. In addition, newer therapies tend to require more sophisticated cooperation from patients in following treatment regimes. Taken together, these factors focused attention on the importance of obtaining a patient's informed consent to treatment.

Such consent is based on three principles: First, the patient must be competent to give consent. Second, consent must be given voluntarily. Third, consent must be based on an adequate understanding of the proposed treatment program. Although the phrase "informed consent" did not achieve legal definition until 1957, the doctrine of informed consent is now recognized in case law or statute in nearly all U.S. jurisdictions. Because individual attitudes toward autonomy or self-determination as applied to medical care differ, the process of giving information and obtaining consent to a treatment plan must be flexible. Although forced, coercive treatment is rare, caregivers can exert undue influence on patients by means of subtle or overt manipulation. The shared decision making required by the ethical imperative of informed consent places special emphasis on the process of communication between caregivers and patients. Much more than simply a laundry list of risks to be recited in an effort to avoid potential complaints or legal problems, informed consent can be a mechanism for facilitating cooperation between a patient and a physician working toward a common goal of optimal health care.

Among the most emotionally charged issues in medical ethics are those that relate to euthanasia (intentionally and actively bringing about the death of a terminally ill person) and forgoing life-sustaining treatment (either by withholding or withdrawing treatment). Questions about the "right to die" have been prominent since the landmark case involving Karen Ann Quinlan during the mid-1970s. What is the proper balance between sustaining life and preventing suffering when further treatment is likely to be futile? What effect do modern life-sustaining technologies have on the quality of patients' lives, particularly in situations involving irreversibly comatose patients or patients in a persistent vegetative state?

The arguments put forward by advocates of euthanasia in support of the notion that human beings have an inherent "right to die" (and, as a corollary, that it ought to be permissible for medical practitioners to assist terminal patients in voluntarily ending their lives painlessly) are being received favorably in many quarters, despite the fact that taking active measures to end someone's life remains a capital crime in the United States. Critics of euthanasia express concerns that a legally sanctioned "right" to die could become an "obligation" to die due to subtle pressures to lessen the burden on loved ones or to lessen the economic impact of terminal care on society at large. Where would one draw the line, they ask, once the slippery slope of euthanasia has been embarked on? Such critics also claim that the infrequent requests for euthanasia are likely to disappear when the pain and depression that accompany terminal disease are treated and the sources of anxiety addressed.

In contrast to the debate over euthanasia, the withholding or withdrawing of treatments considered to be medically useless is an increasingly well-established and accepted practice in American medicine. For virtually any life-threatening condition, some medical intervention is capable of delaying the moment of death. Despite general agreement among medical practitioners as well as among the public that extraordinary interventions need not be used when a patient is hopelessly ill, many areas of uncertainty remain. One difficulty involves arriving at a consensus as to what is meant by the term *extraordinary.* For example, courts in various jurisdictions across the country have dealt with the question of whether the artificial provision of nutrition and hydration constitutes extraordinary medical intervention or ordinary care. Discussions about such issues often revolve around conceptual ambiguities—in this case, those involving the artificial delivery of food and fluids. Although the delivery of such nourishment requires invasive medical procedures and technical skills, feelings about the provision of food and drink and the specter of starving a person to death are deeply rooted in the human psyche.

In the summer of 1990, the U.S. Supreme Court ruled on a petition to end the artificial feeding of Nancy Beth Cruzan, a Missouri woman who had been in a persistent vegetative state resulting from an automobile accident in 1983. In deciding the case, the Court acknowledged that a competent person has a right to refuse life-sustaining medical treatment, but also found that states (in this case, Missouri) could establish procedural requirements for clear and convincing evidence regarding an incompetent patient's wishes. Since Nancy Cruzan had not formally made her wishes known by executing an advance directive (such as the living will), the case was referred back to the Missouri courts (where, after further consideration and new testimony from three of Nancy's friends, it was ruled that the "clear and convincing" standard had been met and permission was granted to remove the tube supplying food and water). The case of Nancy Cruzan pointed up not only the diversity of opinion about what constitutes extraordinary treatment, but also the confusing legal situation that frequently characterizes situations involving ethical issues in medicine. The burden of such uncertainty weighs heavily on families when patients cannot express their own choices—either because they have lost that capacity, as with individuals who are in a coma, or because they have not yet achieved the power to exercise autonomy, as in the case of seriously ill newborns.

Organ transplantation is another area of medicine in which ethical issues have been prominent. Because fewer organs are donated than are needed, physicians are forced to act as gatekeepers, choosing among prospective recipients. The manner in which organs are allocated for transplantation raises important ethical concerns about the rationing of scarce health care resources. How are we to determine the selection criteria for making decisions about who shall live and who shall die?

The practice of organ transplantation has also focused attention on the criteria appropriate for defining death and the standards to be used in determining when death can be said to have occurred. Medical technology now allows physicians to maintain the viability of bodily organs for subsequent transplantation by sustaining certain physiological functions in the body of an individual who has been declared dead. The conventional signs of death—most notably, the absence of heartbeat and respiration—are rendered inadequate when vital processes are maintained artificially. Thus, most efforts to expand the criteria for determining death have focused on the loss of the capacity for bodily integration (popularly known as "brain" death), which is essentially defined as irreversible coma confirmed by a flat electroencephalogram (EEG) reading and unresponsiveness to all external stimuli. Using this approach, a determination of death does not depend on the provision of artificial life support to sustain breathing and heartbeat; rather, the crucial factor has to do with the presence or absence of the capacity for bodily integration. A person whose vital processes are sustained artificially during surgery, for example, is not dead. But a person who has lost the capacity for bodily integration, even though the body's vital processes are maintained artificially, is dead.

Over the course of the past two decades, various forms of legislation have been enacted recognizing the fact that the conventional definition of death is inadequate in certain circumstances in light of present medical practice. By 1988, half of the states had adopted some version of the Uniform Determination of Death Act, which was proposed by a presidential commission on medical ethics. When the vital processes are not supported on a respirator, the need to evaluate brain function does not arise. Thus, irreversible circulatory and respiratory cessation is the obvious and sufficient basis for determining death in the vast majority of cases. For respirator-maintained bodies, on the other hand, the irreversible cessation of all functions of the entire brain, including the brain stem, constitutes death. Although noteworthy suggestions have been put forward regarding the substitution of a "higher-brain" criterion—that is, one focusing on the capacity for consciousness, social interaction, or personhood—in place of the "whole-brain" formulation contained in the Act, there appears, at present, to be relatively little enthusiasm for such a fundamental change in the manner of defining death.

KEY TERMS AND CONCEPTS

artificial feeding

autonomy

beneficence

brain death

cellular death

clinical death

CMO (comfort measures only)

comatose

CPR (cardiopulmonary resuscitation)

death with dignity

DNR (do not resuscitate)

euthanasia

extraordinary measures

Harvard criteria for determining death

Hippocratic oath

informed consent

justice

life-sustaining treatment

neonatal intensive care

organ transplantation

passive management

persistent vegetative state

placebo

right to die

rigor mortis

self-determination

truth telling

Uniform Determination of Death Act

vital signs

QUESTIONS FOR GUIDED STUDY AND EVALUATION

Multiple-choice questions relevant to this chapter can be found in the test bank.

1. Name at least five medical technologies that have contributed to a longer lifespan for some individuals.

2. Evaluate the roles of autonomy, beneficence, and justice in medical decision making.

3. Define the terms *self-determination* and *informed consent* and name the three principles of informed consent.

4. Describe changes in the climate of truth telling since the 1950s.

5. Evaluate the care options for hopelessly ill or comatose patients, keeping in mind ethical considerations.

6. Assess each side of the issue of euthanasia and construct a convincing position statement for each.

7. Develop a position on the question of a seriously deformed infant's right to life, and discuss the ramifications of such a position.

8. Describe the relationship between organ transplantation and the way that death is defined and determined.

9. Contrast traditional methods of defining death with newer definitions.

10. Identify Robert Veatch's four approaches to defining and determining death. Which do you find most helpful and least helpful? Explain your response.

11. Compare and contrast the Uniform Determination of Death Act proposed by the President's Commission with earlier proposals for determining death. Do you think the Commission's proposal is an improvement? Why or why not?

12. Design your own proposal for defining and determining death, pointing out its strengths and weaknesses. Be sure to state who should be involved in making a determination of death.

TEACHING STRATEGIES

1. Divide the class into groups. Have each group imagine it is a hospital ethics committee composed of a hospital administrator, a doctor, a patient advocate from the community, and a member of the clergy. Together, they must judge whether or not a patient should receive life-sustaining treatment. Allow enough time for each participant to choose one of the roles and to begin identifying relevant concerns. Then distribute one of the following questions to each of the groups and instruct students to jointly arrive at answers.

   • A sixty-two-year-old patient who has suffered a heart attack is resuscitated and placed on a respirator. After 24 hours, an electroencephalogram (EEG) shows no brain activity. Should life support be withdrawn?

   • An emergency medical team is called to the scene of a "man down," where they find a seventy-five-year-old resident of a posh district in a major metropolitan city with no vital signs. Is this patient D.O.A. or should resuscitation efforts be started?

   • An emergency medical team is called to the scene of a "man down," where they find a seventy-five-year-old "skid row" derelict with no vital signs. Is this patient D.O.A. or should resuscitation efforts be started?

   • The patient is an anencephalic newborn (with a congenital malformation such that there is no brain development). The parents request that physicians withdraw intravenous feeding. Should the ethics committee consent to the parents' request?

   • The patient is a newborn with Down's syndrome and intestinal blockage. The parents refuse to give their consent to surgery and request that physicians withdraw intravenous feeding. Should the ethics committee consent to the parents' request?

   • A patient dying of AIDS asks to be released from the hospital in order to return home and commit suicide. What is the hospital's responsibility?

   • A newborn is given no medical possibility of living longer than five to seven days because of a congenital, always fatal, condition. The adjacent incubator in the neonatal intensive care unit holds a newborn who will die within 48 hours without a heart transplant. Is it ethical to shorten the first infant's life by a couple of days so that another child has a chance to live? Who should decide?

- A husband and wife are diagnosed, respectively, with Alzheimer's and untreatable, terminal cancer. They mutually decide on a suicide pact, desiring to die as they have lived for the previous six decades—together. Do they have the right to end their lives in this manner?

- A major medical center announces that it wishes to open a special wing to keep the bodies of neomorts (brain-dead corpses) functioning on life support until the organs can be harvested to aid patients with life-threatening conditions. Should the medical center be allowed to proceed with this plan? Who should benefit financially from such harvesting of organs?

- A woman who has received governmental assistance (welfare) for the last forty-five years of her life is killed in an automobile accident. There is no known next of kin, and she did not complete an organ donor card or leave other instructions about the disposition of her remains. Given that the woman was supported by the state for more than four decades of her life, does the state have any "vested interest" in deciding whether her organs can be used for transplantation? Should the hospital ethics committee make such a request of the state?

Encourage students to take strong stands based on the perspectives of their chosen roles. Allow 15 minutes for group discussion and then have each group report to the class and discuss its decision.

2. Make a brief presentation to the class on arguments for and against euthanasia. Then set up a situation whereby students move to one side of the room to indicate a position in favor of euthanasia and to the other side to indicate a position against euthanasia. Within each group have students discuss their individual beliefs to make sure that each student is on the appropriate side of the room. After several minutes, point out how difficult it can be to maintain a highly polarized position as well as how beliefs may change as an issue is understood more completely. Bring the class together to discuss the feelings and insights generated by this activity.

COMMENTS AND CONSIDERATIONS

Ethical Issues and Personal History. Ethical issues can bring up past experiences by which students determine their present stands. Encourage them to relate their experiences to their beliefs.

RESOURCES: FILMS AND VIDEOCASSETTES

Better Off Dead? (videocassette; 60 min.; color; 1984; PBS Video) This award-winning episode of "Frontline" investigates the "Baby Doe" controversy over ethical choices concerning the limits of medical care for damaged newborns.

Born Dying (videocassette & 16 mm.; 20 min.; color; 1983; Research Press) Bioethical issues in determining the treatment of severely handicapped newborns are looked at from many perspectives, including that of parents, grandparents, attending nurses, and physicians.

Code Gray: Ethical Dilemmas in Nursing (videocassette & 16 mm.; 28 min.; color; 1983; Fanlight Productions) Explores the dilemmas of nurses as they face conflicts on a daily basis between what they feel they should be doing and what they are able to do. Allocation of time and energy is one such dilemma. Another involves the struggle with ethical concerns, such as those relating to a newborn baby with serious birth defects, a nursing home patient, and a terminally ill patient.

Dax's Case: Who Should Decide? (videocassette & 16 mm.; 60 min.; color; 1985; Filmakers Library) Documents the situation of Dax Cowart, a burn victim who demanded the right to die and was refused, looking at bioethical, moral, and religious concerns both from his perspective and from the perspective of his family, physicians, and attorneys.

Deception (videocassette; 34 min.; color; 1988; Fanlight Productions) This dramatization deals with the question of whether doctors can ever justify deceiving patients for the patients' own good. Without providing easy answers, the film explores the issues involved and provokes thought.

Decisions of the Heart (videocassette; 8 min.; color; 1989; American Journal of Nursing Co.) Addresses human and ethical issues around the decision whether to resuscitate a seriously ill family member. Explains the nature of resuscitative efforts as well as DNR instructions. Describes the option of palliative care instead of resuscitation.

A Dignified Exit (videocassette & 16 mm.; 26 min.; color; 1981; Filmakers Library) Patients, families, and physicians discuss the ethics of euthanasia, with special attention to the Exit Society in England.

Discussion with Parents of a Malformed Baby (videocassette; 37 min.; color; Case Western Reserve University) This interview with parents of a six-week-old infant with Down's syndrome looks at parenting issues as well as how hospital personnel related to the parents.

Discussions in Bioethics (videocassette & 16 mm.; 107 min.; color; Pyramid Film & Video) This series of eight open-ended dramas dealing with bioethical issues was produced under the guidance of Dr. David J. Roy, Director of the Centre for Bioethics in Montreal. The eight vignettes (each about 15 minutes) are based on actual cases and deal with the subjects of death through benign neglect, the right to refuse treatment, quality of care, allocation of scarce medical resources, prenatal diagnosis, compulsory sterilization, the handicapped newborn, and chemical warfare. Because they offer no pat answers, these eight vignettes stimulate discussion of bioethical issues and encourage thought about difficult questions. The series emphasizes that ethical decisions take place within the context of relationships.

The DNR Dilemma (videocassette; 43 min.; color; 1988; Carle Medical Communications) Who, what, when, where, and why of resuscitation decisions, including an exploration of the specifics concerning DNR guidelines.

Done with Life (videocassette; 43 min.; color; 1989; Films for the Humanities & Sciences) Describes the practice of government-sponsored euthanasia in the Netherlands. With English subtitles.

Dying Wish (videocassette; 52 min.; color; 1989; Films for the Humanities & Sciences) This CBS "48 hours" documentary looks at the ethical questions raised by sophisticated medical technologies.

Esther's Story (videocassette; 33 min.; color; 1984; Health Sciences Consortium, Southern Illinois University School of Medicine) An account of the last weeks in a woman's life and her decision to have her life-support machine removed. Emphasizes the process by which she regained her dignity about the prospect of death and the importance of respecting the rights of patients and families regarding treatment.

Euthanasia (videocassette; 44 min.; color; 1990; Filmakers Library) An important film on the "right to die" issue. Explores the legal, moral, and ethical implications of euthanasia. Includes a segment on the Netherlands, where active euthanasia is socially supported and permitted by the courts.

Extending Life (videocassette & 16 mm.; 15 min.; color; 1976; Phoenix/BFA Films & Video) An overview of bioethical questions regarding the extension of life.

Is This Life Worth Living? (videocassette; 30 min.; color; 1987; Filmakers Library) Stories on the plight of three families with a comatose family member. This documentary explores the complex, and sometimes haunting, ethical questions about sustaining life and making life-death decisions, especially when the patient is incompetent.

Last Rights (videocassette; 60 min.; color; 1987; PBS Video) An "Inside Story" account of Dr. John Kraai, who killed his long-time friend and patient Frederick Wagner, who lay gravely ill in a nursing home. Featuring segments from the Hemlock Society's national convention, this program probes the issues surrounding euthanasia, or mercy killing, and examines the topic of living wills as a means by which individuals can take steps to control their own medical care.

Leon Kass (videocassette; 60 min.; color; 1989; PBS Video) A physician and philosopher, Leon Kass is noted for his contributions to medical ethics. Interviewed by Bill Moyers, Kass shares his insights into science, mortality, and the search for souls in Part I of this program. In Part II, Kass focuses on the moral implications of euthanasia and the new reproduction technologies.

Let My Daughter Die (videocassette; 60 min.; color; 1988; PBS Video) From the "Frontline" series, this video reports on the efforts by the parents of Nancy Cruzan to have artificial feeding removed from their comatose daughter. Explores the legal and ethical issues through interviews with Nancy's caregivers, as well as with her parents and the parents of other comatose patients.

Liver Transplant (videocassette; 29 min.; color; 1988; PBS Video) Kendra Poarch received a new liver for her fourteenth birthday as her only chance of living after being diagnosed with Alagille's Syndrome, a rare and fatal condition. This program explores the lives of organ transplant recipients.

Matter of Life or Death (videocassette; 20 min.; color; 1989; Filmakers Library) Narrated by James Earl Jones, this video examines ethical issues concerning who decides about treatment when a person is admitted to a hospital in critical condition. Excellent discussion starter in a classroom setting. Thought-provoking and stimulating.

Medicine and Mercy (videocassette; 26 min.; color; 1988; Films for the Humanities & Sciences) This program examines the interplay among technology, ethics, and quality of life; the definition of life and death; and the thesis that humans have a right to die. Looks at two court decisions pertaining to the cessation of artificial life support and examines the ethical arguments on both sides of the issue.

Mercy Killing (videocassette; 28 min.; color; 1987; Films for the Humanities & Sciences) Adapted from a Phil Donahue program, this video examines issues of medical ethics through the accounts of a woman who helped her terminally ill mother acquire the drugs to end her life, the daughter of a seventy-six-year-old man who shot his crippled wife to death after she begged him to end her misery, and the mother of Karen Ann Quinlan.

Parents and Children (videocassette & 16 mm.; 24 min.; color; 1979; Research Press) Explores the legal issues for parents related to medical treatment of their children. Includes discussions of informed consent, the difference between an emergency and nonemergency decision, minors who undergo abortions, and child abuse.

Please Let Me Die (videocassette; 30 min.; color; 1974; Videotape Library of Clinical Psychiatric Syndromes) Examines the right to die when a patient faces unbearable pain. A young man has been severely burned over 70 percent of his body, and the film graphically depicts, without comment, an episode of treatment. The second part of the film is a discussion between the patient and his psychiatrist during which the patient, with lucidity and control, says that he wants to die.

Prenatal Diagnosis: To Be or Not to Be (videocassette & 16 mm.; 45 min.; color; 1981; Filmakers Library) With the advent of such prenatal tests as fetoscopy, amniocentesis, and ultrasound, a number of ethical issues arise. Included in this discussion are what such tests reveal and whether to terminate a pregnancy based on the test results.

The Right to Die (videocassette; 19 min.; color; 1985; Carle Medical Communications) Examines the legal, ethical, and emotional issues surrounding a patient's request to disconnect his breathing apparatus, an action resulting in his death.

The Right to Die (videocassette; 28 min.; color; 1987; Films for the Humanities & Sciences) Adapted from a Phil Donahue program, this video examines the question of whether patients have a right to die, or is society (and the medical profession) obligated to keep patients alive as long as possible, regardless of pain, indignity, and cost, even when there is no hope of recovery. These issues are discussed by Governor Richard Lamm of Colorado, a physician attorney, a nurse who disconnected a patient's life support and is facing charges for her actions, and a wife who wants doctors to honor her husband's wish to die.

The Right to Die (videocassette; 25 min.; color; Medcom, Inc. / Trainex Division) Perspectives on the competent patient's request to withdraw life-sustaining treatment are expressed by the physician, the spouse, the primary nurse, and the patient.

The Right to Die (videocassette; 120 min.; color; 1990; PBS Video) The case of Nancy Cruzan is at the center of this "Frontline" special on medical ethics. The issues are discussed by a panel hosted by Fred Friendly and including the Cruzan's attorney, the attorney general of the state of Missouri, ethicists, doctors, scholars, and newspaper columnists. A good presentation of arguments on all sides of the right-to-die issue.

A Time to Die: Who Decides? (videocassette; 34 min.; color; 1988; Churchill Films) A three-part program that looks at three families confronting the issue of euthanasia. The first episode involves a couple's decision to end force feeding of their six-month-old son with an inoperable brain tumor. The second episode involves two sisters with Hodgkin's disease, and the decision by the older sister to arrange for her younger sister's life support to be withdrawn after experimental surgery proves ineffective and she lapses into a coma. The third episode presents the case of Roswell Gilbert, convicted of murder and sentenced to 25 years in prison for killing his wife Emily, who suffered from painful osteoporosis and advanced Alzheimer's disease.

To Hurt and to Heal (videocassette & 16 mm.; 60 min.; color; 1987; UCB Extension Media Center) Two-part program explores ethical issues in the field of neonatology, including the impact of technology.

UCLA Medicine and Society Forum Videocassettes (videocassette; 72 part series, 60 min./program; black & white & color; 1974–1981; UCLA Instructional Media Library) A series of panel discussions on a wide range of topics, many of which include bioethical considerations. Topics include abortion; suicide; battered children; organ transplantation; the Natural Death Act; brain biopsies on children; the law and medicine; patient's rights, including the rights of children; DNA research; genetic screening; unconventional therapies; life-sustaining technologies; definitions of death; informed consent; and the role of the psychiatrist.

University of Virginia Medical Center Videocassettes (videocassette; series of 44 parts, 60 min./segment; black & white & color; 1973–1981; University of Virginia School of Medicine) A series of panel discussions focusing mainly on bioethical considerations. Topics include patient–doctor relations; behavioral genetics; informed consent; children's rights; disciplinary procedures in medicine; ethical problems in clinical training; genetic and fetal research; amniocentesis; *in vitro* fertilization; sperm banks; the right of physicians to strike; organ transplants; hospice care; alternative cancer treatment; relations among health care professionals; recombinant DNA; human experimentation; living wills; and patients' rights, including the right to privacy.

Chapter 11

The Law and Death

OBJECTIVES

1. To evaluate issues concerning advance directives.
2. To describe the stipulations contained in the Uniform Anatomical Gift Act and to assess its pertinence for oneself.
3. To describe the functions of the coroner and the medical examiner.
4. To identify the functions of the death certificate and the purposes of the autopsy.
5. To identify the types, content, and purposes of wills.
6. To explain the processes of probate and to evaluate the consequences of dying intestate.
7. To differentiate between estate and inheritance taxes and to evaluate the usefulness of a comprehensive plan that includes trusts, life insurance, and other death benefits.

CONTENT OVERVIEW

Chapter 11 is a wide-ranging survey of legal and administrative matters pertaining to death and dying. The discussion encompasses advance directives, regulations governing organ donation, the death certificate, the role of the coroner and medical examiner as well as the purposes and procedures involved in autopsies, laws regulating body disposition, the nature and function of wills and probate, and the types of life insurance and other death benefits.

Living wills, natural death directives, and durable powers of attorney—known collectively as advance directives—have become increasingly important in medical decision making. Such directives generally indicate a person's desire that medical heroics be avoided when death is imminent. Used to express preferences about life-sustaining treatment and drafted while the person is able to make informed decisions, such documents can be extremely important in shaping the circumstances of a person's dying. As of 1989, thirty-eight states had enacted some type of "natural death" legislation. For individuals who have completed a living will, the advance proxy directive (or durable power of attorney) represents an added safeguard toward ensuring that his or her preferences relative to life-sustaining treatment will be followed. In the wake of the Nancy Beth Cruzan case, and following enactment of the Patient Self-Determination Act (which requires health care facilities receiving federal Medicare funds to notify patients of their right to refuse treatment), advance directives have not only gained public attention, but have also become part of mainstream institutional health care.

Organ donation is another area of interest to the student of death and dying that reflects the impact of governmental regulation and standardized procedures. The Uniform Anatomical Gift Act, which has been enacted in some form in all fifty states, provides for the donation of the body or specific body parts upon the death of the donor. The Act was revised in 1987 to simplify organ donation by removing requirements that the document be witnessed and that next of kin give consent. Organ donation can be accomplished easily by completing a brief donor card (available from the motor vehicle department of most states). It should be emphasized, however, that even though consent by next of kin is not legally required to effect organ donation, it is nonetheless prudent to discuss one's plans for donation with close relatives to ensure that such wishes are carried out. A central office to help match donated organs with potential recipients was established as part of the National Organ Transplant Act (1984), and most states have enacted "required request" (or routine inquiry) laws that require hospitals to institute procedures encouraging organ donations.

The official registration of death by means of the death certificate is considered to be the most important legal procedure following a death. Though often taken for granted, the death certificate can have far-reaching effects with respect to such diverse matters as distributing property and benefits to heirs, aiding in the detection of crime, tracing family genealogy, and promoting efforts to understand and prevent disease. The modes of death usually recognized by law include natural, accidental, suicidal, and homicidal. Yet the cause of death is not always the same as the mode of death. A death caused by asphyxiation due to drowning, for example, might be classified as an accident, a suicide, or a homicide, depending on the circumstances.

The coroner or medical examiner plays an important role in determining the cause and mode of death in doubtful circumstances. The cause of death is determined by the use of various scientific procedures, possibly including an autopsy as well as other tests, analyses, and studies. Autopsy—the medical examination of a body after death to determine the cause of death or to investigate the extent and nature of changes caused by disease—is an important tool for medical research and training as well.

Wills provide a legal means for expressing a person's intentions regarding the disposition of his or her property after death. As such, the will is a valuable tool for planning one's estate and for conveying property to one's beneficiaries. The conventional document for specifying such intentions is the formally executed will, which is usually completed in consultation with an attorney who is conversant with any requirements established by the laws of the state in which the will is executed. The making and probating of a will can be symbolically significant for both the testator and his or her survivors. During the course of probate, the validity of the will is proved, the matters necessary to settling the estate are carried out by the executor or administrator, and, with the probate court's approval, the decedent's property is distributed to his or her beneficiaries. In the absence of a will, the distribution will be made according to the applicable laws of intestate succession.

Life insurance can provide a basic estate for one's beneficiaries, or it may be part of a more comprehensive estate. Insurance plans can be designed in a variety of ways to suit many different purposes. Unlike some other assets, life insurance benefits usually become available to beneficiaries immediately following the insured's death, thus providing funds and perhaps a sense of security to survivors. Other death benefits may be payable through governmental programs, such as Social Security and the Veterans Administration, or through pension plans resulting from employment.

As the topics covered in Chapter 11 demonstrate, the law and legalities impinge in many ways on our experiences of death and dying. In some cases, laws increase our options; in other cases, they restrict them. Either way, a basic knowledge of the legalities concerning death and dying can provide for more informed choices and potentially more satisfying outcomes.

KEY TERMS AND CONCEPTS

advance directives	laws of succession
autopsy	life insurance
beneficiary	living will
bequest	medical examiner
codicil	mutual will
conditional will	National Organ Transplant Act
coroner	natural death directive
death benefits	next of kin
death certificate	nuncupative will
durable power of attorney for health care	organ donor card
estate	Patient Self-Determination Act
estate/inheritance taxes	postmortem
executor/administrator	probate
forensic pathology	qualified patient
formally executed will	testator
holographic will	trust
intestate	Uniform Anatomical Gift Act

QUESTIONS FOR GUIDED STUDY AND EVALUATION

Multiple-choice questions relevant to this chapter can be found in the test bank.

1. Summarize the contents of an advance directive, such as a living will.

2. Explain the stipulations found in the Durable Power of Attorney for Health Care described in the text or in similar legislation enacted in your state.

3. Take a stand on the living will that will allow you to support or refute each of the letters to the editor reprinted in the text.

4. Prepare a list of reasons that people may express for choosing organ donation.

5. Summarize the information included on a death certificate and analyze its purpose.

6. Trace the duties of the coroner from historical times to the present.

7. Contrast the training and qualifications of coroners and medical examiners.

8. State at least four reasons for performing autopsies.

9. Summarize the laws regulating body disposition.

10. Assess the psychological, social, and economic value of preparing a will.

11. List and describe three legal stages with respect to the financial affairs and other legal matters of a terminally ill patient.

12. Name and define four different kinds of wills. Explain what type of information is generally included in a will and define the term *codicil*.

13. Describe in detail what is meant by the word *probate*.

14. Discuss the duties of the administrator or executor of an estate.

15. Summarize common practices regarding intestate succession.

16. Differentiate between estate and inheritance taxes. Discuss ways of lessening the impact of each on an estate.

17. Look up your state's inheritance tax rates and be prepared to describe them in class. Do these rates seem fair? Why or why not?

18. Differentiate between a mutual insurance company and a stock company and between a term and a whole life policy (ordinary or straight life). Discuss whether you think insurance policies are an important part of estate planning. Why or why not?

19. Describe the role of death benefits in estate planning and give examples of two types.

TEACHING STRATEGIES

1. The coroner's office is usually helpful in educating students in death and dying classes about the activities of a coroner. Such a presentation can include a slide show of various aspects of a coroner's work, an interview by the instructor, and a discussion with the students. The coroner can be asked to talk generally about the function of the office, and you can follow up with an interview, including questions such as the following:

   Q: Your job involves dealing frequently with tragic deaths. How do you cope personally?

Q: How would you describe a typical day's activities?

Q: What is the most difficult part of your job?

Q: What are the most difficult kinds of cases?

Q: What are some of the stereotypes about coroners? How do you handle them? Are you treated differently by your peers?

2. This teaching strategy is an interview that includes the following questions designed to inform students about the activities of an attorney specializing in estate planning and probate. In such an interview, the attorney responds to questions about dying intestate, probate, estate and inheritance taxes, durable power of attorney, education, and personal experience.

Q: We've read about a number of different kinds of wills in our text. Some of us have made wills, but, statistically, seven out of ten people die intestate. Perhaps some of us have not made a will because we have little property to leave our friends and loved ones and so we believe that wills are for others and not for us. Would you describe the average person for whom you draw up a formally executed will? For instance, what is his or her socioeconomic status?

Q: What is contained in a typical will, with respect to both material and nonmaterial considerations? Besides the distribution of the testator's property, what are the benefits of drawing up a will? Is there an emotional value for the testator and for his or her survivors?

Q: Under what circumstances would a mutual will or a conditional will be executed? What about a holographic or a nuncupative will? When would it be appropriate to make one of these types of wills?

Q: What occurs in this state when a person dies without leaving a will? In other words, what are the laws of succession? Let's take a hypothetical case: Suppose a middle-aged corporation officer with two grown children divorces his wife to marry another woman. Then he adopts the new wife's two children from her previous marriage. The next year he dies of a heart attack, intestate. How would his estate be divided? For instance, would the line of succession go from his present spouse to the four children? What about the former wife to whom he may have been married for more than twenty years? If a former spouse is not included in the laws of succession, does she or he have any recourse? How would a court determine the distribution of property in such cases?

Q: In turning to the subject of probate, would you describe the legal procedures that occur when a client dies? What actions do you take? Under what circumstances might you be named as executor? What does an executor or executrix do? What is the cost of probate and is there any way to reasonably avoid it? Are there any pitfalls in trying to avoid probate?

Q: With respect to estate and inheritance taxes, would you briefly describe each and how they differ? What exactly is taxed? How might one reduce or avoid the burden of such taxes?

Q: Are you familiar with living wills or natural death directives? Have you been asked to draw one up? Under what circumstances do you find them to be valuable? Do you believe that having a living will may result in an individual experiencing a "better" death? Is the living will legally enforceable? Are individuals truly able to exercise choice about life support? What do you think are some problems with living wills and similar measures?

Q: What was the most complicated or difficult will for you to draw up? Why?

Q: As a professional, how do you cope with the loss when a client dies? Can you describe any particularly difficult experiences related to the issue of loss?

Q: In your experience, does law school prepare attorneys for dealing with survivors? One might imagine a course called "Survivors 102," for example. If there is some preparation, how is the topic of death dealt with? Has this aspect of your work ever been a problem to you?

3. Using the death certificate published in the text (or one from your own state), have students review all the items and note those that elicit their greatest interest. Have the class discuss the similarities and differences in their responses.

4. Have students fill in the following information:

   - I have signed a living will; it is located at _____
     _____.

   - Any exceptions to the living will would be _____
     _____.

   - I would most like to die at _____ and I would like (who)
     _____ there.

   - If this isn't possible, I would like to die _____
     _____.

   - To prepare before my death, I would like (clergy, close friend, special reading, service, or . . .) _____.

   - My family/loved one may need extra support. Please contact (agency or individual)
     _____.

   - I have a donor card. I would like to donate _____
     _____.

   - I would approve/not approve of an autopsy, if given a choice.

   - Right after my death, please do the following with my body: _____
     _____.

   - Right away, please notify _____.

   - Later, please notify _____.

   - For my children, I have requested (who) _____
     _____ as their guardian.

- My vital statistics, veteran's papers, life insurance and other benefits, deeds, financial records, will, safe deposit box key, are located at _____
_____.

Besides having students discuss their reactions to completing the inventory, you can suggest that they date, sign, and give copies to family members who would need this information.

COMMENTS AND CONSIDERATIONS

1. **An Age-Dependent Inability to Relate to Wills.** Some students may not readily identify with the importance of wills. Making a will may be viewed as a task restricted to later life. Students may not be aware of the form and content of a will, or they may not understand the potential ramifications of dying intestate even at a young age. During the attorney interview, bring out the importance of the nonmaterial aspects of will making, as well as those involving the distribution of material goods. In this way, students who may have felt they had little wealth to distribute (and therefore no reason to make a will) can begin to understand the role and purpose of wills more fully.

2. **Discomfort at Talking About the Very Real Deaths Encountered by the Coroner's Office.** Some students exhibit aversion to exploring such topics as homicide, suicide, and autopsies as they relate to the legal issues surrounding death. In discussing these topics, keep in mind that emotional responses are sometimes triggered by a past experience. Often, however, the aversion results from a lack of information, not too much. It is important to be sensitive to a student's emotional response, but information of itself is not harmful and it may provide relief from the pain an individual feels in connection with a personal experience of death.

3. **Facilitating the Slide Show.** If slides are shown as part of the coroner's presentation, they may include scenes of autopsies, murder, suicide, burn and drowning victims, and the like. When they are graphic, such slides can elicit a very direct awareness of death. Encourage students to hold their questions until the end of the presentation so that no single slide is dwelt on. It is also useful to ascertain whether any student has been recently involved in a coroner's case to offset the awkward possibility that he or she may recognize someone in the slides. If so, that particular case could be deleted from the slide presentation.

RESOURCES: FILMS AND VIDEOCASSETTES

A Country Auction: The Paul V. Leitzel Estate Sale (videocassette & 16 mm.; 58 min.; color; 1984; Pennsylvania State University) The auctioning of a rural estate becomes an occasion for a family's grief and recollection. Deals with the economic as well as emotional issues that frequently accompany coming to terms with loss. The camera follows the family of the deceased as they clean, sort, and prepare for the auction. Family members are shown cooperating, negotiating, and coming to terms with the realities of death and dissolution. Members of the community come to bargain hunt, as well as to share memories. Antique dealers come as merchants, transforming beloved household items into commodities. In the aftermath of the auction, the viewer follows some objects to their new homes in the community while others, now "antiques," are transported to distant parts of the country.

Dead Man (16 mm., no sound; 4 min.; black & white; 1972; Foundation of Thanatology) The body of an old man is viewed in a morgue. Expresses social and cultural attitudes about death.

Dealing with Death (16 mm.; 20 min.; color; 1976; Portland State University) Four police officers are portrayed as they react to different death experiences.

Death Is Different Now (videocassette; 13 min.; color; 1986; Rush-Presbyterian-St. Luke's Medical Center) Intended as a training film for hospital staff, this program urges professional caregivers to be active advocates of organ donation. Offers suggestions for tactfully presenting the donation option to grieving survivors and reviews the procedures involved in organ donation, including obtaining permission, the surgical processes, and the nationwide transplant system.

Death Notification (videocassette; 23 min.; color; 1977; Coronet/MTI Film & Video) A training film for law enforcement officers who will be responsible for notifying relatives about a loved one's sudden death.

Journey's End (16 mm.; 28 min.; color; 1974; UCB Extension Media Center, USC Film Distribution Center) A dramatization of the problems faced by a middle-class family when the father dies intestate and without funeral plans.

Last Rites (videocassette; 58 min.; color; 1989; Carle Medical Communications) Examines the legal issues relative to euthanasia. Contains interviews with family members and health professionals, as well as advocates and opponents of euthanasia.

Requesting Anatomical Gift Donation: A Nursing Perspective (videocassette; 28 min.; color; 1989; American Journal of Nursing Co.) Describes the role of nurses in requesting anatomical donations, including their relationships with potential donors and their families.

Responding to Sudden Death: Support and Coping (videocassette; 25 min.; color; 1985; Boulder County Hospice) Examines how law enforcement officers experience, personally and professionally, the fact of sudden death in their jobs. Especially poignant since the filmmaker herself recently survived the sudden death of her child. Highly recommended.

Where Do I Begin? Approaching Families About Organ and Tissue Donation (videocassette; 27 min.; color; 1987; American Journal of Nursing Co., Carle Medical Communications) Step-by-step instructions for talking with families about donation of body parts, with an emphasis on acknowledging the grief of survivors.

Chapter 12

Environmental Encounters with Death

OBJECTIVES

1. To assess one's level of risk-taking activities.
2. To describe the incidence and extent of accidents and to compare the factors influencing accidents in specific populations.
3. To identify helping strategies for survivors of disaster.
4. To define homicide and distinguish its various categories and types.
5. To identify and explain the cultural standards by which homicidal acts are judged.
6. To evaluate the effects of capital punishment.
7. To develop an alternative model for punishment.
8. To name and give examples of the factors increasing the likelihood of violence.
9. To differentiate between the moral standards of war and peacetime as regards the taking of life.
10. To assess the effects of war and its aftermath on both combatants and noncombatants.
11. To identify the needs and motives that give rise to war and evaluate strategies for reducing conflict.
12. To identify common defense mechanisms used to avoid the truth about nuclear warfare.
13. To explain the mechanism of stress and its effects on health.
14. To describe a healthy response to stress.

CONTENT OVERVIEW

Chapter 12 examines a broad range of environmental encounters with death related to risk taking, accidents, disasters, violence, war, the nuclear threat, and stress. Some of these encounters seem remote from our own lives; others are pervasive, though we may give little conscious attention to them. News reports are filled with accounts of disasters—natural as

well as human-caused. But, until we ourselves confront such a threat to well-being, we may not comprehend all the dimensions of loss it represents. Yet, consciously or not, we risk subtle, and sometimes dramatic, encounters with death as we engage in our life's pursuits.

Indeed, all life involves risk, although the degree of risk we are willing to assume is often subject to personal choice. Individuals can exercise control over risks related to smoking, driving habits, and the kinds of recreational activities they pursue. In many areas of life, steps can be taken to minimize our exposure to risk. Ignoring or denying the risk inherent in an activity does not make the danger disappear, but it may reduce the likelihood of our taking adequate steps to counteract the risk.

As a leading cause of death, especially among young people, accidents deserve our attention, both as individuals and as a society. Although accidents are commonly viewed as events that "just happen," deeper analysis reveals that many accidents are preventable. Instead of being unavoidable, accidents frequently result from carelessness, lack of awareness, or ignorance. Thus, accidents are typically events over which individuals do have varying degrees of control. For example, about half the drivers involved in fatality accidents are under the influence of alcohol. Such accidents represent tragedies that could have been avoided.

Accidents are influenced both by intrinsic factors—a person's own physical and mental qualities—and by extrinsic factors—conditions in the environment. Unsafe conditions in the environment are sometimes called "accidents waiting to happen." In many instances, these conditions are due to negligence. If we view accidents as due solely to chance or fate, then we ignore the significant role of carelessness and neglect. Attention to such factors might well result in constructive actions toward prevention. Although life can never be completely free of risk, steps usually can be taken to minimize it.

Disasters—which can be defined as life-threatening events that affect many people within a relatively brief period of time, bringing sudden and great misfortune—result from both natural phenomena and human activities. Floods and earthquakes are examples of natural disasters; fires, airplane crashes, and chemical spills are examples of disasters resulting from human activities. Population growth and industrialization have increased the exposure to disasters related to human activities. Despite the fact that communities can decrease the risk of injury and death by taking measures to lessen the impact of a potential disaster, the effects of a disaster are difficult to fully anticipate. Adequate warnings of an impending disaster can save lives. Yet necessary information may be withheld because of greed or political expediency, or simply because of uncertainty about the nature and extent of the threat, or because of concern about causing panic. Even with an adequate warning system, however, people do not always respond to the threat prudently. Just as some people ignore the risks associated with smoking or place themselves in situations more prone to accidents, individuals frequently believe themselves immune to the effects of a disastrous situation.

In the aftermath of disaster, meeting the immediate needs of survivors—food and shelter, medical care, vital services—is essential. Important, too, is attending to survivors' emotional needs. Although efforts directed toward coping with disaster tend to be focused on the initial period of emergency, the return to financial and emotional stability may take years. The needs of caregivers who offer supportive services to survivors also need to be acknowledged and met as part of a comprehensive program of disaster postvention.

Violence, one of the most potent and frightening encounters with death, can affect our thoughts and actions even though we ourselves have not been victimized. It is now recognized as a public health problem, and special emphasis has been placed on the prevalence of interpersonal violence. In a recent year, nearly twice as many murders were related to arguments of one kind or another than were related to the commission of a felony. Besides the violence related to interpersonal conflict and criminal activities, many people are concerned about terrorism, which may involve planned as well as indiscriminate killing. Occurring outside the boundaries of the social sanctions that are intended to regulate conduct between individuals and between groups, terrorism is an affront to civilization.

Within the framework of the U.S. judicial system, the circumstances of a particular killing, the relationship between killer and victim, and the killer's motivation and intent are all considered in assessing a homicidal act. Research shows that the legal outcome for a person who kills a close relative is usually quite different from the outcome for a person who combines killing with theft, robbery, or other such criminal or antisocial acts. The most severe penalty is usually reserved as punishment for killing a stranger. The killer who chooses a stranger as his or her victim overtly threatens the preservation of the social order. In this respect, killings carried out by terrorists can be likened to other homicidal acts involving strangers.

Within the context of ordinary human interaction, our moral as well as legal codes stand in strict opposition to killing. In war, however, killing is not only acceptable and necessary, but possibly heroic. Yet, despite society's efforts to convert civilians into warriors, those who face the prospect of kill-or-be-killed in war often pay a high emotional and psychological price as a result of the trauma of war. In addition to the burden it places on combatants, war also creates a "phantom army" composed of the spouses, children, parents, and friends who serve invisibly at home. The mourning of losses accompanies even the most joyous of victory celebrations.

Whether or not war is an inescapable part of the human condition, it is easy to discern a wide variety of needs and motives relating to its onset. To prepare the way for war, we engage in a psychological process of creating the enemy. Dividing the world into "us" and "them" works to devalue and dehumanize the members of the outgroup, thus paving the way for hostile acts against them. In searching for ways to civilize hostilities, therefore, we must investigate the processes that promote or deter war in both the individual psyche and social institutions.

Early warfare had limits; now, civilians as well as combatants are its victims. Technological alienation has been called the central feature of modern warfare; it is exemplified by the mass deaths in Dresden, Hiroshima, and Nagasaki. Exposed to such destruction and death, our self-protective psychological response is to become insensitive, unfeeling, numb. For more than four decades, the threat of nuclear war has cast a shadow over our lives. Although we can be grateful for recently lessened hostility between the keepers of the world's major nuclear arsenals, the nuclear threat has not disappeared. The continuing proliferation of such weapons as well as the possibility of nuclear accident remain cause for concern.

Although less dramatic than other encounters with death discussed in this chapter, stress is also a common component of modern life that can have life-threatening consequences. The conditions of modern living—more complex life-styles, materialistic expectations, and inner discontent—provoke the fight-or-flight response characteristic of stress. The eventual result can be a lowering of the body's resistance to disease. In Japan, occupational stress reportedly causes more than 10,000 deaths a year. The epidemic of heart disease in the developed countries is attributed, at least in part, to the effects of stressful life-styles that derive from high technology and affluence. It is important to recognize, however, that stress does not inevitably lead to bodily deterioration or increased susceptibility to disease. One can learn more effective ways of coping with stress and managing the situations that elicit it. Personal and social problems may need to be confronted and corrected in order to reduce the level of stress in our lives. Conceived of in this way, the symptoms of stress can be a signal that it is time to reexamine our patterns of living. The failure to do so—and indeed to find adequate means of coping with all the encounters with death represented in this chapter—is itself a threat to the survival of both societies and individuals.

KEY TERMS AND CONCEPTS

accident prone
accidents
alarm reaction
capital punishment
combat death
conversion of the warrior
disaster preparedness
environmental pollution
genocide
Holocaust
homicide
industrial accidents
internal war
karoshi
limited war

natural disasters
nuclear threat
nuclearism
occupational hazards
post-traumatic stress
postvention
propaganda
psychic numbing
risk taking
stress
technological alienation
terrorism
total war
violence

QUESTIONS FOR GUIDED STUDY AND EVALUATION

Multiple-choice questions relevant to this chapter can be found in the test bank.

1. Describe patterns of risk taking and suggest ways of managing risk.
2. Identify at least three factors that contribute to accidents.
3. Describe the effects of disaster on those who survive.
4. Explain how differential punishments for homicide may be based on the relationship of the killer to the victim.
5. Evaluate the argument that violence is contagious in American society.
6. List the pros and cons of capital punishment as you see them, and assess your ideas. Are there alternatives? What are they?
7. Provide a concrete example for each of the factors favoring violence given in the text.
8. Describe the effects of war and its aftermath on combatants and noncombatants.
9. Give at least five examples of the needs and motives that contribute to war and suggest strategies that can work to reduce conflict.
10. Explain what is meant by the statement: "Technological alienation is the most characteristic feature of the twentieth century war machine." Give examples.
11. Name six defense mechanisms used to avoid facing the truth about the nuclear threat.
12. Describe the relationship between stress and illness.
13. Complete the Holmes and Rahe Social Readjustment Rating Scale. Total your score. Name at least five positive ways of coping with stress.

TEACHING STRATEGIES

1. At least one week before the material from this chapter is reviewed in class, ask students to go through the newspaper and clip out or photocopy articles concerning incidents of violent death or terrorism. Instruct them to categorize the incidents by kind and frequency, and have them prepare oral reports on their findings for presentation in class.
2. Tell students to list ten high-risk vocations and ten high-risk avocations. Instruct them to note which of the items listed they are most attracted to. Have them rank each item on a scale from 1 to 5, with 1 being the least and 5 the most attractive. Then have students meet in small groups to discuss their lists. Return to the large group and ask students to evaluate their lives in terms of the risks they take.
3. Brainstorm a list of death-related occupations. Direct students to comment on careers such as the following: mortician, doctor, pathologist, ambulance driver, paramedic, nurse, gravestone carver, crematorium employee, grave digger, fire fighter, police officer, clergyperson, bereavement counselor, coroner, and suicide prevention

counselor. Have students write a brief phrase next to each job, indicating what they believe would be the best and the worst aspects of that particular encounter with death.

4. Divide the class in half. Instruct one group to make a list of statements favoring capital punishment and the other group to make a list of statements opposing capital punishment. Then come together as a class and discuss these lists. Have the class come up with a list of ideas that would prevent the need for capital punishment.

COMMENTS AND CONSIDERATIONS

Limiting the Focus. Because of the wide range of topics covered in this chapter, you may wish to focus most discussion or lecture time on only one of the areas covered. Students generally appreciate the opportunity to explore one of these areas in greater depth. This can be done through presentations in class by invited speakers. Possible speakers include Mothers Against Drunk Drivers (MADD), Parents of Murdered Children (POMC), advocates of a nuclear freeze, or Physicians or Educators for Social Responsibility, as well as an individual who is a disaster relief worker, disaster survivor, or member of a high-risk profession.

RESOURCES: FILMS AND VIDEOCASSETTES

Accident (16 mm.; 16 min.; color; 1974; National Film Board of Canada) Heightened appreciation of life is a focus of this account of one man's brush with death in the crash of a light plane.

Acid Rainbows (videocassette; 30 min.; color; 1988; PBS Video) The damaging effects of acid rain, its causes, and what can be done to protect the environment are the subject of this documentary, which focuses particularly on the American West, where serious damage from acid rain is a fairly new phenomenon.

Acts of Violence (videocassette; 60 min.; color; 1985; The Cinema Guild) Examines the high level of deadly violence in American society, focusing on three types of murderers—the mass murderer, the serial murderer, and the political assassin. Includes interviews with victims as well as perpetrators. Commentary by psychiatrists and sociologists offers insights into the personal and social causes of homicidal behavior.

The Arming of the Earth (videocassette; 58 min.; color; 1984; PBS Video) The invention of dynamite, the machine gun, and the airplane would make war too terrible to fight, or so it was believed by many people in the early years of this century. In this program, Bill Moyers examines how each of these inventions led to the development of more devastating weapons, increasing the scope and scale of modern warfare.

The Black Tulip (videocassette; 27 min.; color; 1988; The Video Project) Shows the impact of the Afghan War on Soviet society, particularly its effect on glasnost and perestroika. Soviet soldiers describe the war in words reminiscent of the American experience in Vietnam.

The Bombing of Pan Am 103 (videocassette; 60 min.; color; 1990; PBS Video) This "Frontline" program features interviews with relatives of the victims of the terrorist attack on Pan Am flight 103 over Lockerbie, Scotland. The personal side of this tragedy is explored as family members piece together the few clues they have about the last hours of their loved ones and explain their efforts to seek justice and to ensure safeguards against similar terrorist acts in the future.

Building Bombs (videocassette; 54 min.; color; 1989; The Video Project) Examines the consequences of the arms race by focusing on the Savannah River Plant in South Carolina, where weapons-grade plutonium and tritium are manufactured. The social and environmental impact of the plant is detailed through historical footage as well as personal stories of the residents and workers.

Buster and Me (videocassette; 22 min.; color; 1983; The Video Project) A presentation through puppetry that reveals children's fears and anxieties about nuclear war and offers hope.

Caring for an Endangered Planet (videocassette; 50 min.; color; 1984; Original Face Video) Helen Caldicott of Physicians for Social Responsibility speaks about the personal and social struggles in creating a nuclear-free world.

Chernobyl: Chronicle of Difficult Weeks (videocassette; 54 min.; color; 1986; The Video Project) A film by Vladimir Shevchenko, whose crew was the first into the disaster zone following the meltdown of the Chernobyl nuclear plant. They filmed continuously for more than three months, documenting both the disaster and the efforts to clean up. While the film was being edited, the editor was already fatally ill from exposure to radiation. In Russian with English subtitles.

Counseling the Vietnam Veteran (videocassette; 28 min.; color; 1986; American Journal of Nursing Co.) Scenes from group counseling sessions with Vietnam veterans are used to illustrate the principles of working with veterans diagnosed with post-traumatic stress disorder or other problems of adjustment. Two VA psychiatric nurses describe how the veterans of Vietnam differ from the veterans of previous wars.

Crime and Human Nature (videocassette; 28 min.; color; 1987; Films for the Humanities & Sciences) Explores the nature of criminality and antisocial aggressive behavior. Can adult criminal behavior be predicted in the antisocial behavior of children? Anthropologist Ashley Montague and other experts address such questions in this specially adapted Phil Donahue program.

Cry, Ethiopia, Cry (videocassette; 58 min.; color; 1984; PBS Video) An Emmy-winning documentary about the drought and famine in Ethiopia; investigates why the early warning signals of this natural disaster were ignored by officials who might have helped.

The Day After Trinity: J. Robert Oppenheimer and the Atomic Bomb (videocassette & 16 mm.; 88 min.; color; 1981; Pyramid Film & Video, UCLA Instructional Media Library) Describes the beginnings of the nuclear age.

Deafsmith, A Nuclear Folktale (videocassette; 43 min.; color; 1990; The Video Project) Chronicles the efforts of Deafsmith County residents to prevent all of the nation's high-level nuclear waste from being buried beneath their farms. Homespun, grassroots activism versus the Department of Energy's efforts to portray nuclear waste as the residents' "friend" and the DOE's assurances that everything is "safe" and "under control."

Death and the Mistress of Delay (videocassette; 30 min.; color; 1987; Wombat Productions) This video dealing with the issues surrounding capital punishment focuses on the debate in Florida, where the "mistress of delay," Charlotte Holman, has worked successfully to keep death sentences from being carried out. The arguments on both sides of the death-penalty debate are expressed clearly in this Emmy-winning video.

The Death Penalty (videocassette; 26 min.; color; 1988; Films for the Humanities & Sciences) Examines the research that suggests that death penalties are imposed arbitrarily and that little evidence exists to support the contention that the death penalty is an effective deterrent. Looks at the cases of two men who committed virtually identical murders and were tried in the same courtroom two weeks apart. Includes discussion by prosecutors, lawyers, jurors, and victims.

Death Row and the Death Penalty (videocassette; 14 min.; color; 1984; The Media Guild) Contains interviews with prisoners on death row as well as with spokespeople for and against the death penalty. Includes clips from the feature film *The Executioner's Song* and footage of the death by injection of Charles Brooks.

Death Sentences (videocassette; 30 min.; color; 1980; UCLA Instructional Media Library) Discusses the pros and cons of capital punishment.

A Dialogue for Human Survival Featuring Ram Dass and Daniel Ellsberg (videocassette; 40 min.; color; 1984; Original Face Video) Contrasts the belief systems of two men with different strategies for responding to the threat of nuclear war. A fascinating and provocative discussion.

Doin' Life (videocassette; 60 min.; color; 1980; The Cinema Guild) The moral and philosophical issues of crime and punishment are explored by focusing on five men serving life sentences as well as on the victims of their crimes. Includes commentary by politicians, philosophers, penologists, and prison reformers.

Dr. Strangelove, or How I Learned to Stop Worrying and Love the Bomb (16 mm.; 1 hour & 33 min.; black & white; 1964; Swank Motion Pictures) A comedy about the potentially devastating effects of toying with nuclear war.

Drinking and Driving: The Toll, the Tears (videocassette; 60 min.; color; 1986; PBS Video) The devastating effects of drinking and driving are documented through interviews with accident victims, their families, and drunk drivers themselves. An excellent exploration of alcohol abuse and social responsibility.

Eleven Months on Death Row (videocassette; 17 min.; color; 1984; Journal Film and Video) An extended interview with a prisoner who received a reprieve of his death sentence just moments before he was to be hanged.

The Executioner's Song (videocassette; 157 min.; color; 1982; U.S.A. Home Video) An adaptation of Norman Mailer's book about the last months in the life of convicted murderer Gary Gilmore.

Faces of War (videocassette; 23 min.; color; 1985; The Video Project) Looks at the ravages of war in South America and involvement by North Americans.

Facing Evil (videocassette; 90 min.; color; 1988; PBS Video) Historic events of cruelty and hatred, ranging from personal violence to genocide and the devastation of entire countries, forms the background to this investigation of the problem of evil. Hosted by Bill Moyers, a group of scholars, philosophers, and artists delve into the origins of evil and search for strategies to disarm violence. Participants include poet Maya Angelou, Holocaust scholar Raul Hilberg, choreographer and author Chung-Liang Al Huang, former congresswoman Barbara Jordan, and philosopher Philip Paul Hallie, among others.

Faith, War, and Peace in the Nuclear Age (videocassette & 16 mm.; 28 min.; color; 1984; The Video Project) A religious view of the nuclear age and the threat of nuclear war.

A Family Gathering (videocassette; 60 min.; color; 1989; PBS Video) A documentary account of Masuo Yasui, the patriarch of the Yasui family, who emigrated from Japan to the Hood River Valley in Oregon in the early 1900s. A respected member of the community, five days after the Japanese attack on Pearl Harbor, Yasui was arrested as a "potentially dangerous" enemy alien and interned along with many other Japanese-Americans. This program tells the story of the U.S. internment policy and the Yasui family's battle to reclaim their place as Americans.

Fighting Terrorism: Inside the National Security Council (videocassette; 60 min.; color; 1987; PBS Video) An in-depth look at the NSC's management of a terrorism crisis during a two-day simulation involving a hypothetical scenario that might lead to direct nuclear confrontation between the superpowers. Shows the participants' concern with "positioning" the issues so as to gain the support of American allies and the public.

Genocide (16 mm.; 60 min.; color; 1975; USCAN International) Produced by the Simon Wiesenthal Center, this film describes the devastation of the Holocaust.

Geronimo and the Apache Resistance (videocassette; 60 min.; color; 1988; PBS Video) This account of the nineteenth-century U.S. war against the Apache people highlights the clash of cultures and the legacy of the battles. It portrays the tragedy of a society faced with the loss of its ancestral land and traditions.

Heart of the Warrior (videocassette; 54 min.; color; 1990; The Video Project) Portrays the personal aftermath of war for two men: Bob Sampson, a former U.S. Army paratrooper who fought in Vietnam until his left leg was shot off, and Nikolai Chuvanov, a former paratrooper in the Soviet Army who served in Afghanistan until his right leg was shattered by a bullet. Sampson and Chuvanov travel separately back to Vietnam and Afghanistan, where they relive their combat experiences and meet their former enemies face to face. When the two veterans meet, they share the enduring pain of war with a sense of compassion and comraderie.

Hearts and Minds (videocassette; about 1 hour & 50 min.; color; 1974; Paramount Pictures) A documentary about the psychological repercussions of the Vietnam conflict.

Home on the Range (videocassette; 58 min.; color; 1990; The Video Project) Documents the human cost of the arms race by focusing on the islands of the Kwajelein Atoll, once home to several thousand Pacific islanders. For the last three decades, the atoll has been used as a test range for ballistic missiles, resulting in relocation of the islanders and destruction of their traditional way of life.

How Far Home: Veterans After Vietnam (videocassette; 30 min.; color; 1988; PBS Video) An intimate portrait of the men and women who returned from the Vietnam conflict to find a more personal conflict waiting for them at home. Focuses on the personal lives and social adjustments that many veterans have made since the war. Veterans at the dedication of the Vietnam War Memorial speak emotionally about fallen comrades whose names are etched in the stark granite wall; they offer their own reflections on a turbulent era.

The Hyatt Disaster: The Hidden Victim (videocassette; 51 min.; color; 1981; University of Kansas) The "hidden victims" of a tragic accident that killed 114 people are those who survived. A series of interviews and film footage of the 1981 accident, where two walkways collapsed in a hotel in Kansas City, form the basis of a discussion about the psychological reactions of survivors. Victims comment on how they felt and the care they received; survivor guilt is a common theme.

In Cold Blood (16 mm.; about 2 hours & 10 min.; black & white; 1968; Ambrose Video Publishing, Swank Motion Pictures) A homicide forms the background for an exploration of criminal activity and for questions regarding capital punishment. Based on the book by Truman Capote.

In the Nuclear Shadow: What Can the Children Tell Us? (videocassette & 16 mm.; 25 min.; color; 1983; The Video Project) Children's emotional reactions to nuclear war are explored through interviews.

Juveniles and the Death Penalty (videocassette; 58 min.; color; 1989; Films for the Humanities & Sciences) This program visits Death Row inmates who committed murder before they were eighteen and talks with prosecutors, defense attorneys, and families about the punishment appropriate to criminals who were juveniles when they committed their crimes.

Kristallnacht: The Journey from 1938 to 1988 (videocassette; 60 min.; color; 1988; PBS Video) Witnesses of the Crystal Night recall the horrors of destruction and violence of "the night of breaking glass" that left hundreds of German and Austrian synagogues destroyed and thousands of Jewish businesses vandalized. Also records the efforts of people in Germany and Austria to try to come to terms with their Nazi past.

The Last Epidemic: Medical Consequences of Nuclear Weapons and Nuclear War (videocassette & 16 mm.; 30 min.; color; 1981; The Video Project) From the 1981 National Conference of the Physicians for Social Responsibility, Helen Caldicott and others talk about the hopelessness of medical care in a nuclear war.

License to Kill (videocassette & 16 mm.; 28 min.; color; 1985; The Cinema Guild) Presents perspectives on capital punishment as a worldwide phenomenon. An award-winning program that features interviews with condemned prisoners, bereaved survivors, government representatives, lawyers, and human rights activists.

Losing Control (videocassette; 58 min.; color; 1990; Ideal Communications) Documents the dangers of accidental nuclear war. This award-winning program includes interviews with Robert McNamara, Richard Perle, and Sam Nunn.

Missile (videocassette; 115 min.; color; 1987; Zipporah Films) A documentary by Frederick Wiseman about the 4315th Training Squadron of the Strategic Air Command at Vandenberg Air Force Base in California, which trains officers to man the Launch Control Centers for the Minuteman Ballistic Missiles. Includes discussion of the moral and military issues of nuclear war; the arming, targeting, and launching of the missiles; protection against terrorist attack; and emergency procedures. This fair and hard look at weapons systems brings home the point that nuclear war could really happen.

Mr. Rogers' Special: Robert Kennedy Assassination (16 mm.; 30 min.; black & white; 1968; Family Communications) Precipitated by Robert Kennedy's death, this program examines the impact of violence on children.

Night and Fog (videocassette & 16 mm.; 31 min.; color; 1977; Films, Inc., Mass Media Ministries) With English subtitles, this film depicts a painful journey from the Holocaust to the present through the juxtaposition of current and past film footage.

No Accident (videocassette & 16 mm.; 13 min.; color; 1987; Perennial Education) A film about drinking and driving that describes the circumstances of the death of eight-year-old Brian Robertson, killed by a repeat-offender drunk driver. After serving a brief sentence for Brian's death, the driver went on to cause another accident and serious injury. "No Accident" characterizes the legal system that allows such incidents to continue.

No Other Generation: Twelve Voices from the Thirty-Seventh Year of the Nuclear Age (videocassette; 35 min.; color; 1984; Original Face Video) Spiritual leaders and nuclear activists discuss the nuclear threat.

The Nuclear Nightmare: A Forum for Teen Expression (videocassette; 40 min.; color; 1986; United Learning) Young people, teachers, and experts on nuclear issues conduct a community forum about the feelings engendered by the threat of nuclear conflict and ways of bringing about meaningful change.

The Nuclear Winter: Changing Our Way of Thinking (videocassette; 58 min.; color; 1985; The Video Project) Carl Sagan talks about the impact of nuclear war on the global climate.

An Occurrence at Owl Creek Bridge (videocassette & 16 mm.; 27 min.; color; 1964; Films, Inc.) A classic Civil War story told through flashbacks as a man is being hanged.

The Ox-Bow Incident (16 mm.; 75 min.; black & white; 1943; Films, Inc.) This story about the potential harm of capital punishment centers on the hanging of three innocent men in the old West.

People to People (videocassette; 28 min.; color; 1985; The Video Project) Residents of Seattle, Washington, seeing themselves as a primary target of nuclear weapons, band together and journey to their sister city in the Soviet Union to talk about their mutual concern: possible extinction.

A Place to Begin: An Approach to Nuclear Education (videocassette; 30 min.; color; 1985; Educators for Social Responsibility) Intended primarily for educators, this video describes a model short course on the subject of nuclear issues education. Includes classroom scenes to illustrate the importance of teacher preparation and the need to develop an atmosphere of trust and tolerance in sharing views about nuclear war and nuclear weapons.

A Portrait of Elie Wiesel (videocassette; 60 min.; color; 1988; PBS Video) This interview with the 1986 winner of the Nobel Peace Prize gives us an intimate portrait of a Holocaust survivor and describes his efforts as chairman of the United States Holocaust Memorial Council and as author of more than a dozen books to keep humanity from forgetting the horror of the death camps.

Prophecy (videocassette & 16 mm.; 45 min.; color; 1983; Films, Inc.) Describes the effects of the atomic bombs dropped on Hiroshima and Nagasaki from the Japanese perspective. Documents the deaths from the atomic blast itself and from subsequent radiation poisoning. Scenes showing the scars, disabilities, and continuing medical treatment of the Hiroshima-Nagasaki casualties are intercut with scenes of the "improved" arsenals of the superpowers and weapons tests.

The Probable Passing of Elk Creek (videocassette & 16 mm.; 60 min.; color; 1983; The Cinema Guild) This film tells the story of residents of an Indian reservation in California, who are faced with the destruction of their homes as well as values—heritage, tradition, community—as a result of the construction of a dam that would flood their tribal land.

The Question of Television Violence (videocassette & 16 mm.; 56 min.; color; 1973; Phoenix/BFA Films & Video) Media specialists discuss the effects of television violence on children in this excerpt from the 1972 Senate Hearings on Television Violence.

Radio Bikini (videocassette; 60 min.; color; 1989; PBS Video) Tests of the atomic bomb on the Bikini Islands by the U.S. Navy following World War II exposed thousands of sailors to heavy doses of radiation. The entire native population of the islands was uprooted and, more than four decades later, their homeland is still too contaminated to support human life. This documentary, nominated for an Academy Award, tells the story through the words of eyewitnesses and archival footage.

Remember My Lai (videocassette; 60 min.; color; 1989; PBS Video) An award-winning episode of "Frontline" about the involvement of Charlie Company, a U.S. Army unit, in the 1968 massacre of 500 unarmed men, women, and children in a rural hamlet of Vietnam called My Lai. Contains interviews with American servicemen and Vietnamese survivors.

Reunion (videocassette; 30 min.; color; 1985; PBS Video) This video captures the memories of two people who experienced the Holocaust from different points of view—one a young tank sergeant who helped liberate the Nazi concentration camp Mauthausen; the other a young woman who endured torture, disease, starvation, and forced labor in the camp. Reunited for the first time since the war, the two developed a friendship and began to speak out about their experiences. Descriptions of the camp are interspersed with interviews with other Holocaust survivors and with Judge William Wilkins, who participated in the Nuremberg trials.

The River That Harms (videocassette; 45 min.; color; 1987; The Video Project) Documents the largest radioactive waste spill in U.S. history. Ninety-four million gallons of water contaminated with radioactive mining waste broke through a storage dam in 1979 and poured into the Puerco River in New Mexico—the main water supply for the Navajo who live along the river and a tributary of the major source of water for Los Angeles. Unaware of the danger, Navajo ranchers, their children, and farm animals waded through the contaminated river. This radioactive waste spill continues to take a toll on the Navajo, who have lost the use of the water, and they see the event as a prophetic warning for all humanity.

Safe Harbor (videocassette & 16 mm.; 27 min.; color; 1984; The Media Guild) A hedonistic young man who feels that nothing can be done to alleviate the nuclear threat is challenged when he encounters an elderly Japanese-American survivor of Hiroshima and his granddaughter. They speak to him about the need for hope and for making peace with our own fears so that we can then begin to make peace in the world. This story helps to expose feelings of insecurity and fear, and it suggests a hopeful alternative to selfish acquiescence in the face of nuclearism.

Sandstorm in the Gulf: Digging Out (videocassette; 30 min.; color; 1990; The Video Project) A critical perspective on the Gulf War and its long-term consequences. Looks at policies that contributed to the conflict and problems not solved by the war, as well as the political, economic, and social costs of the war to Americans.

Soldier's Heart (videocassette; 30 min.; color; 1990; The Video Project) The story of Mel Seligman, who stormed the beaches of Normandy in 1944 as part of the D-Day invasion. Returning to the Normandy countryside four decades later, Seligman and his family describe how the horror of combat led to his early discharge for battle fatigue and left him emotionally scarred.

Stereotypes (videocassette; 25 min.; color; 1990; The Video Project) A collaborative effort of U.S. and Soviet filmmakers, this blend of animation and live action parodies the superpowers' traditional views of one another. An unusual look at a global rivalry that resulted in years of dangerous confrontation.

Strategic Trust: The Making of Nuclear-Free Palau (videocassette & 16 mm.; 58 min.; color; 1984; The Cinema Guild) Documents the decision of an independent Pacific nation to declare itself a nuclear-free territory.

Teenagers and the Nuclear Arms Race (videocassette; 30 min.; color; 1987; PBS Video) High school students discuss the possibility of nuclear annihilation and share their feelings about the future.

The Terror Trade: Buying the Bomb (videocassette; 55 min.; color; 1989; Filmakers Library) This film examines the illicit spread of nuclear weapons capabilities via black-market sales of plutonium and other such materials. Sales are made not only to governments outside the so-called "Nuclear Club," but also to well-financed political groups.

Throwaway People (videocassette; 60 min.; color; 1990; PBS Video) Examines a once-proud neighborhood's descent into drugs and death. This "Frontline" report looks at Shaw, a neighborhood in Washington, D.C., that was once the home of Duke Ellington and many prominent Black educators and lawyers, and is now a killing field at the mercy of crack dealers and other perpetrators of wanton violence.

The Triumph of Memory (videocassette & 16 mm.; 30 min.; color; 1989; PBS Video) The accounts of three non-Jewish resistance fighters who were sent to Nazi concentration camps bears witness to the Holocaust and reminds us of the atrocities committed in Mauthausen, Buchenwald, and Auschwitz-Birkenau. The program is narrated by Arnost Lustig, a Jewish survivor of Auschwitz.

TV: The Anonymous Teacher (videocassette & 16 mm.; 15 min.; color; 1976; Ecufilm, Mass Media Ministries) TV violence is one aspect of this presentation about the effects of television on young viewers.

Understanding Psychological Trauma (videocassette; 61 min.; color; 1990; Carle Medical Communications) Survivors of environmental encounters with death—including murder, disaster, accidents, and random violence—share their stories of recovery and healing.

Vietnam Memorial (videocassette; 52 min.; color; 1983; PBS Video) This documentary about the National Salute to Vietnam Veterans, a five-day tribute held in Washington, D.C., in November 1982, contains interviews with veterans as well as with those who stayed home and those too young to remember.

Waiting for Cambodia (videocassette; 60 min.; color; 1988; PBS Video) The human suffering behind a stalemated political situation is seen in the lives of Cambodian refugees living in temporary camps on the Thai–Cambodian border.

We All Live Downstream (videocassette; 30 min.; color; 1990; The Video Project) Explores the problems and stories of people who live along the Mississippi River, which, because of industrial waste, has been called "a 2300 mile toxic waterway." Cancer and mortality rates are among the highest in the nation along the chemical corridor stretching from Baton Rouge to New Orleans.

What Soviet Children Are Saying About Nuclear War (videocassette & 16 mm.; 22 min.; color; 1983; The Video Project) Documents the visit of two American psychiatrists with Soviet adolescents to discuss their attitudes toward the nuclear threat.

When a Woman Fights Back (videocassette; 59 min.; color; 1980; PBS Video) Examines the legal and social questions surrounding the issue of women killing men in self defense in the context of the murder trial of Yvonne Wanrow in Washington state. The reversal of her murder conviction by the Washington State Supreme Court set a precedent that was subsequently applied in three other murder trials. The issues involved included the concept of "reasonable force" and legal standards between men and women. The program also examines how men and women perceive threatening situations differently.

Who's Killing Calvert City? (videocassette; 60 min.; color; 1989; PBS Video) Issues arising from toxic waste and contamination of the environment are focused in this story about Calvert City,

Kentucky, a town of 3000 people situated on the banks of the Tennessee River. The economic benefits brought to the community with the opening of several large chemical plants have been accompanied by pollution that some have characterized as worse than Love Canal or Times Beach. This "Frontline" program includes interviews with cancer victims, former plant workers, environmental activists, and ordinary citizens who fear the plants are jeopardizing their lives, as well as interviews with politicians, businesspeople, plant executives, and workers who insist that the "pollution panic" could ruin the town's economic future.

Women—For America, for the World (videocassette & 16 mm.; 28 min.; color; 1984; The Video Project) Prominent American women speak out about the nuclear threat.

World War II: The Propaganda Battle (videocassette; 58 min; color; 1984; PBS Video) Hosted by Bill Moyers, this program traces the development of mass-media propaganda during World War II and studies the principles and psychological effects of propaganda. Includes interviews with film director Frank Capra, who created the "Why We Fight" series in the U.S., and with chief Nazi filmmaker Fritz Hippler.

Chapter 13

Suicide

OBJECTIVES

1. To identify potential suicide populations.
2. To construct a comprehensive definition of suicide.
3. To describe the sociological and psychological models of suicide.
4. To list and describe four types of suicide and to give examples of each.
5. To explain the risk factors influencing suicide through the lifespan.
6. To describe the various methods of suicide and to analyze them for information regarding the suicidal person's intent.
7. To differentiate between myths and facts about suicide.
8. To create a model of suicide intervention.
9. To plan a suicide postvention strategy.

CONTENT OVERVIEW

Chapter 13 examines suicidal behavior by focusing on theoretical explanations of suicide, types of suicide, risk factors influencing suicide, patterns of suicidal behavior during different stages of the lifespan, methods used in attempting or committing suicide, suicide notes, and efforts related to suicide prevention, intervention, and postvention. Until the late 1960s, suicide rates generally increased directly with age, with the lowest rates among the young and the highest among the aged. More recently, this pattern has shifted, with a decrease in the suicide rate among older persons being offset by an increase among adolescents and young adults. Both of these trends are due largely to changes in the behavior of white males, a group that accounts for the majority of suicides in the United States.

Generally speaking, suicide is listed as the cause of death only when circumstances are unequivocal. This hesitancy about classifying a death as suicide is due largely to the social stigma of suicide, which is commonly viewed as a failure on the part of the person who commits suicide, his or her family and friends, and society as a whole. Many automobile accidents, for example, are believed to be suicides in disguise, as are some victim-precipitated homicides. Thus, the actual extent of suicide is likely to be greater than official statistics suggest.

One of the methods devised to improve the accuracy of suicide statistics is the psychology autopsy, which involves gathering information that sheds light on the general life style of the victim, any stresses that he or she may have been experiencing, and whether any suicidal communications were made prior to the death. In addition to being an investigative tool for correctly classifying deaths, the psychological autopsy is also a valuable research tool that can help to identify risk factors in the lives of suicide victims.

Efforts to explain suicidal behavior have generally looked either to the social context in which it occurs or to the mental and emotional dynamics within the life of the individual victim. Whereas the sociological model focuses on the relationship between the individual and society, the psychological model focuses on the individual's conscious as well as unconscious motivations. Each of these approaches has contributed to our understanding of suicide. Recent efforts to provide a theoretical perspective on suicide usually draw from both approaches and conclude that suicide is best understood as behavior influenced by both culture and personality, as well as by the unique circumstances of an individual's situation.

Our understanding of suicide is also broadened by examining it from various perspectives, such as types of suicide, the nature of risk factors influencing it, and patterns of suicidal behavior throughout the lifespan. For example, when we examine the characteristics of suicidal behavior, we can distinguish at least four types: (1) suicide as escape (as with terminally ill persons who see no other exit from unremitting suffering), (2) suicide resulting from psychotic illness or depression, (3) subintentional and chronic suicide (in which the victim plays a partial or subliminal role in his or her own demise, perhaps over a period of time by reason of an unhealthy life style), and (4) suicide as a "cry for help" (a form of communication intended to elicit some change, but which can have lethal consequences). Similarly, in examining the risk factors influencing suicide, we find that they generally comprise four broad areas—culture, personality, the individual situation, and biological factors—some or all of which may overlap when we consider an individual instance of suicidal behavior. Finally, in looking at suicide from a lifespan perspective, we find that various motives and influences are relatively more or less important at the different stages of life—childhood, adolescence and young adulthood, middle adulthood, and late adulthood.

Over the course of the past several decades, as suicide has become increasingly a matter of public discussion and concern, various activities related to suicide prevention, intervention, and postvention have become widespread. Much can be done to reduce suicide risk, and education is an essential element in any program of suicide prevention. Such education generally emphasizes two key points: (1) Since life is complex, all of us will inevitably experience disappointment, failure, and loss at some time in our lives; (2) we can learn to deal with such experiences by developing appropriate coping techniques, including a healthy sense of humor. Whereas the goal of suicide prevention is primarily to eliminate or minimize suicide risk, the goal of suicide intervention is to reduce the lethality of a particular suicidal crisis. The emphasis of intervention is on short-term care and treatment of persons in crisis. The cardinal rule is to do something—take the threat seriously, answer cries for help by offering support and compassion, and provide constructive alternatives to suicide. Suicide postvention refers to the assistance given to survivors, including those who survive suicide attempts as well as the families, friends, and associates of those who commit suicide.

KEY TERMS AND CONCEPTS

acute suicidal crisis

altruistic suicide

ambivalence

anomic suicide

assisted suicide

attempted suicide

chronic suicide

cluster suicides

crisis suicide

cry for help

depression

dyadic nature of suicide

egoistic suicide

fatalistic suicide

intrapsychic pressures

neurobiologic markers

order of lethality

psychodynamic model of suicide

psychotic suicide

rational suicide

referred suicide

romantic suicide

seppuku

sociological model of suicide

subintentioned suicide

suidical success syndrome

suicide intervention

suicide notes

suicide pacts

suicide postvention

suicide prevention

surcease suicide

suttee

telephone hotlines

unintentioned suicide

QUESTIONS FOR GUIDED STUDY AND EVALUATION

Multiple-choice questions relevant to this chapter can be found in the test bank.

1. Cite at least two statistics concerning the frequency of suicide.

2. Evaluate the four definitions of suicide given in the text.

3. Summarize the three types of suicide in the sociological model postulated by Emile Durkheim.

4. Describe the psychological model of suicide with attention to the role of ambivalence and its implications for caregivers.

5. List and analyze at least three cultural and three individual meanings of suicide.

6. Differentiate among intentioned, unintentioned, and subintentioned deaths, identifying at least two specific patterns in each category.

7. Identify and explain at least four possible motives for suicidal behavior.

8. Identify at least three motives for suicide at each stage of the lifespan: childhood, adolescence and young adulthood, middle adulthood, and late adulthood.

9. Name at least four possible reasons for the increase in childhood and adolescent suicide.

10. Interpret the various meanings and factors influencing choice of suicidal method.

11. Describe the progression toward lethality of various methods of suicide.

12. Distinguish among suicide prevention, intervention, and postvention.

13. List and refute at least eight myths about suicide.

14. Assume that you are confronted by a person who tells you he or she is contemplating suicide. Make a list of the information you would like to obtain and discuss your plan of action for responding to this individual.

TEACHING STRATEGIES

1. As an introduction to the topic of suicide, have students respond to the following statements, indicating true or false and explaining the reasons for their answers:
   - People who talk about suicide do not commit suicide.
   - Improvement in a suicidal person means the danger has passed.
   - Once a suicide risk, always a suicide risk.
   - Suicide is inherited.
   - Suicide affects only a specific group or class of people.
   - Suicidal behavior is insane.
   - Suicidal people are fully intent on dying.
   - The motive for suicide is always clearly evident.

   Have students compare their answers and explanations to those given in the text.

2. An investigation of coroner's duties allows students to look at types of suicides, how they are handled by the coroner's office, and how they affect survivors (see Chapter 11, teaching strategy 1). Have students divide into small groups and, based on the coroner's accounts, talk about which suicide seemed most offensive to them and which they could easily forgive. Come together as a class to discuss their thoughts.

3. Arrange for an in-class interview with a person who has attempted suicide, focusing on the social and psychological impact. How did relationships with others change? What kinds of feelings were evoked as a result?

COMMENTS AND CONSIDERATIONS

Various Responses to Suicide. Students' responses to suicide—whether the particular suicide evokes feelings of anger or forgiveness—will depend in part on cultural, religious, and psychological backgrounds. Help them to distinguish these components of understanding. Take time to identify from which part of their belief system and background their responses arise.

RESOURCES: FILMS AND VIDEOCASSETTES

Childhood's End: A Look at Adolescent Suicide (videocassette & 16 mm.; 28 min.; color; 1980; Brigham Young University, Filmakers Library) Looks at the complexities of adolescent suicide, focusing on two suicide attempters and the friends of an eighteen-year-old suicide victim.

Dangerous Years (videocassette; 29 min.; color; 1989; Coronet/MTI Film & Video) Examines the incidence of violence and suicide among adolescents.

Dead Serious (videocassette & 16 mm.; 23 min.; color; 1987; Coronet/MTI Film & Video) An award-winning film on adolescent suicide that focuses on being aware of the warning signs and learning how to respond to them when a peer is contemplating suicide. Based on the book by Jane Mersky Leder.

Deadline (videocassette & 16 mm.; 47 min.; color; 1985; The Media Guild) When Jeff, a high school student, writes a suicide note to the school newspaper, it triggers a search by his fellow students for the writer. In the process, they—and the viewers of this video—learn some important lessons about adolescent suicide. This dramatization is well acted and professionally produced.

Death of a Porn Queen (videocassette; 58 min.; color; 1987; PBS Video) This documentary from the "Frontline" series tells the tragic story of Colleen Applegate who, at age eighteen, left Farmington, Minnesota, to seek success in Hollywood. Becoming involved in the porn industry, a world where she could "feel like a queen," she developed a cocaine addiction and ended her life at age twenty. Examines the effect of environment on a young person's search for identity and self-esteem.

Depression: A Study in Abnormal Behavior (videocassette & 16 mm.; 27 min.; color; 1973; CRM Films) Dramatization of a young professional woman's thwarted suicide threats.

Depression and Suicide (videocassette; 30 min.; color; 1988; PBS Video) An award-winning program about adolescent suicide that includes a visit to two high schools that each recently experienced a suicide by one of its students. Identifies the signs that may be exhibited by people at risk of suicide and suggests procedures for intervention. Positive ways of coping with depression and stress are also considered.

Depression and Suicide (videocassette & 16 mm.; 26 min.; color; 1976; The Cinema Guild) Examines the role of depression in adolescent suicide. Looks at causes as well as means of coping with depression.

Did Jenny Have to Die? Preventing Teen Suicide (videocassette; 41 min.; color; 1985; Batesville Management Services, Sunburst Communications) A three-part series which looks at suicide prevention. Part 1, *Road to Nowhere,* looks at the motivation for Jenny's suicide. Part 2, *Behind the Smiles,* examines the warning signs of suicide. Part 3, *A Foundation for Living,* explores ways of preventing teenage suicide.

Elderly Suicide (videocassette; 28 min.; color; 1987; Films for the Humanities & Sciences) Examines the incidence of suicide among the elderly as an alternative to chronic disease and pain, waning physical and mental powers, economic stress, and fear of helplessness and total dependence. Adapted from a Phil Donahue show.

Ernie and Rose (videocassette & 16 mm.; 29 min.; color; 1983; Filmakers Library) Issues relative to suicide among the elderly are the focus of this film about the last days of a couple of Army buddies, now sharing a house and caring for each other in their old age. With a healthy dose of humor and an strong sense of human dignity, the two characters discuss the infirmities of age and their option of willingly "stepping aside" rather than waiting for death.

Everything to Live For (videocassette; 52 min.; color; 1987; Films for the Humanities & Sciences) This documentary on adolescent suicide features the stories of four youngsters who attempted suicide, two of whom survived. The families and the two surviving teens discuss the causes or presumed causes of the suicidal behavior and the warning signs of suicide.

Fragile Time (videocassette; 13 min.; color; 1988; Perennial Education) Through the use of three case studies, this program focuses on adolescent suicide, emphasizing the need for effective intervention. Two of the individuals profiled received help and are able to tell their story; the third, eighteen-year-old Andy, ended his life.

Harold and Maude (16 mm.; about 1-1/2 (1,2) hours; color; 1971; Paramount Pictures) A humorous film about suicide and funerals starring Ruth Gordon.

I Want to Die (16 mm.; 25 min.; color; 1977; The Media Guild, University of Illinois) Examines the motivations behind one young man's suicidal tendencies.

The Inner Voice in Suicide (videocassette; 32 min.; color; 1984; The Glendon Association) Interviewed by Dr. Robert Firestone, a psychologist, Susan, age thirty-eight, talks about the thought processes and the "inner voice" that led up to her serious suicide attempt. She describes the progression from self-hatred to hopelessness as the "voice" insisted: "You don't matter to anyone anyway."

Permanent Record (videocassette; 92 min.; color; 1988; Baker and Taylor Video) The suicidal death of an apparently happy and successful high school student causes his peers to struggle to understand what went wrong.

Rational Suicide (videocassette & 16 mm.; 15 min.; color; 1981; Carousel Film & Video) Deals with surcease suicide, contrasting the ideas of Cecily Saunders, founder of St. Christopher's Hospice, with those of Derek Humphry, founder of the Hemlock Society, who helped his wife end her struggle with cancer through suicide.

The Shootist (16 mm.; 1 hour & 40 min.; color; 1976; Paramount Pictures) John Wayne portrays a gunfighter who chooses to die in his own way rather than face terminal cancer.

Suicide (videocassette; 13 min.; color; 1982; Batesville Management Services) Based on a book by Earl Grollman, this film discusses issues realistically and emphasizes the need for education about suicide.

Suicide: Teenage Crisis (videocassette & 16 mm.; 10 min.; color; 1981; CRM Films) Counselors from a suicide prevention center discuss the dynamics of suicide and its prevention.

Suicide: The Warning Signs (16 mm.; 14 min.; color; 1974; Portland State University) Three suicidal teenagers are portrayed in this dramatization.

Suicide—But Jack Was a Good Driver (videocassette & 16 mm.; 15 min.; color; 1974; CRM Films, Portland State University, UCB Extension Media Center) The motives and warning signs of teenage suicide are explored as Jack's high school friends begin to suspect that his death may have been suicide.

Suicide Clinic: A Cry for Help (videocassette & 16 mm.; 28 min.; black & white; 1969; Indiana University, UCLA Instructional Media Library) Examines motives for suicide and the services provided by a suicide clinic.

Teenage Depression (videocassette; 30 min.; color; 1987; PBS Video) Focuses on the self-doubt, alienation, and general malaise that are frequently associated with the years of adolescence. Examines the role of depression in teen suicide and offers methods for dealing constructively with depression.

Teenage Suicide (videocassette; 19 min.; color; 1987; Films for the Humanities & Sciences) Explores the reasons adolescents commit suicide and the behavior patterns to which families and friends should be alerted. A young man who attempted suicide describes his calls for help and how he hoped they would be heeded.

Teenage Suicide: An Approach to Prevention (videocassette; 50 min.; color; 1987; Perennial Education) A two-part program featuring Dr. Frank Walton that focuses on recognizing the warning signals and positive intervention. The segments are entitled *Recognizing the Problem* and *How to Help*.

Teenage Suicide: The Ultimate Dropout (videocassette; 29 min.; color; 1979; PBS Video) Fourteen-year-old Arizona teen Dee Dee White talks candidly and in detail about her attempted suicide and the feelings that led to it. Dee Dee's mother, and other parents, discuss their own feelings of frustration and guilt, and how they sought help for family problems. Psychiatrists and social workers offer advice to families facing a potential suicide crisis.

Teens Who Chose Life: The Suicidal Crisis (videocassette; 45 min.; color; 1986; Batesville Management Services, Sunburst Communications) A three-part series that looks at suicide survivors. Part 1, *Keith Chooses Life,* investigates depression as a motivation for suicide and explores some of the possible warning signs. Part 2, *Gail Chooses Life,* looks at how death may seem impermanent and romantic to teenagers. Part 3, *Erica Chooses Life,* looks at losses, especially divorce, as possible motivation for suicide.

Why Suicide? (videocassette; 30 min.; color; 1987; PBS Video) Focusing on adolescent suicide, this program deals with the question of why some teens are able to cope with the pressures of adolescence and others are not. Four teens who attempted suicide share their experiences, noting that they tried to end their lives when they were lonely, depressed, and craving attention.

Chapter 14

Beyond Death/After Life

OBJECTIVES

1. To compare and contrast the views of immortality in the Hebrew, Hellenistic, Christian, Islamic, and secular traditions.
2. To compare and contrast Eastern religious views of life after death.
3. To describe the central features of near-death experiences.
4. To analyze the alternative interpretations of near-death experiences.
5. To summarize death-related experiences resulting from the use of psychedelic drugs and their therapeutic application.
6. To demonstrate how beliefs about what follows death influence a person's understanding of death and how such beliefs evidence themselves in choices regarding care of the dying as well as in daily life.

CONTENT OVERVIEW

Chapter 14 explores the major philosophical, religious, and parapsychological views concerning immortality. Such an exploration can lead to a more coherent appreciation of both life and death, making possible a congruence of hopes and perceptions. The notion that earthly existence continues on in some form following death is one of the oldest concepts held by human beings, as attested to by discoveries made in the earliest known graves. In traditional societies, death usually represents a change of status for the deceased, some kind of transition from the land of the living to the land of the dead.

In the West, our views about immortality have been influenced by the Hebrew, Hellenistic, and Christian traditions, as well as by the secular ideas of the modern era. At the risk of oversimplifying, a capsule statement of the conventional Western view is that human beings live a single life, that the individual soul survives the death of the body, and that conduct during earthly life determines the ultimate fate of the soul. For the most part, the emphasis on survival of the individual soul is a later development, having been preceded by an emphasis on some type of corporate survival involving the continued existence of the community as a whole. Even so, the emphasis on one's conduct in the present life as a determinant of some future state is ancient and is shared by many cultures worldwide. The concept of immortality in the Islamic tradition shares many features with the other Abrahamic traditions, Judaism and Christianity. Although neither the Bible nor the Qur'an provides a systematic treatment of death, the subject is not ignored. Rather, the emphasis is on living righteously and on moral accountability.

For many people, death has been divorced from its mythic and religious connotations. The underpinnings for traditional beliefs no longer carry the same weight in a culture that emphasizes scientific method and empirical verification. Although the present milieu is one in which secular alternatives to religion are widespread and indeed pervasive, it is not unusual for a person to hold several competing world views at the same time, combining a vague religious faith (perhaps carried over from childhood) with a more secular faith in scientific modes of knowledge and humanitarian ideals of conduct. Despite the option of unbelief, most people still affirm belief in God and, to a somewhat lesser degree, belief in more or less conventional notions of heaven and hell. It may be that, for persons steeped in the materialist culture of the modern West, religious beliefs about the afterlife represent a comforting backdrop to more concrete forms of immortality found in the biological continuity represented by one's children or the social continuity represented by creative work or heroic deeds.

Whereas Western thought is noted for its tendency to make distinctions, point up contrasts, and establish differences, Eastern philosophies and religions typically seek to discover the unity that lies behind apparent opposites. Distinctions are subsumed within a holistic "both/and" perspective. The Eastern view is that life and death are complementary aspects of an essentially undivided reality. This viewpoint informs both Hinduism and Buddhism, and it is reflected throughout the holy books of the East, although individual sects exhibit a diversity of opinion with respect to how these insights should be applied in daily life. The doctrine of reincarnation, for example, can be understood as referring to *physical* transmigration (the passing of the soul from one body to another at death) as well as to *continuous* transmigration (the insubstantial and ineffable process of psychophysical events that constitute moment-to-moment experience). Either way, the aim is to know the unconditioned state beyond both birth and death.

Stories of travel to another realm beyond the earthly existence can be found in virtually all cultures. Near-death experiences (NDEs) represent a modern variation of such otherworld journeys. These accounts by persons who have reportedly glimpsed the afterworld, or the path that leads to it following death, have been interpreted variously. Some believe these journeys are proof of personality survival after death. Others view them as nothing more than a psychological or neurophysiological response to the stress of life-threatening danger. An individual's own model of reality is likely to favor one or the other of these differing interpretations. Each requires a form of faith. In the fragmented religious situation that characterizes modern society, the accounts that derive from near-death experiences (and experiences resulting from the ingestion of LSD and other psychedelic substances) remind us of the universal human need to make meaning of life and death. Whether we view death as a wall or as a door, our beliefs about the nature of the cosmos and our place in it exert a powerful influence on how we choose to live and on how we care for and relate to persons who are dying or bereaved.

KEY TERMS AND CONCEPTS

after-death states	Buddhism
afterlife	Christianity
ancestor-gods	Day of Reckoning
bardo	dualism
Hebraic tradition	panoramic life review
Hellenistic concepts	positivism
Hinduism	rebirth
humanitarianism	reincarnation
immortality	resurrection
Islam	*samsars*
Judgment Day	secularization of death
karma	soul
LSD (lysergic acid diethylamide)	*Tao*
NDE (near-death experience)	transcendence
nirvana	transmigration of the soul

QUESTIONS FOR GUIDED STUDY AND EVALUATION

Multiple-choice questions relevant to this chapter can be found in the test bank.

1. Contrast the Hebrew and Hellenistic concepts of life after death.
2. Compare Pythagoras, Socrates, and Plato with respect to their views of life after death.
3. Trace the historical changes in the concept of life after death in the Christian tradition.
4. Summarize the main elements of Islamic belief about life after death.
5. Describe what is meant by the secularization of death, and give at least three examples of a secular understanding of immortality.
6. Summarize the Eastern view of immortality and describe how it differs from Western views.
7. Identify the central themes of the Hindu view of life after death.
8. Describe the Buddhist perspective of death, paying particular attention to the different meanings of karma, the two types of death, and transmigration.
9. Describe the composite picture of NDEs and discuss the frequency with which the various elements are experienced.

10. Explain at least three possible models for interpreting near-death experiences.

11. Summarize Russell Noyes and Raymond Kletti's three stages of NDEs.

12. Describe the therapeutic use of LSD with terminally ill patients.

13. Evaluate the "wall/door" metaphor and its implications. Which seems more correct to you? Why?

TEACHING STRATEGIES

1. Distribute five-by-eight cards to students. Explain that people generally hold beliefs about death that are somehow useful to them; in other words, beliefs serve a purpose. Then ask students to write on the cards their answers to each of the following questions:

   • Side 1: What do you believe happens at and shortly after the moment of death?

   • Side 2: How does that belief serve you?

   When students have finished writing, instruct them to pass the cards (with side 1 showing) to the third person on their right. Ask them to imagine that they have had a dramatic change of mind or spiritual conversion, and that the card they now have states their new belief. Have them consider how that belief would function to serve them. Ask for a volunteer who has a card describing a very different belief from his or her own, and have that person read the belief on side 1 and offer a guess about how that belief would be useful. Then have the volunteer read side 2 of the card aloud. As a class, discuss how the views expressed by the writer of the card differ from or are the same as what was suggested by the volunteer. This activity can be repeated several times to reinforce learnings about the connection between a belief and the purpose it serves.

2. There are many ways of thinking about immortality. Besides various religious and parapsychological ideas, immortality can be associated with achievements such as writing books, performing human services, and otherwise contributing to society. Many believe that children are a form of immortality. Have students list three to five ways in which their beliefs relate to this kind of immortality. How would they like to be remembered? What values would they like to leave as a legacy through their achievements or otherwise? Discuss their ideas as a class.

3. Guest speakers who are knowledgeable about particular topics or traditions discussed in this chapter can be invited to give a brief presentation and answer students' questions. For example, a Buddhist priest could describe that religion's understanding of immortality, or a person who had undergone a near-death experience could describe what it was like. Have students formulate specific questions beforehand to make optimal use of class time.

COMMENTS AND CONSIDERATIONS

1. **Defensiveness.** Some students are possessive about their beliefs and feel they must defend them. By this time in the course, they may feel less threatened, but it can be important to talk briefly about why it is useful to examine one's beliefs. One insight gained from teaching strategy 1 is the awareness that there are many different beliefs that can serve people well, and that beliefs can be examined in a nonjudgmental way to expand awareness.

2. **Ideal Versus Real.** Students may want to have two cards for teaching strategy 1, one containing information about actual beliefs and the other about desired beliefs. Differences between the two can be important information since they form the basis for appropriate change and reflect the recognition that what served us well at one point in our lives may not always serve us equally well.

RESOURCES: FILMS AND VIDEOCASSETTES

Afterlife (videocassette & 16 mm.; 7 min.; color; 1978; National Film Board of Canada) An animated film using myths and cross-cultural beliefs to depict one person's idea about afterlife.

The Awakening of Nancy Kaye (videocassette; 46 min.; color; 1985; Filmakers Library) One woman's story, as told by family and friends, of lifelong disability (spina bifida) and her spiritual awakening as she faces death.

Back from Light (videocassette; 28 min.; color; 1989; Filmakers Library) Interviews with men and women who have experienced NDEs.

Encounter with Garvan Byrne (videocassette; 30 min.; color; 1990; Gateway Films) This encounter with a twelve-year-old boy in the last year of his life is an example of the power of religious faith in the face of death. Garvan says: "Death isn't really dying. It's going through an old door into a new door—into a new room, and Jesus will be there."

In Search of Life After Death (videocassette & 16 mm.; 24 min.; color; 1977; Pyramid Film & Video) Leonard Nimoy narrates dramatizations of people who describe their near-death experiences. One man in particular talks about how he reevaluated and changed his life after the experience.

Islam (videocassette; 60 min.; color; 1989; PBS Video) From the series "Smithsonian World," this program provides an introduction to Islam and offers a perspective on this ancient religion as its confronts modern society. Explores what it means to be a Muslim.

The Lion's Roar (videocassette & 16 mm.; 50 min.; color; 1985; Barr Films) A presentation of Tibetan Buddhist beliefs about life and death.

Living and Death (16 mm.; 29 min.; black & white; 1971; Indiana University) Looks at fear in daily life in the context of Indian philosophy.

The Mystery That Heals (videocassette & 16 mm.; 30 min.; color; 1972; Films, Inc.) Examines the Jungian concept of life after death.

The Near-Death Experience Video (videocassette & 16 mm.; 60 min.; color; 1985; Howard Mickel) Interviews with five people about their near-death experiences. Included with the video are a teacher's guide, workbook, and *The Near-Death Experiences: A Basic Introduction.*

A Plain Pine Box (16 mm.; 25 min.; color; 1977; Committee on Congregational Standards) A film valued both for its presentation of Jewish rituals surrounding the dead and for its look at Jewish religious beliefs in general. In it we see the functions of a Jewish burial society: building the plain pine coffin, preparing the body for burial, and counseling the bereaved. Members of the society talk about their commitment to performing this service for their community and the value of their participation in helping them face the reality of death.

Return from Death: The Near Death Experience (videocassette; 52 min.; color; 1990; Filmakers Library) Interviews with eleven persons who have returned after being pronounced clinically dead, giving their accounts of what took place in the minutes before resuscitation.

Spark of Life (videocassette & 16 mm.; 24 min.; color; 1977; Bhaktivedanta Book Trust) Hindu beliefs are examined through the doctrines of the Hari Krishna group, including a discussion of transmigration of the soul.

Theology of Suffering, Health and Healing—Buddhism (videocassette; 60 min.; color; 1978; Learning Resources Center) Examines Buddhist beliefs about suffering.

Theology of Suffering, Health and Healing—Evil and the God of Love (videocassette; 60 min.; color; 1978; Learning Resources Center) Explores how combining Western and non-Western (Buddhist) views can help alleviate suffering.

Theology of Suffering, Health and Healing—New Testament (videocassette; 60 min.; color; 1979; Learning Resources Center) A look at the Christian view of suffering.

Theology of Suffering, Health and Healing—Old Testament (videocassette; 60 min.; color; 1979; Learning Resources Center) Explores the view of suffering found in the Hebrew scriptures.

Though I Walk Through the Valley (videocassette & 16 mm.; 29 min.; color; 1972; Pyramid Film & Video) Focuses on a devoutly Christian middle-aged professor facing impending death and the importance of his religious faith.

Vishnu's Maya (videocassette; 30 min.; color; 1977; Phoenix/BFA Films & Video) Examines the concept of "maya" in Indian philosophy as an element of classical Hindu culture. Shows Hindu worship and marriage ceremonies, as well as the daily activities of village life in India.

Chapter 15

The Path Ahead:
Personal and Social Choices

OBJECTIVES

1. To identify and evaluate the social and personal consequences of studying death and dying.
2. To assess the current state of death education and to suggest concerns that should be addressed.
3. To analyze speculation about attitudes and practices related to death in the future and to assess the potential effects of these changes on individuals and society.
4. To identify and appraise for oneself the qualities associated with an appropriate death.

CONTENT OVERVIEW

Chapter 15 brings our survey of death and dying to a close with opportunities for reflection on the topics discussed throughout the text. Acknowledging the impact of death in our lives can awaken us to just how precious life is and lead us into a greater appreciation of relationships. One of the benefits gained through an exploration of death and dying lies in the new choices such study offers. Death is taken out of the closet and scrutinized from a variety of perspectives. The close examination of death often brings insights that help to dissipate or resolve feelings of guilt or blame related to grief over a loved one's death. New and more comforting perspectives may shed light on experiences that were previously unsettling.

Many people discover that their study of death and dying has application not only to personal or professional concerns, but also to issues facing society at large. Questions concerning such issues as the allocation of scarce health care resources, care for dying patients and for the elderly, and the use of life-sustaining medical technologies require an informed public, individuals who can participate knowledgeably in the shaping of public policy. Confronting the meaning of death in social as well as personal contexts may alter our political consciousness and offer a deeper dimension of reality to issues involving public safety, disarmament, environmental pollution, and violent crime.

Death education is a young discipline, one in which curricula and standards for measuring outcome are still being defined. As the tag line of virtually every journal article, regardless of discipline, states: "More research is needed." It is perhaps especially so in the field of thanatology. Students who undertake further work in the discipline will find innumerable opportunities to make significant contributions. Because thanatology deals with both scientific and humanitarian concerns, the qualities of objectivity and caring are both necessary. Needed, too, is a dedication to maintaining communication among theorists, researchers, and practitioners.

The field of thanatology—and, by extension, death education and the death awareness movement—has already made important contributions to the quality of our communal life with respect to humanizing medical relationships, advancing appropriate care for the dying, and calling attention to the essential human values that sustain us through experiences of loss and grief. The compassionate acts of service that have been encouraged and promoted thus far are founded on a recognition of the identity and worth of each human being.

As we look to the future, and as the field of death education continues to mature, new questions and issues will demand our attention. It has been estimated that there will be 2.6 million deaths annually by the year 2000, less than a decade away. This represents an increase of about one-third over the present number of deaths each year. Will care of the dying become big business? Or will dying be brought back into the personal realm of the individuals and families who are closest to a particular death? Individuals who have become sensitive to issues of terminal care as a result of studying death and dying will be equipped to make meaningful choices and to share information with others as they work toward the goal of ensuring compassionate care. The pace of social change is such that most people devote little time to the rituals of celebration and gathering together that were so central to traditional communities. If we believe that funerals are a time-honored means for facilitating the expression of grief and coping with loss, how can the essential features of such ritual be maintained or altered in such a way that the therapeutic importance of the ritual remains intact? Again, individuals who have gained some understanding of the meaning of funeral ritual and the process of grief will be in a position to make personally meaningful choices as well as to share their insights with others.

Death is an intensely human experience. In beginning to make room for loss and change in our lives, we may find it useful to balance our fears with openness, our anxieties with trust. But in gaining more familiarity with death, we ought to be wary about becoming overly casual about it—or it might turn out that we have confronted only our image of death, not death itself. In facing death, perhaps we should let go of our desire for a "good" death and attend rather to the possibility of an *appropriate* death. In the context of such a death, the social and emotional needs of the dying person are met to the fullest extent possible, and suffering is kept to a minimum. There is no place for dehumanizing or demeaning procedures. An appropriate death is the death that someone would choose for himself or herself—if there were a choice.

KEY TERMS AND CONCEPTS

apocalyptic scenarios
appropriate death
Armageddon
death anxiety
death awareness movement
death education

grief clinics
horrendous death
humanizing death
hydrostatic models of grief
planetary death
thanatology

QUESTIONS FOR GUIDED STUDY AND EVALUATION

Multiple-choice questions relevant to this chapter can be found in the test bank.

1. Compare and contrast your own feelings about taking a course in death and dying with those expressed by the students quoted in the text.

2. Suggest and evaluate at least three societal applications of death education.

3. Summarize the current state of death education and suggest areas that you think deserve further study.

4. Summarize the conditions associated with an appropriate death.

5. Interpret the poem "The Angel of Death," and explain what you think the author is saying about the relationship of death to life.

TEACHING STRATEGIES

1. Instruct students to imagine themselves as anthropologists arriving on Earth from another planet in the year 2020. Have them describe what they envision. What kinds of life-threatening illnesses prevail? How are the dying treated? How is death defined? Does the imagined future include "neomorts," bodies in suspended animation from which parts are taken when needed? What kinds of death rituals are observed? Encourage students to be imaginative in their responses. Then, on the basis of their imagined data, have them extrapolate and describe the beliefs that would be present in such a future society.

2. Have students form small groups and discuss what they believe would be a good or appropriate death for themselves. Then come back together as a class and discuss the variety of dying states that were proposed.

3. Divide the class into two groups. One group will pretend to be people who were granted immortality a thousand years ago. The other group consists of people who are mortal and have a normal lifespan. The second group is faced with the choice whether or not to allow science to produce a new drug that would give them immortality. Have them interview members of the first group by asking questions such as the following:

- How does it feel to live forever?
- Do you wish you could die?
- What changes have you lived through in the last thousand years?
- Are you bored or lonely?
- How valuable is each day when you do not have limits on your time?

Afterwards, have students write their reflections on the learning generated by this activity. [Adapted from *Death Out of the Closet: A Curriculum Guide to Living with Dying*, by Gene Stanford and Deborah Perry (New York: Bantam, 1975), p. 105. Reprinted by permission.]

COMMENTS AND CONSIDERATIONS

Technology versus Humanism. When engaged in teaching strategy 1, students may find themselves in one of two camps. Some may see death as becoming less familiar because of technology, whereas others see the development of a more humane approach to death and dying. This presents an excellent opportunity to encourage a discussion of how this dichotomy can be reconciled.

RESOURCES: FILMS AND VIDEOCASSETTES

Before It's Too Late (videocassette; 3 min.; color; 1979; Batesville Management Services) With a musical theme, this film addresses the importance of death education.

Coma (16 mm.; about 1 hour & 50 min.; color; 1978; Films, Inc.) The technological future at its worst is presented in this science fiction drama about the removal of body parts from comatose patients.

Soylent Green (16 mm.; about 1 hour & 40 min.; color; 1973; Films, Inc.) A futuristic look at life and death in urban New York with euthanasia as a primary focus; stars Edward G. Robinson and Charlton Heston.

Appendix A

Course Papers

These two papers are assigned at the beginning of the term and students are encouraged to make notes for them as the course progresses. The first paper is due at the end of the first quarter of the term; the second at the end of the term.

ASSIGNMENT 1

Deathography. Ask students to review their experiences with loss and death during childhood, adolescence, and adulthood. Have them inventory and describe each influential loss experience, analyzing its impact on their attitudes toward death. Instruct them to write a paper, of approximately six typed, double-spaced pages, highlighting the important death-related events in their lives and connecting these to their beliefs today. The following excerpt is an example:

> In examining my somewhat ambiguous feelings about ground burial, I began to get an idea of how conflicting notions arose in my experience. Memories of my mother's response to my digging up a long-buried goldfish join in my mind with the childhood rhyme, "The worms crawl in, the worms crawl out, the worms play pinochle on his snout." No wonder I am ambivalent about burial.

Collect, collate, and bind these papers. Then about midterm, have students read one another's deathographies. We find the college library to be a convenient location for the bound deathographies, which are placed on two-hour reserve. Supply students with a list of questions to be completed as they read the deathographies. Since there is only one bound copy, they should plan their reserve reading time carefully. Tell students to come to class prepared with written answers to the following questions:

1. Which death experiences seem like ones that might be especially difficult for you to survive?
2. What similarities do you notice between the death experiences you have written about and those of your classmates?

3. Select at least two examples from the writings of your classmates that describe ways of thinking about a death that seem especially useful to you.

4. Note descriptions of death rituals that you believe would be helpful to you as a survivor.

5. From the experiences of your classmates, identify what you believe to be a high-grief death.

During the class discussion of the deathography assignment, students are encouraged to report on both the experience of reading other students' papers and the writing of their own (see Chapter 7, teaching strategy 1).

ASSIGNMENT 2

I Learned Final Paper. This paper is designed to be a review of students' learnings during the term. Direct them to recall the various topics covered in the course and organize them sequentially. Ask students to choose at least three personal learnings and three learnings of broader social import. For example, a student's personal learning could involve a new understanding of previously unresolved or unsettled issues related to a family member's illness or death. A learning with social import could involve a greater awareness of the options for terminal care and a desire to expand the choices available to the community. Each learning should be supported by examples from readings, class discussions, activities, field trips, guest speaker's presentations, films, and videocassettes. It is important for students to identify, with specific examples, the sources and extent of their learnings. The paper should be written in the form of "I" statements: I learned, I relearned, I noticed, I was surprised, I can see, I feel, I tuned into, I got a handle on, and so on. In summary, this paper is a course review, eliciting those learnings most useful to students.

Appendix B

Examinations

PART 1: OBJECTIVE TEST QUESTIONS

The following (from Chapter 14) is a sample of objective test questions. The complete test bank is available in printed form or on computer disk from Mayfield Publishing Company. Refer to the preface for information about obtaining either format. The relative difficulty of the items is indicated according to the following scale:

1 = easy (recall facts)
2 = moderately easy (comprehend facts)
3 = moderately difficult (apply concepts)
4 = difficult (differentiate concepts)

Multiple Choice

Answer: B
Difficulty: 2

1. The notion that life continues after death
   a. originated in early Greece.
   b. is one of the oldest human concepts.
   c. is a relatively recent idea.
   d. originated in Egypt.

Answer: D
Difficulty: 3
   2. Which of the following statements is most in keeping with traditional Hawaiian beliefs about the afterlife?
      a. "The afterlife is nonexistent."
      b. "There is a place in heaven for everyone."
      c. "We cannot change the fate chosen for us by the gods."
      d. "Wrongdoers will suffer eternal punishment."

Answer: B
Difficulty: 2
   3. Traditional Hawaiian beliefs about death emphasize the
      a. young.
      b. clan.
      c. individual.
      d. old.

Answer: B
Difficulty: 3
   4. The ancient Hebrews advocated righteous conduct in the present life because
      a. it guarantees future rewards for the individual.
      b. it leads to harmony in the present life.
      c. they feared eternal damnation.
      d. they feared the physical pain of dying.

Answer: B
Difficulty: 3
   5. The books of the Bible reflect ideas about death that are
      a. unchanging over long periods of time.
      b. modified over long periods of time.
      c. based on the concept of damnation.
      d. based on individual destiny.

Answer: A
Difficulty: 3
   6. The Hebrew word *She'ol* refers to
      a. the underworld of the dead.
      b. hell.
      c. the resurrection of the body into heaven.
      d. everlasting life.

Answer: D
Difficulty: 3
   7. Traditional Hebrew doctrine views the "soul" as
       a. taking over the body.
       b. nonexistent.
       c. an entity that will be reincarnated.
       d. virtually indistinguishable from the body.

Answer: C
Difficulty: 3
   8. Which of the following statements would the Biblical writers most likely have said?
       a. "We have a right to an afterlife."
       b. "Because there is no afterlife, we must make the most of this life."
       c. "The afterlife is God's gift."
       d. "Eternal damnation is inevitable."

Answer: B
Difficulty: 1
   9. Weighing the soul against the feather of truth is associated with the concept of judgment after death in which culture?
       a. Greek
       b. Egyptian
       c. Hindu
       d. Hebrew

Answer: C
Difficulty: 3
  10. The ancient Greeks stressed the survival of the
       a. individual.
       b. fittest.
       c. group.
       d. ruling class.

Answer: A
Difficulty: 3
  11. Christian beliefs about death emphasize
       a. the destiny of the individual soul.
       b. the nonexistence of an afterlife.
       c. that death brings eternal damnation for all.
       d. that death is not something to be concerned with during life.

Answer: A
Difficulty: 3
12. Qur'anic teachings about death emphasize:
   a. that God determines a person's lifespan.
   b. that God is powerless; it is the individual who determines his or her fate.
   c. the existence of hell.
   d. the nonexistence of an afterlife.

Answer: B
Difficulty: 4
13. According to the Islamic tradition, what role do Munkar and Nakir play in death?
   a. They punish wrongdoers with death.
   b. They interrogate the deceased.
   c. They represent the devil.
   d. They inspire the deceased's family.

Answer: C
Difficulty: 4
14. According to orthodox Islamic tradition, the funeral
   a. is an occasion for a large celebration.
   b. should be elaborate.
   c. should be simple.
   d. is an occasion for intense grief.

Answer: A
Difficulty: 1
15. What is "positivism?"
   a. It reflects the belief that religious modes of knowing are imperfect and that knowledge must be based on observation and scientific methods.
   b. It centers on human values and interests, emphasizing the use of optimistic reasoning.
   c. It is a philosophy of the afterlife that, based on the teachings of the ancient Greeks, stresses the use of logic to solve complex questions about the afterlife.
   d. It is the belief that, depending on one's conduct during earthly existence, the afterlife will be either pure torment or pure bliss.

Answer: A
Difficulty: 4
16. In *Without God, Without Creed*, James Turner discusses
    a. changes in society and religion that have given rise to the possibility of not believing in God.
    b. the resurgence of Islam as an increasingly prominent religion throughout the world.
    c. the Abrahamic religious traditions and their unchanging concepts of life and the afterlife.
    d. humanitarianism and its focus on empirical knowledge in proving there is indeed life after death.

Answer: B
Difficulty: 3
17. With respect to Eastern philosophical and religious thought, the characteristic view of reality is
    a. dualistic.
    b. holistic.
    c. pessimistic.
    d. materialistic.

Answer: D
Difficulty: 3
18. The concept of reincarnation has its roots in
    a. Islam.
    b. Christianity.
    c. Western thought.
    d. Eastern thought.

Answer: B
Difficulty: 4
19. *Samsara* refers to
    a. the passing of the soul from one body to another at the time of death.
    b. the linking of incarnational experiences.
    c. the Hindu holiday observing the death of Arjuna.
    d. the Islamic belief that all lives will be reviewed and each person will answer for his or her deeds.

Answer: C
Difficulty: 3
20. Buddhism emphasizes the
    a. unchanging substantiality of the soul.
    b. turmoil of the present life.
    c. impermanence of the self.
    d. restfulness of the afterlife.

Answer: D
Difficulty: 1
21. *Nirvana* literally means
    a. liberation.
    b. deification.
    c. illumination.
    d. extinction.

Answer: B
Difficulty: 4
22. Hinduism and Buddhism are similar in that both
    a. view death as negative and life as positive.
    b. emphasize transmigration.
    c. view God as powerless.
    d. emphasize the absence of an afterlife.

Answer: D
Difficulty: 3
23. Which of the following is NOT a form of the "otherworld journey" identified by Carol Zaleski?
    a. the journey to the underworld
    b. the ascent to higher worlds
    c. the fantastic voyage
    d. the visit to purgatory

Answer: D
Difficulty: 3
24. According to the text, which of the following is NOT an element commonly found in near-death experiences?
    a. feelings of peace and well-being
    b. entry into a dark tunnel
    c. separation from the body
    d. weakened self-confidence

Answer: A
Difficulty: 3
25. Psychoanalytic pioneer Oskar Pfister attributed the near-death experiences of skiers and climbers in Albert Heim's study to
    a. psychological defense mechanisms.
    b. the Oedipal complex.
    c. separation anxiety experienced in childhood.
    d. beliefs in God and eternal afterlife.

Answer: B
Difficulty: 4
26. According to the psychological model associated with Noyes and Kletti, life review often involves
    a. detachment from one's individual existence.
    b. affirmation of the meaning of one's existence.
    c. the recognition of imminent danger and struggle against it.
    d. the acceptance of death as unavoidable.

Answer: A
Difficulty: 4
27. With respect to care of the dying, why does one need to be cautious about a too-ready acceptance of near-death experiences?
    a. Dying persons need attention and concern at the present time.
    b. Talk of near-death experiences may cause unnecessary fear in the dying patient.
    c. Research has shown that near-death experiences are merely hallucinations.
    d. Talk of near-death experiences gives a false sense of hope to dying persons.

Answer: B
Difficulty: 3
28. The therapeutic use of lysergic acid diethylamide (LSD), pioneered by Eric Kast in the early 1960s, sought to
    a. study the deterioration of the minds of dying patients due to drug use.
    b. decrease physical pain and alter attitudes toward death.
    c. comfort persons who had suffered the loss of a loved one.
    d. increase understanding of near-death experiences by relating them to drug-induced hallucinations.

Appendix B | *Examinations* 137

Answer: C
Difficulty: 4
29. Death has been characterized as a "door" or a "wall." In the context of the discussion in this chapter, Christians would most likely characterize death as
a. a door.
b. a wall.
c. both a door and a wall.
d. neither a door nor a wall.

Answer: A
Difficulty: 4
30. Death has been characterized as a "door" or a "wall." In the context of the discussion in this chapter, Hindus would most likely characterize death as
a. a door.
b. a wall.
c. both a door and a wall.
d. neither a door nor a wall.

True/False

Answer: False
Difficulty: 2
31. The notion of the afterlife is a relatively new concept.

Answer: False
Difficulty: 2
32. The books of the Bible provide a systematic theology of death and the afterlife.

Answer: True
Difficulty: 3
33. The ancient Greeks believed that conduct during earthly life determined the destiny of the soul after death.

Answer: False
Difficulty: 3
34. The Islamic holy book, the Qur'an, provides a systematic treatment of death and the afterlife.

Answer: False
Difficulty: 2

35. A 1991 survey found that religion is of declining importance among twentieth-century Americans.

Answer: True
Difficulty: 2

36. Death holds a central place in the teachings of Buddhism.

Answer: False
Difficulty: 2

37. Parapsychologists emphasize that, to understand near-death experiences, scientifically verifiable evidence must be obtained.

Answer: False
Difficulty: 1

38. Beliefs about life after death are generally the same across cultures.

Answer: True
Difficulty: 3

39. To investigate one's true nature, Zen master Hakuin advised meditation on the word *shi*, the character for death.

Answer: False
Difficulty: 2

40. Researchers of near-death experiences have reached the consensus that such experiences are merely the result of psychological defense mechanisms.

Answer: False
Difficulty: 1

41. A Gallup poll conducted during the 1980s reported that about one-fifth of all adult Americans answered yes to the question, "Do you believe in life after death?"

Answer: True
Difficulty: 2

42. According to the text, what we believe about death and the afterlife can influence the actions taken when we near death.

Matching

Difficulty: 4
Answers: 43-B, 44-A, 45-C, 46-E
Listed below are various traditions discussed in the text and brief descriptions of the traditions. Match each tradition with the most appropriate description.

43. Eastern thought   A. Life represents affirmation, and death represents negation.

44. Western thought   B. Death and life are seen as complementary facets of an underlying process.

45. Hebrew thought   C. *Gehinom* and *Pardes* play a role in this tradition.

46. Islamic thought   D. Death serves to foster mindfulness of the importance of choosing wisely in the present life.

E. For the believer, death is a release from the sorrows and troubles of life.

PART 2: ESSAY EXAMINATION CONSTRUCTION

In reviewing the sample essay examination included in Part 3 of this Appendix, notice that questions have been drawn from throughout the text. The sections of the *Instructor's Guide* entitled "Key Terms and Concepts" and "Questions for Guided Study and Evaluation" have been used as a basis for constructing the comprehensive essay examination. The design of the examination provides a means of determining students' learning at varying levels—including knowledge, comprehension, application, analysis, synthesis, and evaluation. The following model, which includes key terms for use in constructing questions, is useful in distinguishing the levels of response required from students relative to the material being tested.

Knowledge (to become acquainted with, to recognize or recall information from memory). Key terms: List, define, name, identify, state. Responses should give information within context; facts should be clear and specific.

Comprehension (to interpret, paraphrase, or restate information, to reorganize information to show understanding, to extrapolate trends). Key terms: Explain, describe, interpret, summarize, illustrate, tell in your own words, give an example. Responses should illustrate by quotation, logically extend the facts, and be stated in a framework appropriate to student-level comprehension.

Application (to put information to use, to apply concepts in new situations, to solve problems). Key terms: Compute, apply, demonstrate, solve, use, prepare, construct, estimate. Responses should link process to method, theory to study or observation. Appropriate rules of application (theory) should be stated with reference to examples or case studies.

Analysis (to separate ideas into their component parts, to use logic and critical thinking skills, to examine relationships). Key terms: Analyze, determine, point out, distinguish, associate, differentiate. Responses should demonstrate application of a model, concept, or set of principles to a particular setting, environment, or situation.

Synthesis (to combine ideas, to associate, to create new classifications and innovative applications). Key terms: Plan, compose, design, create, organize, develop, modify. Responses should demonstrate recognition of differences as well as the ability to develop new criteria and engage in divergent thinking.

Evaluation (to make judgments using self-produced criteria or established standards). Key terms: Judge, assess, appraise, compare, contrast, conclude, evaluate. Responses should review merits of the item or situation under evaluation and state criteria for judgment.

PART 3: SAMPLE ESSAY EXAMINATION

Directions: This examination is designed to sample your learning during the course. You will find questions that tap knowledge, comprehension, application, analysis, synthesis, and evaluation levels of understanding. Each level requires more thought and better verbal ability. The levels of the questions asked are identified, and the points assigned to each question reflect the increasing complexity of thought required in the response. Present your responses in a typewritten, double-spaced, 10–15 page paper.

Knowledge Level: 10 points

Define 10 of the following terms briefly and completely. Each response is worth 1 point.

1. Epidemiologic transition
2. *El día de los Muertos*
3. Magical thinking
4. Palliative care
5. Metastasis
6. Columbarium
7. Linking objects
8. Anticipatory grief
9. Bibliotherapy
10. Awareness contexts
11. Beneficience
12. Nuncupative will
13. Probate
14. *Karoshi*

15. Psychic numbing
16. Suicidal success syndrome
17. *Samsara*
18. *Nirvana*
19. Appropriate death

Comprehension: 12 points

Choose two of the following and answer them briefly but completely. Each response is worth 6 points.

1. Discuss the role of funerals in society. Be sure to explain at least three different purposes that can be served by funerals. Contrast traditional funeral rites with those of memorial societies as discussed in your text.
2. Describe at least three different life-style possibilities for aged persons, commenting on the impact of illness and institutionalization.
3. List *and* refute at least three myths about suicide.

Application: 20 points

Choose two of the following. (*Note:* The detail of your responses is important.) Each response is worth 10 points.

1. Your neighbor's wife is dying. She is thirty-one years old and has a ten-year-old girl, a five-year-old-boy, and a two-year-old girl. Your neighbor comes to you and asks *what* and *how* he should tell the children about their mother's condition and eventual death. Your response should be broken down into three parts, one for each child. You should also recommend at least three specific references that you would urge the father to use in talking with the children. Finally, you should explain to him why each child will need different explanations, referring to the theories discussed during class and covered in the textbook.
2. Contrast Geoffrey Gorer's model of the phases of grief with those of James Kavanaugh, Beverly Raphael, and William Worden. Then present your own model for helping adults work through the grief process.
3. Compare and contrast the traditional hospital treatment of dying patients with that of hospice care. Be sure to specify at least three major differences. Then present your own detailed plan for caring for dying patients, incorporating the strengths of both hospital and hospice approaches.

Analysis: 16 points

Answer one of the following questions.

1. Using the principles of the scientific method, analyze the material in Chapter 14 of the text (as well as any material covered in class and any other readings you have done) on the subject of near-death experiences. What do we *know* about these experiences? What are the possible causes of these experiences? Are such experiences "real"? What does the *body of evidence* suggest? What other evidence should be accumulated? Are there other ways of testing the reality of NDEs?

2. Briefly review the modern necessity for an accurate definition of death, giving at least three reasons. Consider three definitions of death given in the text. Examine their components. Discuss the strengths, weaknesses, and practicality of each. Finally, suggest the ideal definition of death in our modern age.

Synthesis: 20 points

Discuss the changes in longevity across the century. Be sure to include at least five factors that have contributed to increased life span. Then, utilizing all you knew before this course and all you have learned during the course, predict what the average life expectancy might be in 2020, discussing specific problems associated with such a longevity pattern.

Evaluation: 22 points

Choose one of the following questions and answer it briefly but *completely.*

1. Review the changing meanings of death historically. (Be sure to incorporate Ariès' work into your discussion.) Suggest at least four major changes within this century that have had an impact on our view of death. Then, comparing our current view with past views, evaluate which period had the healthiest attitudes toward death; support your choice.

2. Summarize the current state of death education based on your reading in the text (as well as any other materials). Be sure to give enough detail to make clear what age groups and levels you are discussing. Compare and contrast your own feelings about taking a course in death and dying with those expressed by students in Chapter 15 of the text. Suggest *and evaluate* at least *three* societal applications of death education.

Appendix C

Further Readings: Teaching Strategies and Resources

This bibliography of books, articles, and periodicals related to death education for children and adults includes both seminal works and recent literature. The readings cover many topics, including pedagogical techniques and philosophies, curricula, learning activities, and course outlines.

BOOKS AND ARTICLES

Ainsa, Trisha. "Teaching the Terminally Ill Child." *Education* 101 (1981): 397–401.

Anderson, Herbert. "Learning and Teaching About Death and Dying" (with course outline). In *The Role of the Minister in Caring for the Dying Patient and the Bereaved*, edited by Brian O'Connor, Daniel J. Cherico, and Austin H. Kutscher. New York: Irvington, 1976.

Bailis, Lawrence, and William Kennedy. "Effects of a Death Education Program Upon Secondary School Students." *Journal of Educational Research* 71 (November/December 1977): 63–66.

Barton, David, and Miles K. Crowder. "The Use of Role Playing Techniques as an Instructional Aid in Teaching About Dying, Death, and Bereavement." *Omega: Journal of Death and Dying* 6 (1975): 243–250.

Beineke, John A. *Death and the Secondary School Student*. Lanham, Md.: University Press of America, 1979.

Benoliel, Jeanne Quint, ed. *Death Education for the Health Professional*. New York: Hemisphere, 1982.

Bloch, S. "Instruction on Death and Dying for the Medical Student." *Medical Education* 10 (1976): 269–273.

Bloom, Sholom. "On Teaching an Undergraduate Course on Death and Dying." *Omega* 6 (1975): 223–226.

Bluebond-Langner, Myra. "Wither Thou Goest?" *Omega* 18 (1987–1988): 257–263.

Bordewich, Fergus M. "Mortal Fears: Courses in 'Death Education' Get Mixed Reviews." *The Atlantic* 261 (February 1988): 30–34.

Bryant, Ellen Huntington. "Teacher in Crisis: A Classmate Is Dying." *Elementary School Journal* 78 (1978): 233–241.

Bugen, Larry A. "Coping: Effects of Death Education." *Omega* 11 (1980–1981): 175–183.

————. *Death and Dying: Theory/Research/Practice.* Dubuque, Iowa: William C. Brown, 1979.

Bugenthal, James F. T. "Confronting the Existential Meaning of 'My Death' Through Group Exercises." *Interpersonal Development* 4 (1973–1974): 148–163.

Butler, Robert N. "A Humanistic Approach to Our Last Days." *Death Education* 3 (1980): 359–361.

Colton, Arthur E., Darwin E. Gearhart, and Richard P. Janaro. "A Faculty Workshop on Death Attitudes and Life Affirmation." *Omega* 4 (1973): 51–56.

Corr, Charles A. "A Model Syllabus for Death and Dying Courses." *Death Education* 1 (1978): 433–458.

————. "What Is Philosophical in the Death and Dying Course?" *Death Education* 1 (1977): 93–112.

————. "Workshops on Children and Death." Essence 4 (1980): 5–18.

Crase, Darrell. "Black People Do Die, Don't They?" *Death Studies* 11 (1987): 221–228.

————. "Death Education: Accountability Through Scholarly Inquiry." *Journal of the American College Health Association* 27 (1979): 257–260.

————. "Death Education: Its Diversity and Multidisciplinary Focus." *Death Studies* 13 (1989): 25–29.

————. "Death Education Resources." *Journal of School Health* 50 (1980): 411–415.

————. "Profiling the Death Education Student." *Thanatos* 12 (1987): 20–23.

Crase, Darrell, and Dixie R. Crase. "Attitudes Toward Death Education for Young Children." *Death Education* 3 (1979): 31–40.

————. "Emerging Dimensions of Death Education." *Health Education* 10 (January/February 1979): 26–33.

Crase, Darrell, and Dan Leviton. "Forum for Death Education and Counseling: Its History, Impact, and Future." *Death Studies* 11 (1987): 345–359.

Davis, Gary, and Arne Jessen. "An Experiment in Death Education in the Medical Curriculum: Medical Students and Clergy 'On Call' Together." *Omega* 11 (1980–1981): 157–165.

Degner, Leslie F., and Christina M. Gow. "Evaluations of Death Education in Nursing." *Cancer Nursing* 11 (1988): 151–159.

Durlak, Joseph A., and Lee Ann Riesenberg. "The Impact of Death Education." *Death Studies* 15 (1991): 39–58.

Eddy, James M., and Wesley F. Alles. *Death Education.* St. Louis: Mosby, 1983.

Eddy, James M., R. St. Pierre, W. Alles, and R. Shute. "Conceptual Areas of Death Education." *Health Education* 1 (1980): 14–15.

Eiser, Christine. "How Leukemia Affects a Child's Schooling." *British Journal of Social and Clinical Psychology* 19 (1980): 365–368.

Engel, George L. "A Group Dynamic Approach to Teaching and Learning About Grief." *Omega* 11 (1980–1981): 45–59.

Engelman, Ralph M., and Robert S. Smith. "Dealing with Death: An Exercise in Thematic Programming and Development of Community." *NASPA Journal* 13 (1976): 52–56.

Farrell, James J. "The Dying of Death: Historical Perspectives." *Death Education* 6 (1982): 105–123.

Feifel, Herman. "Psychology and Death: Meaningful Rediscovery." *American Psychologist* (April 1990): 537–543.

Fulton, Robert, Jerry Carlson, Karl Krohn, Eric Markusen, and Greg Owen. *Death, Grief and Bereavement: A Bibliography, 1845–1975.* New York: Arno, 1976.

Fulton, Robert, and Greg Owen. "Death and Society in Twentieth Century America." *Omega* 18 (1987–1988): 379–395.

Glass, J. Conrad, Jr. "Changing Death Anxiety Through Death Education in the Public Schools." *Death Studies* 14 (1990): 31–52.

Glass, J. Conrad, Jr., and Curtis Trent. "Death Education: An Adult Concern." *Lifelong Learning: The Adult Years* (January 1982): 24–30.

Gordon, Audrey, and Dennis Klass. "The Facts of Life—And Death: The Role of Schools in Teaching About Death." *American Teacher* 60:8 (1976): 8–10.

———. "Goals for Death Education." *School Counselor* 24 (May 1977): 330–347.

———. *They Need to Know: How to Teach Children About Death.* Englewood Cliffs, N.J.: Prentice-Hall, 1979.

Green, Betty R., and Donald P. Irish, eds. *Death Education: Preparation for Living.* Cambridge, Mass.: Schenkman, 1971.

Gurfield, Mitchell. "On Teaching Death and Dying." *Media and Methods* 13:6 (1977): 56–59.

Harris, Audrey P. "Content and Method in a Thanatology Training Program for Paraprofessionals." *Death Education* 4 (1980): 21–27.

Harris, W. H. "Some Reflections Concerning Approaches to Death Education." *Journal of School Health* 48 (1978): 163–165.

Hoelter, J. W., and R. J. Epley. "Death Education and Death-Related Attitudes." *Death Education* 3 (1979): 67–76.

Kalish, Richard, and David Reynolds, eds. *Death and Ethnicity.* Farmingdale, N.Y.: Baywood, 1981.

Kastenbaum, Robert J. "Death Education, 1975." *Omega* 6 (1975): 179–181.

———. "Theory, Research, and Application: Some Critical Issues for Thanatology," *Omega* 18 (1987–1988): 397–410.

———. "We Covered Death Today." *Death Education* 1 (1977): 85–92.

Kastenbaum, Robert J., and Beatrice Kastenbaum, eds. *Encyclopedia of Death.* Phoenix: Oryx Press, 1989.

Klingman, Avigdor. "Teacher's Workshop in Death Education: The Effects of Simulation Game and Bibliotherapy-Oriented Methods." *Death Studies* 11 (1987): 25–33.

Knott, J. Eugene. "Death Education for All." In *Dying: Facing the Facts*, edited by Hannelore Wass. New York: Hemisphere, 1979. Pp. 385–403.

Knott, J. Eugene, and Richard W. Prull. "Death Education: Accountable to Whom? For What?" *Omega* 7 (1976): 177–181.

Knott, J. Eugene, Mary C. Ribar, Betty M. Duson, and Marc R. King. *Thanatopics: Activities and Exercises for Confronting Death.* Lexington, Mass.: Lexington, 1989.

Kopel, Kenneth, Walter O'Connell, Joyce Paris, and Peter Girardin. "A Human Relations Laboratory Approach to Death and Dying." *Omega* 6 (1975): 219–221.

Kurlychek, Robert T. "Death Education: Some Considerations of Purpose and Rationale." *Educational Gerontology* 2 (1977): 43–50.

Laube, Jerri. "Death and Dying Workshop for Nurses: Its Effect on Their Death Anxiety Level." *International Journal of Nursing Studies* 14 (1977): 111–120.

Leviton, Dan. "A Course on Death Education and Suicide Prevention: Implications for Health Education." *Journal of the American College Health Association* 19 (1971): 217–220.

———. "Death Education." In *New Meanings of Death*, edited by Herman Feifel. New York: McGraw-Hill, 1977. Pp. 253–272.

———. "Education for Death, or Death Becomes Less a Stranger." *Omega* 6 (1975): 183–191.

———. "Education Toward Love and Peace Behaviors." *Journal of Clinical Child Psychology* 5 (1976): 14–17.

———. "The Scope of Death Education." *Death Education* 1 (1977): 41–56.

Leviton, Dan, and Eileen C. Foreman. "Death Education for Children and Youth." *Journal of Clinical Child Psychology* 3 (1974): 8–10.

Leviton, Dan, and William Wendt. "Death Education: Toward Individual and Global Well-Being." *Death Education* 7 (1983): 369–384.

Liston, Edward H. "Education on Death and Dying: A Neglected Area in the Medical Curriculum." *Omega* 6 (1975): 193–198.

Lockard, Bonnie Elam. "Immediate, Residual, and Long-Term Effects of a Death Education Instructional Unit on the Death Anxiety Level of Nursing Students." *Death Studies* 13 (1989): 137–159.

Meagher, David K., and R. Debra Shapiro. *Death: The Experience.* Minneapolis: Burgess, 1984.

Mills, Gretchen C., Raymond Reisler, Jr., Alice E. Robinson, and Gretchen Vermilye. *Discussing Death: A Guide to Death Education.* Homewood, Ill.: ETC, 1976.

Morgan, Ernest. *Dealing Creatively with Death: A Manual of Death Education and Simple Burial.* 11th ed. Burnsville, N.C.: Celo Press, 1988.

Morgan, Mary Ann. "Learner-Centered Learning in an Undergraduate Interdisciplinary Course About Death." *Death Studies* 11 (1987): 183–192.

O'Connell, Walter E., Kenneth Kopel, Joyce Paris, Peter Girardin, and William Batsel. "Thanatology for Everyone: Developmental Labs and Workshops." *Death Education* 1 (1977): 305–313.

Pacholski, Richard A. "Death Themes in Music: Resources and Research Opportunities for Death Educators." *Death Studies* 10 (1986): 239–263.

———. "Death Themes in the Visual Arts: Resources and Research Opportunities for Death Educators." *Death Studies* 10 (1986): 59–74.

———. "Teaching Nuclear Holocaust, The Basic Thanatological Topic." *Death Studies* 13 (1989): 175–183.

Pine, Vanderlyn R. "The Age of Maturity for Death Education: A Socio-Historical Portrait of the Era 1976–1985." *Death Studies* 10 (1986): 209–231.

———. "A Socio-Historical Portrait of Death Education." *Death Education* 1 (1977): 57–84.

Rosenthal, Nina Ribak. "Adolescent Death Anxiety: The Effect of Death Education." *Education* 101 (1980): 95–101.

————. "Attitudes Toward Death Education and Grief Counseling." *Counselor Education and Supervision* 20 (1981): 203–210.

————. "Death Education: Help or Hurt?" *The Clearing House* 53 (January 1980): 224–226.

————. "Teaching Educators to Deal with Death." *Death Education* 2 (1978): 293–306.

Rosenthal, Nina Ribak, and Care Terkelson. "Death Education and Counseling: A Survey." *Counselor Education and Supervision* 18 (1978): 109–114.

Rosner, Aria C. "How We Do It: An Interdisciplinary Approach to Death Education." *Journal of School Health* 44 (1974): 455–458.

Ryerson, M. S. "Death Education and Counseling for Children." *Elementary School Guidance and Counseling* 11 (1977): 165–174.

Sadwith, J. "An Interdisciplinary Approach to Death Education." *Journal of School Health* 44 (1974): 455–457.

Scott, Frances. "When a Student Dies . . . ." *English Journal* 70:2 (1981): 22–24.

Simpson, Michael A. "The Do-It-Yourself Death Certificate in Evoking and Estimating Student Attitudes Toward Death." *Journal of Medical Education* 50 (1975): 475–478.

————. *Dying, Death, and Grief: A Critically Annotated Bibliography.* New York: Plenum, 1979.

————. *Dying, Grief, and Death: A Critical Bibliography.* Pittsburgh: University of Pittsburgh, 1987.

Sinacore, James M. "Avoiding the Humanistic Aspect of Death: An Outcome From the Implicit Elements of Health Professions Education." *Death Education* 5 (1981): 121–133.

Stanford, Gene, and Deborah Perry. *Death Out of the Closet.* New York: Bantam, 1976.

Stevenson, Rogert G. "The Eye of the Beholder: The Media Look at Death Education." *Death Studies* 14 (1990): 161–170.

Stillion, Judith M. "Association for Death Education and Counseling: An Organization for Our Times and for Our Future." *Death Studies* 13 (1989): 191–201.

————. "Where Thanatos Meets Eros: Parallels Between Death Education and Group Psychotherapy." *Death Education* 7 (1983): 53–67.

Thomas, James L., ed. *Death and Dying in the Classroom.* Phoenix, Ariz.: Oryx, 1984.

Thompson, Mary Langer. "Symbolic Immortality: A New Approach to the Study of Death." *Essence* 13:6 (1977): 60–64.

Ulin, Richard O. *Death and Dying Education: Developments in Classroom Instruction.* Washington, D.C.: National Education Association, 1977.

————. "A Treatment of Death in the Classroom." *English Education* 11 (1980): 162–168.

Warren, W. G. "Personal Construction of Death and Death Education." *Death Education* 6 (1982): 17–28.

Wass, Hannelore. "Aging and Death Education for Elderly Persons." *Educational Gerontology* 5 (1980): 79–90.

Wass, Hannelore, and Charles A. Corr. *Helping Children Cope with Death: Guidelines and Resources.* Washington, D.C.: Hemisphere, 1982.

Wass, Hannelore, Charles A. Corr, Richard A. Pacholski, and Cameron S. Forfar. *Death Education II: An Annotated Resource Guide.* New York: Hemisphere, 1985.

Wass, Hannelore, Charles A. Corr, Richard A. Pacholski, and Catherine M. Sanders. *Death Education: An Annotated Resource Guide.* New York: Hemisphere, 1980.

Wass, Hannelore, M. David Miller, and Gordon Thornton. "Death Education and Grief/Suicide Intervention in the Public Schools." *Death Studies* 14 (1990): 253–268.

Wass, Hannelore, R. Stephen Richarde, Susan Angenendt, Martha Fitch, Donna Drake, and James Stergios. "Effectiveness of Short-Term Death Education Programmes for Adults." *Essence* 4:2 (1980): 49–55.

Watts, P. R. "Evaluation of Death Attitude Change Resulting from a Death Education Instructional Unit." *Death Education* 1 (1977): 187–194.

Weeks, Duane. "Death Education for Aspiring Physicians, Teachers, and Funeral Directors." *Death Studies* 13 (1989): 17–24.

Weiner, Hannah B. "Living Experiences with Death—A Journeyman's View Through Psychodrama." *Omega* 6 (1975): 251–274.

Whelan, W. Michael, and William M. Warren. "A Death Awareness Workshop: Theory, Application and Results." *Omega* 11 (1980–1981): 61–71.

White, Douglas K. "An Undergraduate Course in Death Education." *Omega* 1 (1970): 167–174.

Wilcox, Sandra Galdieri, and Marilyn Sutton. *Understanding Death and Dying.* 3d ed. Palo Alto, Calif.: Mayfield, 1985.

Worden, J. William, and William Proctor. *Personal Death Awareness.* Englewood Cliffs, N.J.: Prentice Hall, 1976.

PERIODICALS

Advances in Thanatology, Foundation of Thanatology, Box 1191, Brooklyn, New York, New York 11202. (718) 858-3026.

American Journal of Hospice Care, Prime National Publishing, 470 Boston Post Road, Weston, Massachusetts 02193. (617) 899-2702.

Bulletin of the Park Ridge Center, Suite 450, 676 North St. Clair, Chicago, Illinois 60611. (312) 266-2222. Medical ethics.

Concern for Dying: Society for the Right to Die Newsletter, 250 West 57th Street, New York, New York 10107. (212) 246-6973.

Crisis: International Journal of Suicide and Crisis Studies, Hogrefe & Huber, Publishers, 14 Bruce Park Avenue, Toronto, Ontario M4P 2S3, Canada. Sponsored by the International Association for Suicide Prevention. (416) 482-6339.

Death Studies, Hemisphere Publishing, 79 Madison Avenue, New York, New York 10016. (212) 725-0772; (800) 821-8312.

Emotional First Aid: A Journal of Crisis Intervention, American Academy of Crisis Interveners, c/o James L. Greenstone, Editor, Box 670292, Dallas, Texas 75367.

The Forum: Newsletter of the Association for Death Education and Counseling, 638 Prospect Avenue, Hartford, Connecticut 06105. (203) 232-4825.

Hastings Center Report, 255 Elm Road, Briarcliff Manor, New York 10510. (914) 762-8500. Medical ethics.

H E C Forum: An Interdisciplinary Journal on Hospitals' Ethical and Legal Issues, Pergamon Press, Maxwell House, Fairview Park, Elmsford, New York 10523. (914) 592-7700.

Hospice Journal: Physical, Psychosocial, and Pastoral Care of the Dying, Haworth Press, 10 Alice Street, Binghamton, New York 13904. (800) 342-9678.

Hospital Ethics, American Hospital Association, 840 North Lake Shore Drive, Chicago, Illinois 60611. (312) 280-6232.

Journal of Community Health Nursing, Lawrence Erlbaum Associates, 365 Broadway, Hillsdale, New Jersey 07642. (201) 666-4110.

Journal of Medical Humanities, Human Sciences Press, 233 Spring Street, New York, New York 10013. (212) 620-8000.

Journal of Palliative Care, Centre for Bioethics, 110 Pine Street, Montreal, Quebec H2W 1R7, Canada. (514) 987-5619.

MADDvocate: A Magazine for Victims and Their Associates, Mothers Against Drunk Driving, Suite 700, 511 East John Carpenter Freeway, Irving, Texas 75062. (214) 744-6233; (800) 438-MADD.

Omega: Journal of Death and Dying, Baywood Publishing Company, Box 337, Amityville, New York 11701. (516) 691-1270.

Second Opinion, Park Ridge Center, Suite 450, 676 North St. Clair, Chicago, Illinois 60611. (312) 266-2222. Medical ethics.

Share Newsletter, 211 South Third Street, Belleville, Illinois 62222. (618) 234-2415.

Suicide and Life-Threatening Behavior, Guilford Publications, Fourth Floor, 72 Spring Street, New York, New York 10012. (212) 431-9800. Sponsored by the American Association of Suicidology.

Thanatology Librarian: News of Books on Death, Bereavement, Loss and Grief, Center for Thanatology Research and Education, 391 Atlantic Avenue, Brooklyn, New York 11217. (718) 858-3026.

Thanatos, Florida Funeral Directors Association, c/o Jan Scheff, Editor, Box 6009, Tallahassee, Florida 32314. (904) 224-1969.

Appendix D

Organizations

This listing includes a broad spectrum of organizations related to death and dying. When the purpose of an organization is not immediately obvious by its title, a brief description follows. Because organizations move, merge, and disband, we have included phone numbers, when known.

AIDS Information Line, Centers for Disease Control, Atlanta, GA 30333. (800) 342-AIDS.

Alliance for Cannabis Therapeutics, P.O. Box 23691, L'Enfant Plaza Station, Washington, DC 20024. (202) 483-8595.

Alzheimer's Disease and Related Disorders Association, Suite 600, 70 East Lake Street, Chicago, IL 60601. (800) 621-0379; (800) 572-6037 (in IL).

AMEND (Aiding Mothers and Fathers Experiencing Newborn Death), 4324 Berrywick Terrace, St. Louis, MO 63128. (314) 487-7582.

American Association of Suicidology, Central Office, 2459 South Ash Street, Denver, CO 80222. (303) 692-0985. Nonprofit organization dedicated to understanding and preventing suicide.

American Cancer Society, National Office, 90 Park Avenue, New York, NY 10016. (212) 599-8200.

American Cemetery Association, Suite 1111, Three Skyline Place, 5201 Leesburg Pike, Falls Church, VA 22041. (703) 379-5838.

American Citizens Concerned for Life, 6127 Excelsior Boulevard, Minneapolis, MN 55416. (612) 925-4395. Anti-abortion.

American Civil Liberties Union, 22 East 40th Street, New York, NY 10016. Death penalty information.

American Council of Life Insurance, 1850 K Street, Northwest, Washington, DC 20006. Compiles statistics and maintains a library relative to health issues and concerns.

American Cryonics Society, P.O. Box 761, Cupertino, CA 95015. (408) 446-4425; (800) 523-2001.

American Ex-Prisoners of War, c/o Sally M. Morgan, 3201 East Pioneer Parkway, #40, Arlington, TX 76010. (817) 649-2979. Widowed person's assistance.

American Heart Association, 7320 Greenville Avenue, Dallas, TX 75231.

American Hospital Association, 840 North Lake Shore Drive, Chicago, IL 60611. (312) 280-6000.

American Institute of Commemorative Art, 2446 Sutter Court, Northeast, Grand Rapids, MI 49505. (616) 361-7827. Memorials and cemetery monuments.

American Life Lobby, P.O. Box 490, Stafford, VA 22554. (703) 659-4171. Opposed to abortion; advocates "Human Life Amendment" to U.S. Constitution to legally recognize personhood of the unborn.

American Medical Association, Order Department, 515 North State Street, Chicago, IL 60610. Can provide Uniform Donor Cards. (312) 464-5000.

American Monument Association, 6902 North High Street, Worthington, OH 43085. (614) 885-2713.

American Sudden Infant Death Syndrome Institute, 275 Carpenter Drive, Northeast, Atlanta, GA 30328. (404) 843-1030.

American Trauma Society, P.O. Box 13526, Baltimore, MD 21203. (800) 556-7890.

Associated Funeral Directors Service, International, 810 Stratford Avenue, P.O. Box 7476, Tampa, FL 33603. (813) 228-9105.

Association for Death Education and Counseling, 638 Prospect Avenue, Hartford, CT 06105. (203) 232-4825.

Barr-Harris Center for the Study of Separation and Loss During Childhood, The Institute for Psychoanalysis, 180 North Michigan Avenue, Chicago, IL 60601. (312) 726-6300.

Batesville Management Services, P.O. Drawer 90, Batesville, IN 47006. (812) 934-7788; (800) 622-8373. Literature for the bereaved.

Befrienders International Samaritans Worldwide, 228 Bishopsgate, London, England EC2M 4QD. 71-377-8968. Composed of volunteers from 44 countries who befriend suicidal and other lonely, anxious, or depressed people.

Bereaved Families of Ontario Ottawa-Carleton, P.O. Box 648, Orleans, Ontario K1C 3V9. An association of families who have lost a child by death.

Big Brothers/Big Sisters of America, 220 Suburban Station Building, Philadelphia, PA 19103. Help for children who are without a parent due to divorce or death.

Boulder County Hospice, 2825 Marine Street, Boulder, CO 80303. (303) 449-7740.

Brass Ring Society, Suite 103, 7020 South Yale Avenue, Tulsa, OK 74136. (918) 496-2838. Dedicated to fulfilling the wishes of dying children.

Cancer Information Service, National Cancer Institute, Building 31, Room 10A24, 9000 Rockville Pike, Bethesda, MD 20892. (800) 4-CANCER; (800) 524-1234 (within Hawaii); (800) 638-6070 (within Alaska).

The Candlelighters Childhood Cancer Foundation, Suite 200, 1312 18th Street, Northwest, Washington, DC 20036. (202) 659-5136; (800) 366-2223. International support and educational group for parents of children with cancer.

Casket Manufacturers Association of America, 708 Church Street, Evanston, IL 60201. (312) 866-8383.

Center for Attitudinal Healing, 19 Main Street, Tiburon, CA 94920. (415) 435-5022. Help for adults and children with life-threatening illnesses.

Center for Crime Victims and Survivors, Inc., P.O. Box 6201, Clearwater, FL 34618. (813) 535-1114.

Center for Death Education and Research, 1167 Social Science Building, University of Minnesota, 267 19th Avenue South, Minneapolis, MN 55455. (612) 624-1895; (612) 624-4300 (messages).

Center for Loss and Life Transition, Alan Wolfelt, Ph.D., 3735 Broken Bow Road, Fort Collins, CO 80526. (303) 484-1313.

Center for Studies in Criminal Justice, University of Chicago Law School, 1111 East 60th Street, Chicago, IL 60637. (312) 702-9493. Research on capital punishment, homicide, violence, and other topics in criminology.

Center for Thanatology Research and Education, 391 Atlantic Avenue, Brooklyn, NY 11217. (212) 858-3026.

Centering Corporation, P.O. Box 3367, Omaha, NE 68103. (402) 553-1200. Perinatal losses.

The Centre for Living with Dying, 305 Montague Expressway, Santa Clara, CA 95054-1702. (408) 434-6969. Volunteer organization for those facing life-threatening illness and their families.

Children's Hospice International, Suite 131, 1101 King Street, Alexandria, VA 22314. (703) 684-0330; (800) 242-4453.

Coalition for the Medical Rights of Women, 1638-B Haight Street, San Francisco, CA 94117. (415) 621-8030. Pro-choice organization.

Committee to Halt Useless College Killings (C.H.U.C.K.), P.O. Box 188, Sayville, NY 11782. (516) 567-1130. Compiles and provides data on hazing incidents, deaths, and injuries on American colleges and universities.

The Compassionate Friends, Inc., P.O. Box 3696, Oak Brook, IL 60522. (312) 990-0010. International support organization for bereaved parents.

Concern for Dying, Suite 831, 250 West 57th Street, New York, NY 10107. (212) 246-6962.

Continental Association of Funeral and Memorial Societies, Inc., Suite 530, 2001 South Street, Northwest, Washington, DC 20009. (202) 745-0634.

Cremation Association of North America, Suite 600, 111 East Wacker Drive, Chicago, IL 60601. (312) 644-6610.

Crysalis Center, P.O. Box 26367, St. Louis, MO 63136. (314) 869-3040. Provides information and resources on bereavement follow up to funeral directors and mortuary firms.

The Elisabeth Kübler-Ross Center, South Route 616, Head Waters, VA 24442. (703) 396-3441.

Foundation of Thanatology, 630 West 168th Street, New York, NY 10032. (212) 694-3685. Publications and seminars focusing on death education.

Fred Hutchinson Cancer Research Center, 1124 Columbia Street, Seattle, WA 98104. (800) 4-CANCER.

Gerontological Society of America, Suite 350, 1275 K Street, Northwest, Washington, DC 20005.

Gold Star Wives of America, c/o Rachel A. Bunn, 600 Bethell Street, Northeast, Leeds, AL 35094. (205) 699-8327. Widows of servicemen who died from service-related causes.

Good Grief Program, Judge Baker Guidance Center, 295 Longwood Avenue, Boston, MA 02115. Resource program for school and community groups to assist bereaved children.

Gray Panthers, Suite 601, 311 South Juniper Street, Philadelphia, PA 19107. (215) 545-6555. Dedicated to promoting positive attitudes toward aging.

HAND (Helping After Neonatal Death), P.O. Box 341, Los Gatos, CA 95031. (408) 732-3228.

The Hastings Center, 255 Elm Road, Briarcliff Manor, NY 10510. (914) 762-8500. Programs and publications concerning issues of medical ethics.

Health Resources and Services Administration, Department of Health and Human Services, Rockville, MD 20857.

Heartbeat, 2015 Devon Street, Colorado Springs, CO 80909. (719) 596-2575. Grief support for persons who have lost a loved one to suicide.

Helping Other Parents in Normal Grieving, Edward W. Sparrow Hospital, 1215 East Michigan Avenue, Lansing, MI 48909. (517) 483-2344. Support for miscarriage, stillbirth, and neonatal death.

Hemlock Society, P.O. Box 11830, Eugene, OR 97440. (503) 342-5748. Supports euthanasia for terminally ill persons.

H.O.P.I.N.G., 3288 Moanalua Road, Honolulu, HI 96819. (808) 834-5333, Ext. 9903. Perinatal loss.

Hospice Association of America, 519 C Street, Northeast, Washington, DC 20002. (202) 546-4759.

Hospice Education Institute, P.O. Box 713, Essex, CT 06426. (203) 767-1620; (800) 331-1620.

Huntington's Disease Society of America, Sixth Floor, 140 West 22nd Street, New York, NY 10011. (800) 345-4372.

Illinois Coalition Against the Death Penalty, Sixteenth Floor, 20 East Jackson Street, Chicago, IL 60604. (312) 427-7330. Promotes abolition of the death penalty.

Indian Health Service, Room 5A-43, 5600 Fishers Lane, Rockville, MD 20857. (301) 443-2546. Concerns include high rate of suicide among Native Americans.

Institute for Studies of Destructive Behaviors, Suicide Prevention Center, 1041 South Menlo Avenue, Los Angeles, CA 90006. (213) 386-5111; (213) 381-5111 (24 hours).

International Alert, 379-381 Brixton Road, London, England SW9 7DE. 71-978-9480. Research and activities concerning the prevention of mass violence and genocide.

International Association for Near-Death Studies, Box U-20, 406 Cross Campus Road, University of Connecticut, Storrs, CT 06268.

International Association of Pet Cemeteries, P.O. Box 606, Elkhart, IN 46515. (219) 294-2211.

International Association for Suicide Prevention, Institut für Medical Psychologie, Severingasse 9, Vienna, Austria A-1090. 222-483568.

International Federation of Telephonic Emergency Services, Pannenweg 4, Siebengewald, Netherlands NL-5853. 31-885-21448. Facilitates exchange of information among providers of telephone help-lines in 20 countries.

International Reference Organization in Forensic Medicine and Sciences, c/o William G. Eckert, M.D., Editor, Box 8282, Wichita, KS 67206. (316) 689-3707.

Jewish Funeral Directors of America, Suite 1120, 122 East 42nd Street, New York, NY 10168. (212) 370-0024.

Joseph and Rose Kennedy Institute of Ethics, Georgetown University, 3520 Prospect Street, Northwest, Washington, DC 20057. (202) 625-2383. Involved in research, consulting, and disseminating information about medical ethics.

KARA, 457 Kingsley Avenue, Palo Alto, CA 94301. (408) 321-KARA. Emotional support services for people with life-threatening illness, limited life expectancy, or grief.

King's College, c/o John Morgan, Ph.D., 266 Epworth Avenue, London, Ontario, Canada N6A 2M3. (519) 432-7946. Sponsors annual conferences on topics of interest to death educators, counselors, and caregivers.

Laughter Therapy, 2359 Nichols Canyon Road, Los Angeles, CA 90046. (213) 851-3394. Supplies tapes of "Candid Camera" to patients, nursing homes, doctors, hospices, and clinics.

Legal Defense and Educational Fund, 10 Columbus Circle, New York, NY 10019. Capital punishment information.

Lifeforce Foundation, P.O. Box 3117, Vancouver, B.C., Canada V6B 3X6. (604) 299-2822. Concerned with environmental problems and social responsibilities.

Living Bank, P.O. Box 6725, Houston, TX 77265. (800) 528-2971. Information regarding organ donation.

Make-A-Wish Foundation, Suite 205, 4601 North 16th Street, Phoenix, AZ 85016. (602) 234-0960. Grants last wishes of terminally ill children.

Make Today Count, National Headquarters, P.O. Box 222, Osage Beach, MO 65065. Support group for persons with life-threatening illnesses.

Medic Alert, P.O. Box 1009, Turlock, CA 95380. Information about organ donation.

Medicine in the Public Interest, Suite 304, 65 Franklin Street, Boston, MA 02110. (617) 482-3288. Nonprofit corporation concerned with public health and welfare, including concerns with bioethics.

Milwaukee Bereavement Center, Suite 300, 250 North Sunnyslope Road, Brookfield, WI 53005. (414) 785-8111.

Monument Builders of North America, 1612 Central Street, Evanston, IL 60201. (312) 869-2031.

Mothers Against Drunk Driving (MADD), Suite 700, 511 East John Carpenter Freeway, Irving, TX 75062. (214) 744-6233; (800) 438-MADD. Support and educational group related to deaths caused by drunk drivers.

National Abortion Federation, 900 Pennsylvania Avenue, Southeast, Washington, DC 20003. (202) 546-9060; (800) 772-9100. Pro-choice organization.

National Abortion Rights Action League, Third Floor, 1424 K Street, Northwest, Washington, DC 20005. (202) 347-7774.

National AIDS Network, Suite 601, 1012 Fourteenth Street, Washington, DC 20005. (202) 347-0393.

National Association of Atomic Veterans, P.O. Box 707, Eldon, MO 65026. (314) 392-3361.

National Association of Cemeteries, Suite 409, 1911 North Forst Meyer Drive, Arlington, VA 22209.

National Association for Home Care, 311 Massachusetts Avenue, Northeast, Washington, DC 20002. Information about patient home care.

National Association of Military Widows, 4023 25th Road, North, Arlington, VA 22207. (703) 527-4565.

National Association of Patients on Hemodialysis and Transplantation, Suite 301, 211 East 43rd Street, New York, NY 10017. (212) 867-4486.

National Association of Radiation Survivors, 78 El Camino Road, Berkeley, CA 94705. (415) 652-4400.

National Burn Victim Foundation, Metcalf Building, 308 Main Street, Orange, NJ 07050.

National Catholic Cemetery Conference, 710 North River Road, Des Plaines, IL 60016.

National Center for Death Education, New England Institute of Applied Arts & Sciences, 656 Beacon Street, Boston, MA 02215. (617) 536-6970. Education related to the mortuary sciences, thanatology, grief, and counseling.

National Center for Nursing Research, Building 38A, Room B2E17, National Institutes of Health, Bethesda, MD 20894. (301) 496-0526.

National Citizens' Coalition for Nursing Home Reform, Suite L2, 1424 16th Street, Northwest, Washington, DC 20036. (202) 797-0657.

National Coalition to Ban Handguns, 100 Maryland Avenue, Northeast, Washington, DC 20002. (202) 544-7190.

National Committee on the Treatment of Intractable Pain, P.O. Box 9553, Friendship Station, Washington, DC 20016. (301) 983-1710.

National Committee on Youth Suicide Prevention, 825 Washington Street, Norwood, MA 02062. (617) 769-5686.

National Council on the Aging, West Wing—#100, 600 Maryland Avenue, Southwest, Washington, DC 20024. (202) 479-1200.

National Council of Guilds for Infant Survival, P.O. Box 3586, Davenport, IA 52808. (319) 322-4870.

National Council for Homemaker and Home Health Aid Services, 67 Irving Place, New York, NY 10003.

National Foundation of Funeral Services (NRIC), 1614 Central Street, Evanston, IL 60201. (312) 328-6545. Publishes information about death and dying.

National Funeral Directors Association (NFDA), 11121 West Oklahoma Avenue, P.O. Box 27641, Milwaukee, WI 53227. (414) 541-2500.

National Home Caring Council, 235 Park Avenue South, New York, NY 10003. Information about patient home care.

National Hospice Organization, Suite 901, 1901 North Moore Street, Arlington, VA 22209. (703) 243-5900.

National Institute of Child Health and Human Development, United States Department of Health and Human Services, Building 31, Room 2A32, Bethesda, MD 20892.

National Interfaith Coalition on Aging, P.O. Box 1924, 298 South Hull Street, Athens, GA 30603. (404) 353-1331.

National Kidney Foundation, 2 Park Avenue, New York, NY 10016. (212) 889-2210. Sponsors Gift of Life organ donation program.

National Library of Medicine, 8600 Rockville Pike, Bethesda, MD 20894. (301) 496-6308.

National Organization for Victims Assistance (NOVA), 918 Sixteenth Street, Washington, DC 20006. (202) 265-5042.

National Reference Center for Bioethics Literature, Georgetown University, Washington, DC 20057. (800) MED-ETHX.

National Right to Life Committee, Suite 402, 419 7th Street, Northwest, Washington, DC 20004. (202) 626-8800.

National Selected Morticians (NSM), 1616 Central Street, Evanston, IL 60201. (312) 475-3414.

National Self-Help Resource Center, 2000 South Street, Northwest, Washington, DC 20009. Referral service for the bereaved.

National Sudden Infant Death Syndrome Clearinghouse, Suite 600, 8201 Greensboro Drive, McLean, VA 22102. (703) 821-8955.

National Victim Center, Suite 1001, 307 West 7th Street, Fort Worth, TX 76102. (817) 877-3355.

National Voluntary Organizations for Independent Living for the Aging, Suite 504, 1828 L Street, Northwest, Washington, DC 20036.

Neptune Society, 4922 Arlington Avenue, Riverside, CA 92504. Memorial society.

New Dimensions Radio, P.O. Box 410510, San Francisco, CA 94141. (415) 621-1126. Disseminates information about human values; sponsors a program about death and dying.

New Orleans Jazz Club, Suite 265, 828 Royal Street, New Orleans, LA 70116. (504) 455-6847. Devoted to historical preservation and performance of jazz developed from the music accompanying Black funeral processions.

Northern California Transplant Bank Institute for Medical Research, 751 South Bascom Avenue, San Jose, CA 95128. Information about organ donation.

The OGR Service Corporation, Order of the Golden Rule, P.O. Box 3586, Springfield, IL 62708. Funeral directors who provide publications and films.

Oncology Nursing Society, Third Floor, 1016 Greentree Road, Pittsburgh, PA 15220. (412) 921-7273.

Pain Consultation Center, Mount Sinai Medical Center, 4300 Alton Road, Miami, FL 33140. Help for the control of pain.

Pain Treatment Center, Scripps Clinic and Research Foundation, La Jolla, CA 92037. Help for the control of pain.

Parents of Murdered Children, Inc. (POMC), Unit B-41, 100 East Eighth Street, Cincinnati, OH 45202. (513) 721-5683.

Parents of Suicides, Second Floor, 15 East Brinkerhoff Avenue, Palisades Park, NJ 07650. (201) 585-7608.

Park Ridge Center, Suite 450, 676 North St. Clair, Chicago, IL 60611. (312) 266-2222. Programs and publications concerning issues of medical ethics.

Peace Project, 511 Cayuga Street, Santa Cruz, CA 95062. (408) 425-5061. Information on religious and spiritual approaches to peace.

Pearl Harbor Survivors Association, Space 28, 867 North Lamb Boulevard, Las Vegas, NV 89110. (702) 452-5820.

People Animals Love (PAL), c/o MacArthur Animal Hospital, 4832 MacArthur Boulevard., Northwest, Washington, DC 20007. (202) 337-0120. Provides pets (including veterinary care and food) to elderly, widowed, and institutionized persons.

Planned Parenthood Federation of America, 810 Seventh Avenue, New York, NY 10019. (212) 603-4637. Pro-choice organization.

Plays for Living, Division of Family Service America, 254 West 31st Street, New York, NY 10010. Offers theatrical performances on issues of aging, death, and dying; distributes production kits.

Pregnancy and Infant Loss Center, Suite 22, 1415 East Wayzata Boulevard, Wayzata, MN 55391. (612) 473-9372.

Reproductive Rights National Network, 17 Murray Street, New York, NY 10007. (212) 267-8891. Pro-choice organization.

Resolve Through Sharing, Gundersen/Lutheran Medical Center, 1910 South Avenue, LaCrosse, WI 54601. (608) 785-0530, Ext. 3675. Perinatal loss.

Saint Francis Center, 1768 Church Street, Northwest, Washington, DC 20036. (202) 234-5613. Support for dying or bereaved adults and children.

St. Mary's Grief Support Center, 407 East Third Street, Duluth, MN 55805. (218) 726-4402. Support services for bereaved adults and children.

Samaritans, Kenmore Square, 500 Commonwealth Avenue, Boston, MA 02215. (617) 247-0220. Formerly known as "Lifeline"; composed of volunteers who befriend the suicidal, the despairing, and the lonely.

Seasons: Suicide Bereavement, c/o Tina Larson, P.O. Box 187, Park City, UT 84060. (801) 649-8327.

Shanti Project, 525 Howard Street, San Francisco, CA 94105. (415) 777-2273. Counseling support service for persons with AIDS, their families, and loved ones.

SIDS Alliance, Suite 420, 10500 Little Patuxent Parkway, Columbia, MD 21044. (301) 964-8000; (800) 221-SIDS. Formerly the National Sudden Infant Death Syndrome Foundation.

Society for the Right to Die, 250 West 57th Street, New York, NY 10107. (212) 246-6973. Focus on death with dignity and living wills.

Starlight Foundation, Suite 785, 10100 Santa Monica Boulevard, Los Angeles, CA 90067. (213) 557-1414. Organization to help meet the wishes of terminally and chronically ill children.

Suicide Information and Education Centre, Suite 201, 1615 Tenth Avenue, Southwest, Calgary, Alberta, Canada T3C 0J7. (403) 245-3900.

Sunshine Foundation, 2842 Normandy Drive, Philadelphia, PA 19154. (215) 743-2660. Volunteer organization dedicated to fulfilling the wishes of dying children.

Telephase Society, 1333 Camino Del Rio, San Diego, CA 92108. (619) 299-0805. Cremation and burial at sea.

THEOS, Suite 410, Office Building, Penn Hills Mall, Pittsburgh, PA 15235-3383. Self-help organization for the widowed.

The Tissue Bank, Naval Medical Research Institute, National Naval Medical Center, Bethesda, MD 20014. Information about organ donation.

To Life, P.O. Box 9354, Charlotte, NC 28299-9354. (704) 322-LIFE. Educational and support services for people with life-threatening illness, the bereaved, and others.

Transplantation Society, Room 040, T-19, State University of New York, Stony Brook, NY 11794. Information about organ donation.

United Network for Organ Sharing (UNOS), Suite 500, 1100 Boulders Parkway, Richmond, VA 23225. (800) 243-6667. Coordinates distribution of organs for transplantation.

University of Southern California Comprehensive Cancer Center, Room 205, 1721 Griffin Avenue, Los Angeles, CA 90031. (800) 4-CANCER.

We Tip, Inc., P.O. Box 1296, Rancho Cucamonga, CA 91730. (714) 987-5005. Formerly "Witness Anonymous Program"; citizen self-help program to eliminate drug trafficking and major crimes.

Widow-to-Widow Program, Needham Community Council, Needham, MA 02192.

Widowed Persons Service, 1909 K Street, Northwest, Washington, DC 20049. (202) 728-4450. Sponsored by the American Association for Retired Persons.

World Federation for Cancer Care, 44 Ladbroke Road, London, England W11 3NW. 71-7274808.

Yad Tikvah Foundation, Union of American Hebrew Congregations, 838 Fifth Avenue, New York, NY 10012. (212) 249-0100. Provides resources concerning teen suicide.

Yad V'Kidush Hashem / House of Martyrs, 4200 Sheridan Avenue, Miami Beach, FL 33140. (305) 532-0363. Holocaust-related.

Youth Suicide National Center, 445 Virginia Avenue, San Mateo, CA 94402. (415) 347-3961.

Appendix E

Distributors of Resources

This list is current and complete as this volume goes to press. Since distributors move, merge, and sell their collections, we have included telephone numbers so that you can obtain current information. You also can refer to *AV Market Place: The Complete Business Directory of Audio, Audiovisual, Computer Systems, Film, Video, and Programming, with Industry Yellow Pages* (New York: R. R. Bowker) for annually updated listings of distributors.

University libraries with large audiovisual holdings are good sources for films and videocassettes that are no longer available for sale or rental from the original sources. Contact information for a number of university audiovisual libraries is printed at the beginning of the resource listings.

To ensure that the film or videocassette you want is available through a particular distributor, be sure to write or call well in advance of the desired viewing date.

UNIVERSITY AUDIOVISUAL LIBRARIES

Boston University, Krasker Memorial Film/Video Library, 565 Commonwealth Avenue, Boston, MA 02215. (617) 353-3272.

Indiana University Audiovisual Center, Bloomington, IN 47405-5901. (812) 855-2103; (800) 552-8620.

Pennsylvania State University Audiovisual Services, Special Services Building, University Park, PA 16802. (814) 865-6314; (800) 826-0132.

South Dakota State University Media Center, Pugsley Hall, Box 2218A—PC101, Brookings, SD 57007-1199. (605) 688-5115.

University of California Extension Media Center, 2176 Shattuck Avenue, Berkeley, CA 94704. (415) 642-5578; (415) 642-0460.

University of Michigan Film and Video Library, University Library, 400 Fourth Street, Ann Arbor, MI 48103-4816. (313) 764-5360; (800) 999-0424.

University of Vermont Media Services, Pomeroy Hall, Burlington, VT 05405. (802) 656-1947.

University of Wisconsin Extension, Bureau of Audiovisual Instruction, P.O. Box 2093, Madison, WI 53701-2093. (608) 262-1644; (800) 362-6888.

GENERAL LISTING: DISTRIBUTORS OF RESOURCES

AIMS Media, 90710 DeSoto Avenue, Chatsworth, CA 91311-4409. (818) 773-4300; (800) 367-2467.

Altschul Group Corporation, 930 Pitner Avenue, Evanston, IL 60202. (800) 323-9084.

Ambrose Video Publishing, Inc., Suite 2241, 1290 Avenue of the Americas, New York, NY 10104. (212) 265-7272; (800) 526-4663.

American Cancer Society, National Office, Creative Services, 1599 Clifton Road, Northeast, Atlanta, GA 30329. (404) 320-3333.

American Journal of Nursing Co., Educational Services Division, 555 West 57th Street, New York, NY 10019-2961. (212) 582-8820; (800) 223-2282. (Information.)

American Journal of Nursing Co., West Glen Communications, 1430 Broadway, New York, NY 10018. (800) 225-5256. (Rentals.)

Baker and Taylor Video, 501 South Gladiolus, Momence, IL 60954. (800) 435-5111; (800) 892-1892 in Ill..

Barnes, Daniel, Access Group, 4 Cielo Lane, #4D, Novato, CA 94949. (415) 883-6111.

Barr Films, P.O. Box 7878, 12801 Schabarum Avenue, Irwindale, CA 91706-7878. (818) 338-7878; (800) 234-7879.

Batesville Management Services, P.O. Drawer 90, Batesville, IN 47006. (812) 934-7788; (800) 622-8373. (Purchases only.)

Beacon Films, 930 Pitner Avenue, Evanston, IL 60202. (800) 323-9084; (800) 322-3307.

Benchmark Films, 145 Scarborough Road, Briarcliff Manor, NY 10510. (914) 762-3838.

Bhaktivedanta Book Trust, 3764 Watseka Avenue, Los Angeles, CA 90034. (213) 559-4455.

Biomedical Communications, University of Texas Cancer Center, M.D. Anderson Hospital and Tumor Institute, P.O. Box 126, 1515 Holcombe Boulevard, Houston, TX 77030. (713) 792-7287.

Boulder County Hospice, 2825 Marine Street, Boulder, CO 80303. (303) 449-7740; (303) 651-3922.

Brigham Young University, Audiovisual Services, Fletcher Building, Room 101, Provo, UT 84602. (801) 378-2713.

Carle Medical Communications, 110 West Main Street, Urbana, IL 61801-2700. (217) 384-4838.

Carousel Film & Video, Room 705, 260 Fifth Avenue, New York, NY 10001. (212) 683-1660.

Case Western Reserve University, Educational Media Center, 2919 Abington Road, Cleveland, OH 44106. (216) 368-2026.

Churchill Films, 12210 Nebraska Avenue, Los Angeles, CA 90025. (213) 207-6600; (800) 334-7830.

The Cinema Guild, Room 802, 1697 Broadway, New York, NY 10019. (212) 246-5522.

Colorado SIDS Program, Suite 134, 1330 Leyden Street, Denver, CO 80220. (303) 320-7771.

Committee on Congregational Standards, United Synagogue of America, 155 Fifth Avenue, New York, NY 10010. (212) 533-7800.

Concern for Dying, 250 West 57th Street, New York, NY 10107. (212) 246-6962.

Coronet/MTI Film & Video, 108 Wilmot Road, Deerfield, IL 60015. (312) 940-1260; (800) 621-2131.

Creative Marketing, Human Services Division, 2631 North Grand East, Springfield, IL 62702. (217) 528-1756.

CRM Films, Suite F, 2233 Faraday, Carlsbad, CA 92008. (800) 421-0833.

Daniel Arthur Simon Productions, P.O. Box 49811, Los Angeles, CA 90049.

Disney Educational Productions, 500 South Buena Vista Street, Burbank, CA 91521. (818) 972-3410; (800) 621-2131.

Documentaries for Learning, c/o Pennsylvania State Audiovisual Services, University Park, PA 16803. (800) 826-0132.

Ecufilm, 810 12th Avenue South, Nashville, TN 37203. (615) 242-6277.

Educators for Social Responsibility, 23 Garden Street, Cambridge, MA 02138. (617) 492-1764.

Elisabeth Kübler-Ross Center, South Route 616, Head Waters, VA 24442. (703) 396-3441.

Encyclopaedia Britannica Educational Corporation, Department 10A, 310 South Michigan Avenue, Chicago, IL 60604. (312) 347-7900; (800) 554-9862.

Family Communications, Inc., 4802 Fifth Avenue, Pittsburgh, PA 15213. (412) 687-2990.

Fanlight Productions, 47 Halifax Street, Boston, MA 02130. (617) 524-0980.

Filmakers Library, Suite 901, 124 East 40th Street, New York, NY 10016. (212) 808-4980.

Films, Inc., 5547 North Ravenswood, Chicago, IL 60640. (312) 878-7300; (800) 323-4222.

Films for the Humanities & Sciences, P.O. Box 2053, Princeton, NJ 08543. (609) 452-1128; (800) 257-5126.

Foundation of Thanatology, 630 West 168th Street, New York, NY 10032. (212) 928-2066.

Fritsch, Julie, 607 Harriett Avenue, Aptos, CA 95003. (408) 688-7990.

Gateway Films / Vision Video, Box 540, 2030 Wentz Church Road, Worchester, PA 19490. (215) 584-1893.

The Glendon Association, Suite 3000, 2049 Century Park East, Los Angeles, CA 90067. (213) 552-0431.

Great Plains National Instructional Television Library, P.O. Box 80669, Lincoln, NE 68501. (402) 472-2007; (800) 228-4630.

Grove Press, Film Division, 196 West Houston Street, New York, NY 10014. (212) 614-7850.

Guidance Associates, Communications Park, P.O. Box 3000, 90 South Bedford Road, Mt. Kisco, NY 10549. (914) 666-4100; (800) 431-1242.

Health Sciences Consortium, Distribution Department, 201 Silver Cedar Court, Chapel Hill, NC 27514. (919) 942-8731.

Hospice Institute, 61 Burban Drive, Branford, CT 06405. (203) 481-6231.

Ideal Communications, 35 Downing Street, New York, NY 10014. (212) 727-8872; (202) 833-4567.

IFEX Films, 201 West 52nd Street, New York, NY 10019. (212) 582-4318.

Indiana University, Audio-Visual Center, Bloomington, IN 47405. (812) 855-8087; (800) 552-6820.

International Film Bureau, 332 South Michigan Avenue, Chicago, IL 60604. (312) 427-4545; (800) 432-2241.

International Tele-Film Enterprises, Ltd., 47 Densley Avenue, Toronto, Canada M6M 5AB. (416) 241-4483.

Journal Film and Video, 930 Pitner Avenue, Evanston, IL 60202. (312) 328-6700; (800) 323-9084.

King Features, Educational Division, 235 East 45th Street, New York, NY 10017. (212) 455-4000; (800) 526-KING.

LaGrand, Louis E., Department of Health and Physical Education, State University College of Arts and Science, Potsdam, NY 13676. (315) 267-2309.

La Mariposa Press, P.O. Box 6117, Mesa, AZ 85206. (602) 981-8747.

Lawren Productions, Inc., 930 Pitner Avenue, Evanston, IL 60202. (312) 328-6700; (800) 323-9084.

Learning Corporation of America, Tenth Floor, 130 East 59th Street, New York, NY 10022. (212) 755-8600; (800) 323-6310.

Learning Resources Center / Bio-Information Center, Creighton University, 28th and Burt, Omaha, NE 68178. (402) 280-2700.

Lefkowitz, Deborah, 44 Hancock Street, Somerville, MA 02144. (617) 864-3316.

Lifecycle Productions, P.O. Box 183, Newton, MA 02165. (617) 964-0047; (800) 242-1520.

Martha Stuart Communications, Inc., 147 West 22nd Street, New York, NY 10011. (212) 255-2718.

Mass Media Ministries, 2116 North Charles Street, Baltimore, MD 21218. (301) 727-3270.

Medcom, Inc., Trainex Division, Box 3225, Garden Grove, CA 92642. (714) 891-1443; (800) 232-2505.

The Media Guild, Suite E, 11722 Sorrento Valley Road, San Diego, CA 92121. (619) 755-9191.

Medical College of South Carolina, 80 Barre Street, Charleston, SC 29401. (803) 792-2300.

Michigan Media, Film & Video Library, 400 Fourth Street, Ann Arbor, MI 48103-4816. (313) 764-5360; (800) 999-0424.

Mickel, Howard, Theta Project, P.O. Box 20132, Wichita, KS 67208. .

National Audiovisual Center, Attention: Order Section, 8700 Edgeworth Drive, Capitol Heights, MD 20743-3701. (301) 763-1891; (800) 638-1300.

National Film Board of Canada, 16th Floor, 1251 Avenue of the Americas, New York, NY 10020. (212) 586-5131; (800) 542-2164.

NBC Educational Enterprises, Room 412, 30 Rockefeller Plaza, New York, NY 10020. (212) 664-4754.

New Day Films, Room 902, 121 West 27th Street, New York, NY 10001. (212) 645-8210.

New Dimension Media, 85803 Lorane Highway, Eugene, OR 97405. (503) 484-7125.

New Film Company, Inc., 7-A Mystic Street, Arlington, MA 02174. (617) 641-2580.

New Line Cinema Corporation, 16th Floor, 575 Eighth Avenue, New York, NY 10018. (212) 239-8880.

OGR Service Corporation, P.O. Box 3586, Springfield, IL 62708. (217) 793-3322.

Original Face Video, P.O. Box 165, 6116 Merced Avenue, Oakland, CA 94611. (415) 339-3126.

Paramount Pictures, 5555 Melrose Avenue, Los Angeles, CA 90038. (213) 468-5000.

PBS Video, 1320 Braddock Place, Alexandria, VA 22314. (800) 424-7963.

Pennsylvania State University, Audio Visual Services, Special Services Building, University Park, PA 16802. (814) 865-6314; (800) 826-0132.

Perennial Education, 930 Pitner Avenue, Evanston, IL 60202. (312) 328-6700; (800) 323-9084.

Phoenix/BFA Films & Video, Tenth Floor, 468 Park Avenue South, New York, NY 10016. (212) 684-5910; (800) 221-1274.

Polymorph Films, 118 South Street, Boston, MA 02111. (617) 542-2004.

Portland State University, Continuing Education Film Library, P.O. Box 1383, 1633 Southwest Park Avenue, Portland, OR 97207. (503) 229-3537; (800) 547-8887.

Prairie Lark Press, P.O. Box 699, Springfield, IL 62705.

Professional Research, Inc., 930 Pitner Avenue, Evanston, IL 60202. (312) 328-6700; (800) 421-2363.

Pyramid Film & Video, P.O. Box 1048, Santa Monica, CA 90406. (213) 828-7577; (800) 421-2304.

RCA/Columbia Pictures Home Video, 3500 West Olive Avenue, Burbank, CA 91506. (818) 953-7900.

Research Press, P.O. Box 3177, Champaign, IL 61826. (217) 352-3273.

Rush-Presbyterian St. Luke's Medical Center, Organ and Tissue Bank, 1753 West Congress Parkway, Chicago, IL 60612. (312) 942-6242.

St. George's Hospital Medical School, *Attn:* Mrs. Freda Macey—Psychiatry of Mental Handicap, Cranmer Terrace, London SW 17 ORE, England.

Sandoz Pharmaceuticals, Film Department, East Hanover, NJ 17936. (201) 503-7500.

Scripps Memorial Hospital Cancer Center Films, P.O. Box 28, 9888 Genessee Avenue, La Jolla, CA 92038. (619) 457-6756.

SIDS Alliance, Suite 420, 10500 Little Patuxent Parkway, Columbia, MD 21044. (301) 964-8000; (800) 221-7437.

Social Work Oncology Group, Sidney Farber Cancer Institute, 35 Binney Street, Boston, MA 02115. (617) 732-3000.

Southern Illinois University School of Medicine, P.O. Box 19230, Springfield, IL 62794. (217) 782-7420.

Stanford University School of Medicine, Division of Instructional Media—M 207, Palo Alto, CA 94305. (415) 723-2300.

Sunburst Communications, 39 Washington Avenue, Pleasantville, NY 10570. (914) 769-5030; (800) 431-1934.

Swank Audio-Visuals, Inc., 211 South Jefferson Avenue, St. Louis, MO 63103. (314) 543-1940.

Tricepts Productions Film Lab, 445 West Main Street, Wyckoff, NJ 07481. (201) 891-8240.

UCB Extension Media Center, University of California, 2176 Shattuck Avenue, Berkeley, CA 94704. (415) 642-0460; (415) 642-5578.

UCLA Instructional Media Library, Powell Library, Room 46, University of California, Los Angeles, CA 90024. (213) 825-0755.

Umbrella Films, 60 Blake Road, Brookline, MA 02146. (617) 277-6639.

United Artists Pictures, 1000 West Washington Boulevard, Culver City, CA 90232. (213) 280-6080.

United Learning, 6633 West Howard Street, Niles, IL 60648. (312) 647-0600; (800) 323-9468.

University of Arizona, Health Sciences Center, Division of Biomedical Communications, Tucson, AZ 85724. (602) 621-1735.

University of Illinois, Film/Video Center, 1325 South Oak Street, Champaign, IL 61820. (800) 367-3456.

University of Kansas, Media Services, Continuing Education Building, Lawrence, KS 66045-2630. (913) 864-3352.

University of Minnesota, AV Library Service, Suite 108, 1313 Fifth Street, Southeast, Minneapolis, MN 55414. (612) 627-4270; (800) 847-8251.

University of Virginia School of Medicine, The Claude Moore Health Sciences Library, P.O. Box 395—Medical Center, Charlottesville, VA 22908. **(804) 924-5839.**

University of Washington, Health Sciences Center for Educational Resources, T-281, SB 56, Seattle, WA 98195. **(206) 545-1186.**

University of Washington Press, P.O. Box 50096, Seattle, WA 98145. **(206) 543-4050; (800) 441-4115.**

U.S.A. Home Video, 7920 Alabama Avenue, Canoga Park, CA 91304-4991. **(818) 888-3040; (800) 423-5558.**

USC Film Distribution Center, Division of Cinema, University Park, Los Angeles, CA 90007. **(213) 740-2311.**

USCAN International, 110 West Hubbard Drive, Chicago, IL 60610. **(312) 828-0500.**

The Video Project, Suite 101, 5332 College Avenue, Oakland, CA 94618. **(415) 655-9050.**

Videotape Library of Clinical Psychiatric Syndromes, University of Texas, Medical Branch, Galveston, TX 77550. **(409) 761-1281.**

Viewfinders, P.O. Box 1665, Evanston, IL 60204. **(708) 869-0600.**

WHA-TV, Marketing Department, University of Wisconsin, 821 University Avenue, Madison, WI 53706. **(608) 263-2121.**

Willowgreen Productions, 509 West Washington Boulevard, Fort Wayne, IN 46802. **(219) 424-7916.**

Wintergreen Press, 3630 Eileen Street, Maple Plain, MN 55359. **(612) 476-1303.**

Wise-Currant Productions, 1137 Bay Street, #3, Santa Monica, CA 90405. **(213) 450-5548.**

WKYC-TV, Public Affairs Department, 1403 East Sixth Street, Cleveland, OH 44114. **(216) 344-3300.**

Wombat Productions, Suite 2421, 250 West 57th Street, New York, NY 10019. **(212) 315-2502.**

Zipporah Films, Unit 4, One Richdale Avenue, Cambridge, MA 02140. **(617) 576-3603.**

Appendix F

Excerpt from The Bog
by Michael Talbot

Directions: As you read this excerpt from *The Bog,* a contemporary paperback horror novel, think about your readings from *The Last Dance.* After you read the excerpt, respond to the review questions assigned by your instructor.

Tuck wiped the tears from his eyes as he pondered this. "Daddy?"

"Yes, Tuck?"

"Are we still going to move?"

"Not for the time being. Maybe in a little while."

Tuck fiddled with a button on his shirt. "I'm glad we didn't leave," he returned. "You know why?"

"Why?"

"Because that would have meant that we were leaving Ben behind." After this remark Tuck continued to fumble distractedly with his shirt button, gazing meditatively off into space. David drew in his breath, grateful at least that Tuck had not phrased the remark in the form of a question, and hugged his son tighter. Nonetheless, a moment later David noticed that Tuck's expression had taken on a darker cast, and as he continued to stare off into the distance some inner voice seemed to be speaking to him, prodding him with things he found painful.

"Daddy?"

"Yes, Tuck?"

"Is Ben ever coming back?"

David closed his eyes as he embraced his son tighter still. It was the question he had been dreading. As long as he himself had been ignorant of Ben's fate it had been easy to be evasive, to postpone confronting the matter. But now that he knew the truth he was left in a quandary. The last thing in the world he wanted to do was tell Tuck the truth, for he feared it would send Tuck even further into his ever-increasing depressions. But after what he had said about Mrs. Comfrey he felt he had no right to lie. He took a deep breath.

"No, Tuck. Ben isn't coming back."

Tuck remained absolutely motionless, absorbing the information with no visible sign of distress.

174

"Why not?" he asked.

David took another deep breath. "Do you know how every fall the flowers die and the leaves fall off the trees? Do you know why they do that?"

Tuck shook his head in the negative. "Cause winter's coming?" he offered tentatively.

"Partly because the winter's coming," David returned. "But partly because they have to make room for the new flowers and leaves. You see, that's the way nature works. Everything has a beginning and an end. If it didn't the world would become stagnant, like a bucket of water that you just let sit and sit. Can you imagine what the world would be like if everything lasted forever? Just think about it. Every bee that ever lived, every tree and every person would still be here, and what a crowded place it would be. The only problem is that it's painful when things we love go away. We miss them and that's okay. But what's not okay is to think that it's bad that things have to go away, because it's not bad. It's a very important thing. It's what allows new flowers to grow, and new leaves to replace the old, and the world to renew itself."

"And Ben went away?"

"Yes, Ben went away."

"Where did he go?"

"To heaven," David replied.

Tuck's lower lip started to quiver. "But why did he have to go to heaven?"

"Because it was his time to go."

A large tear rolled down Tuck's cheek and hit David's arm, and he gave his son another reassuring hug. "Hey, now, I don't want you to be upset about this. I told you the truth about Ben because I don't want you to be afraid when things have to go to heaven. Too many people in this world spend too much time being afraid of that, and it's just silly. When something goes to heaven it's a scary thing, and it's a painful thing. But you've got to be brave about it. Things don't go to heaven very often, but when they do, you've got to face it like a man."

Tuck wiped the tear from his eye. "I've got to have moxie, huh, Dad?"

David smiled. He had forgotten about that. "Yes, Tuck. You've got to have moxie."